LITERARY CONTEXTS

English Romantic Literature

Literary Contexts recognises that literature is always rooted in its social milieu and that we need to study literary cultures in all their complexity and connections. It offers the thrill of locating a text within its context and seeing a context reflected in a literary/cultural text.

Each of the books in the series offers students of English and other literatures concise, informative insights into the history of ideas embodied in literary texts, authors and movements. Organised around themes and ideas with extensive examples from literary and cultural texts, the books enable students to understand how the "literary" takes shape in an intellectual milieu and discover manifestations of abstract ideas in literary texts. Written by scholar-teachers who have taught and researched literature for several years, each volume in the series is a stand-alone reference book for students and teachers alike.

Series editor

Pramod K. Nayar, FEA, FRHistS, teaches at the Department of English, University of Hyderabad, where he also holds the UNESCO Chair in Vulnerability Studies. His most recent books include *Life/Writing* (Orient BlackSwan, 2023), *Nuclear Cultures* (2023), *Alzheimer's Disease Memoirs* (2022), *The Human Rights Graphic Novel* (2021), *Indian Travel Writing in the Age of Empire, 1830–1940* (2020) and *Ecoprecarity* (2019), besides the edited six-volume collection, *The Imperial Archives* (2022).

Also in the series

Shakespeare
American Literature
Modern English Literature, 1890–1960
Victorian Literature
Postcolonial Literatures
Eighteenth-century English Literature
Postmodern Literatures

LITERARY CONTEXTS

English Romantic Literature

Neeraja Sundaram

Series Editor
Pramod K. Nayar

Orient BlackSwan

ENGLISH ROMANTIC LITERATURE

ORIENT BLACKSWAN PRIVATE LIMITED

Registered Office
3-6-752 Himayatnagar, Hyderabad 500 029, Telangana, India
e-mail: centraloffice@orientblackswan.com

Other Offices
Bengaluru, Chennai, Guwahati, Hyderabad, Kolkata,
Mumbai, New Delhi, Noida, Patna, Visakhapatnam

First published 2023

ISBN 978 93 5442 400 7

037590

Typeset in Adobe Caslon Pro 11.5/13.5 *by*
Shine Graphics, Delhi 110 094

Printed at
Yash Printographics, Noida 201301

Published by
Orient Blackswan Private Limited
3-6-752, Himayatnagar, Hyderabad 500 029, Telangana, India
e-mail: info@orientblackswan.com

Contents

Series Editor's Preface

The idea that the literature of every age is rooted in its social milieu is a truism. Mapping the contours of this milieu often requires, for the student, to read through several specialised texts. Titles in *Literary Contexts*, by bringing together the key contexts – both general and specialised – into one volume, offer the student of English and other literatures short, prescient and informative studies that provide the history of ideas embodied in literary texts, authors and movements.

Intellectual history or the history of ideas has always been intertwined with the cultural practices and shifts within them in every age. Therefore titles in the series track the intellectual history of every age through social and historical contexts, whether these were contexts of imperial voyages, "Westward expansion", the Reformation of the Church, great scientific discoveries or nationalist movements. Considerable attention is paid to the contexts of class, literacy, gender relations, the state and its functions in every age.

The series' titles demonstrate how certain dominant ideas in any age operated. To this end, every title in the series draws upon and cites numerous examples from literary texts. This enables the student to get a sense of the literary themes' origins in the intellectual milieu, and discover manifestations of abstract ideas, such as "exceptionalism", "hybrid and displaced identity" or "division of powers of Church and State", in literary texts.

The authors do not seek to establish a direct correspondence between the literary text and the dominant idea of the age, but they offer the student a sense of the dense exchanges between the idea and the literary text. Each title maps ideas across cultural texts – popular forms, high culture, and scientific and philosophical texts – so that it demonstrates how ideas are mobile and cut across genres and domains. The titles in the series also document the conflicts and tensions in every age so that the student is made aware of the complicated nature of both, the history of ideas and the literary expressions of the same, and is alerted to the messy nature of cultural history of any age, in any nation.

Written by scholar-teachers who have taught and researched literature for several years, *Literary Contexts* is student-friendly, being both jargon-free and incisive.

Pramod K. Nayar

Acknowledgements

I am grateful for the support of several individuals who were central to the successful completion of the present work. Thanks are due to Professor Pramod K Nayar for the opportunity to contribute to this series and for his close attention and timely feedback at various stages of this book. Sreenath Sreedharan and Aditi Jha at Orient BlackSwan ensured a thorough editing process and saw the manuscript through to its current form.

At Azim Premji University, Venu Narayan and SV Srinivas enabled a relaxation in teaching duties that gave me much-needed time to meet research and writing deadlines for the book. My colleagues in the School of Arts and Sciences deserve a special mention for their encouragement, intellectual engagement and support throughout the writing process: Alex Thomas for several engaging discussions on eighteenth-century England and the process of creating student resources, Usha Rajaram and Tarangini Sriraman for sharing crucial texts and materials, Divya Uma and Sravanti Uppaluri for making time for regular check-ins during our hectic semesters. I teach a course on the English Romantics at APU and since its first iteration for a small group of undergraduate Honours students in 2018, have learned immensely from the pedagogical experiences that emerged here. Many thanks are due to the students I have met in this course over the years for their enthusiasm, thoughtful questions and criticisms of the key writings from the period that we unpacked together.

Rahul De makes as many accommodations (often unplanned and most inconvenient to him) as needed to ensure that our professional and academic commitments can always be given priority. I am grateful for his support and many sacrifices.

Hemalatha Sundaram and Charumathi Sundaram have been a source of strength even through very difficult times, especially over the last year. Their affection and care have sustained me through all previous academic ventures, including this one. Ranjan De and Anuradha De were generous in their encouragement and gave me timely pep-talks and reminders that helped overcome what seemed like insurmountable challenges to completing deadlines. Rohit De extended swift and gracious help with locating resources I couldn't access. Padmavati Kasi fuelled my academic ambitions with her impossible faith in my abilities. This book is dedicated to her memory with immense gratitude for her many kindnesses, blessings and good wishes.

Introduction

The terms "Romantic" and "Romanticism" give rise to a range of contemporary associations, many of which may not have to do with a specific period in the history of literature produced in England. A common association for instance is with the romance genre – the recurring central pattern of stories in which individuals fall in love – or its historical antecedent – medieval tales of adventure, courtly life and chivalry.[1] This book assumes a degree of familiarity with the existing history of associations while attempting to introduce yet another. There is, at present, a wealth of material that introduces the uninitiated to a history of debates that surround the term in its aesthetic sense: as a movement involving all the arts, not confined to literature, that would spread throughout Europe from around mid-eighteenth to mid-nineteenth century and encompass certain norms of composition and their study.[2] This book will focus instead on understanding Romantic literature as a literary-historical term applied to the study of writing emerging in the late-eighteenth and early-nineteenth centuries in England. The aim here is to demonstrate to students of literary studies, the difficult task of establishing a context in which to read a poem or political cartoon rather than claim a universal mode for making sense of Romanticism. Illustrations from writers and modes of writing considered Romantic are confined to England with references to other regions only when significant appearances/influences are apparent in *English* writing and culture. In this book, I define context as undertaking a certain amount of work to make sense of a historically particular mode of being in the world as expressed in writing Context, for the purposes of this book, will encompass key sociopolitical and cultural events, the mechanics of how texts are interpreted and significant intellectual debates. At the same time, a single source cannot provide a comprehensive overview of contexts, and readers are urged to return to anthologies, critical companions and literary encyclopaedias, which have the bandwidth necessary to showcase the richness of writing in any age.

With the narrowing of focus on a region, another problem is immediately apparent: how does one decide where differences across a period manifest to the degree that they demonstrate a decisive break (or less rigidly, "a movement away") from existing convention, ideas and modes of making sense of the world? In the case of England, Romanticism is thought to have been inaugurated through the decisive declaration in Wordsworth and Coleridge's *Lyrical Ballads* in 1798, that their poetry unseated the conventions of predecessors. An earlier moment, though still identifying the late-eighteenth century as a point of origin for a new period of writing, is the start of the French Revolution in 1789 and the impact it would have on those living in England at the time. This book seeks to inspect these and other transformations of varying degrees that necessitate the Romantic label for a forty-odd year period that intersects with others like eighteenth-century writing and Victorian literature. Chapters have been organised to illustrate some of these undeniable markers of change in writing and thought at this time.

The many revolutions in this age would question social and political divisions such that certain forms of writing and media – like the pamphlet, periodical or political cartoon – become as important to study as the poem and the novel in an earlier age. Poetry too, as evidenced by Wordsworth and Coleridge's *Lyrical Ballads*, would seek out different principles of composition and evaluation in an age where hierarchies of all kinds – those between a monarch and his subjects and authors and readers – were being challenged. The periodical industry, though already consolidated by the late-eighteenth century in England, would facilitate the emergence of several professions of interest to literature students today: the critic, professional writers and editors. It is in this context that several ideas we recognise as Romantic would emerge. Debates about what constitutes an author, ideal standards for major literary genres and labels such as "genius" or "celebrity" applied to some individuals have their roots in this period and continue to be relevant for literary studies today. Perhaps the most recognisable Romantic trait is the close attention to the theme of nature in writing. The book situates this theme in the context of enclosures, growing industrialisation and new ways of making sense of life in a changing world Rural life in England would transform rapidly at this time in response to demands for labour in the cities and the focus on improving agricultural yields to feed a growing population. Several writers, sensitive to change, sought to capture its impact on disadvantaged populations and memorialised vanishing spaces like the village commons in their work.

Sensitivity to others is a central Romantic concern and manifests in writings seeking justice for those wronged by the progress of empire and those as yet unrecognised in this period's many movements to guarantee rights for citizens of newly constituted nations. Slave rebellions would erupt in the wake of a universal declaration of rights for all men in revolutionary France and inspire other demands for recognition, several of which are recorded in writing. Writers, especially women, would participate in the movement to abolish slavery in Britain and create enduring images of suffering slaves, wicked masters and benevolent social activists. Others sought to re-evaluate their nation's policies towards the poor, the elderly, war veterans and workers at a time when England was very critical of its government and its institutions. An anxious monarchy and aristocracy in England would retaliate through censorship and legal action and very often, through conservative pamphleteering and writing of their own. Self-criticism is one of many modes through which a peculiarly late-eighteenth and early-nineteenth-century English character emerged in writing. This period witnessed an increase in writing that focused on one's own life, aspirations, failures and excesses. A heightened sensitivity to the plight of others co-exists comfortably in this period with a market that demanded and supplied self-centred writing in the form of biographies and autobiographies.

It is impossible to read and teach the Romantics in the present as distinct from the body of academic scholarship that surrounds them. The chapters on gender and science in the context of Romantic writing benefit from and illustrate methods of revisiting the corpus of texts considered representative of any age. Recent studies expose a bias in later nineteenth-century projects representing the Romantics where greater focus was placed on a few male writers and the literary forms and themes they favoured. They also illustrate novel ways to contextualise and understand gender in literary studies: looking closely at material circumstances of writers, their choice of form and thematics, and public debates about gender conduct, among others. The chapter on science allows us to see an example of historical variations in associations between knowledge domains. Science in the eighteenth century, though not institutionally organised in the same sense as the present, was a companion domain to literature rather than the distinct field it is today. Scientists or natural philosophers shared many values with poets, artists and thinkers – a desire for simplifying scientific knowledge to make it accessible to all, anxieties over aristocratic and government patronage for scientific experimentation, and sensitivity toward contemporary articulations for rights and justice. Eighteenth-century scientific thought would also contribute to how Romantic writers saw their world organised differently than those in a previous age. Newtonian science, new applications for electricity, the isolation of gases and geological recalculations for the Earth's age would all impact how writers represented themselves and others in relation to natural phenomena.

Where relevant, chapters also illustrate the importance of an inclusive approach to historical epochs when tracking the emergence and sustenance of transformations in ideas and ways of life. For example, when discussing English imperial expansion, the market for printed materials or even the proliferation of the poetic form, chapters also pay attention to evidence of similar or related conditions in earlier times. Similarly, the impact and significance of events like the French and Industrial Revolutions, the American War for Independence and the passage of the 1832 Reform Act would not diminish in England even in the nineteenth and twentieth centuries.

This book can serve as a useful teaching aid while preparing a syllabus and class plan for teaching English Romantic Literature. It can work alongside several excellent resources that take a more inclusive approach to determining the contours of the Romantic period in England. Some notable examples are anthologies like Duncan Wu's *Romanticism: An Anthology* (1994), Mellor and Matlak's *British Literature 1780–1830* (1996) and online teaching resources like *The British Library's* "Discovering Literature" pages. Even as Romantic literature occupies a central place in university syllabi, curating a representative set of ideas and texts continues to be a teaching challenge. Contemporary scholarship, an intellectual history of ideas and notable samples of writing all jostle for space in a single course over a two- or three-year-long programme in English literature. Important considerations like cultural and linguistic diversity in contexts of teaching and interpreting Romantic literature may often be sidelined amidst anxieties over featuring the most representative texts from any period.[3] While this book certainly possesses greater bandwidth than a course and cannot be comprehensively unpacked in a classroom setting, it can still offer suggestions for modes of organising material. For instance, the sense of a whole period of writing cannot emerge without demonstrating the literary–historical work of uncovering how and why ideas and writers can be productively grouped together. How we group and pair writers in any age (The Lake Poets, Charles and Mary Lamb, Dorothy and William Wordsworth, William Wordsworth and Samuel Coleridge, William Blake and Thomas Paine, The Lunar Circle, etc.) can reveal a great deal about professional life, intellectual disagreements and successful collaborations. Individual chapter frameworks can also serve as a theme or question that encourages students to unpack an assumed homogeneity within groups in the period. Dorothy Wordsworth and John Clare featured together in a Romantic course can thus allow for the questioning of an assumed homogeneity in writers' social backgrounds, opportunities and social aspirations. This book also stimulates teachers and students to consider a broad range of texts that allow a sense of the period to emerge: bio-notes, letters, pamphlets and ephemera like advertisements in periodicals, political cartoons and satirical prints, to name a few. Terms like literature, authorship, criticism and literary value are as yet undefined in this period which teaches us additional lessons of not treating these as historically immutable. A detailed study of contexts, this book hopes to demonstrate, is not extraneous to the literature syllabus and classroom.

Works Cited

Ferber, Michael. *Romanticism: A Very Short Introduction*. Oxford University Press, 2010.

Watson, Alex and Laurence Williams, editors. *British Romanticism in Asia: The Reception, Translation and Transformation of Romantic Literature in India and East Asia*. Palgrave Macmillan, 2019.

Notes

1. Another likely association for the student of literature in India is names of authors labelled as such by biographers and teachers – William Wordsworth, Samuel Taylor Coleridge, Percy Shelley, John Keats, Alfred Tennyson and W. B. Yeats. These are among

the most anthologised poets in our school English syllabi and comprise most students' introduction to the idea of a Romantic writer.

2. See for instance Michael Ferber's *Romanticism: A Very Short Introduction* for a concise overview of uses (and abuses) of the term over the last two centuries. Ferber also introduces ways of seeing evidence for a conceptual use of "Romanticism" in companion arts like painting and music and in regions outside England. Also see Watson and Williams' *British Romanticism in Asia* which seeks to understand the term in a more global context.
3. As a student and teacher of the Romantics, I have found it very useful to make cultural contexts explicit in the classroom. Some interesting possibilities are the inclusion of material or assessments that can compare/extend arguments about Romanticism in England and other parts of the world.

ONE

Revolutions and Rights

Bliss was it in that dawn to be alive,
But to be young was very heaven! O times,
In which the meagre, stale, forbidding ways
Of custom, law, and statute, took at once
The attraction of a country in romance!

(Wordsworth, *The Prelude*, Book XI, lines 108–12)

The French Revolution is arguably the most significant of the sociopolitical events that characterises the period classified as "Romantic" in English literary studies. The event would change the political organisation of France at the time in radical ways and influence debates about political ideology in Europe and the rest of the world well into the present century. Eric Hobsbawm, speaking of the French Revolution's impact, said that it provided the "first great example, the concept and the vocabulary of nationalism" (73–74). In 1789, the French successfully dismantled their traditional monarchy and began the process of reimagining France as a new political entity – a "nation" in which all sovereignty was invested, rather than in a monarch. While the eighteenth century was marked by several revolutions,[1] the French example would have the most enduring influence on the political ideas and sensibilities of this period in England and the rest of Europe. The term "revolution" itself would now come to mean a radical transformation of the present and a complete break from tradition.

In eighteenth-century England, a burgeoning periodical industry and mass readership ensured immediacy in reporting the events in France locally and internationally, and a conducive terrain thus existed for the formation and exchange of ideas. Governments like those in England that continued with monarchical rule were naturally anxious about the periodical industry and news about the Revolution that it carried. As we will see, however, over the course of the late eighteenth and early nineteenth century, the English government and the country's educated elite would fear a French contamination of a growing reading public but would come to rely on this very public for counter-revolutionary measures. The spread of patriotic and royalist zeal, and the recruitment of citizens in the eventual war against France would not have been possible without the structures for sharing and engaging with ideas that had developed in England at this time. What is significant for us in the context of literary studies is that writing and reading were particularly contentious activities in this period. Propaganda and pamphlets arguing for and against particular modes of governance, for instance, were among the most widely circulated and most severely censured forms of literary output in this period. This unique political climate, characterised by the French Revolution, resulted in the close association in this period between writing and rebellion, and the individual and social transformation, that are now seen as some of the core features of Romantic literature.

The Revolution in France

The series of events constituting the French Revolution are by now iconic. France was characterised by acute socioeconomic inequality in the eighteenth century and in the years preceding the Revolution, and reforms to address this had failed in the face of an entrenched system of absolute monarchy. Absolute monarchy manifested through various measures to curb the nobility's political and economic power, pushing this group to rely more heavily on their estates for income. Therefore, nearly every man in possession of an estate would look to enforcing feudal privileges of exacting money from the peasants (the landless majority in France) in the absence of any other source of substantial revenue. Having to spend nearly all of their meagre income on taxes, feudal dues and expensive grain, the situation of the peasants at this time was deplorable. To add to this existing socioeconomic conflict, a nearly bankrupt monarchy supported the American War of Independence against England, thereby pushing the country into further debt. This was the state amidst which the French Revolution began, with the first event comprising the aristocrats' attempted takeover of the monarchy. The aristocrats' attempt at takeover was stalled on account of their miscalculation of the needs and demands of the Third Estate – a body that claimed to represent everyone in France who did not belong to the clergy or nobility. This Third Estate, comprising lawyers and businessmen in addition to peasants and labourers, was anxious to gain equal representation to match the voting powers of the clergy and nobility. They would eventually break away, anticipating the suppression of their rising power by the king and nobility, to form the National Assembly with the aim of recasting the Constitution. Given France's state of socioeconomic distress and the middle class' frustration with the entrenched powers of the nobility and clergy, support for the National Assembly grew even in the face of the king's displeasure.

This state of tension would find culmination in the iconic event now titled the "storming of the Bastille prison", which signalled the start of "revolution" in the sense of common people taking up arms against their rulers. On 14 July 1789, armed Paris citizenry forcibly entered and took control of the Bastille prison after overwhelming the royal soldiers and the governor stationed there. The governor was subsequently stabbed and beheaded by the armed crowds, his head mounted on a spike and paraded on the Paris streets, thus emboldening further acts of armed violence and successfully intimidating the already unpopular French rulers. Even though the Bastille was decommissioned at the time, it was still symbolic of the oppressive French monarchy and its takeover was thus hailed as a victory for the common people.[2]

The Impact in England: Printing, Reading and Writing

The storming of the Bastille and subsequent events would have a big impact in England, aided spectacularly by advances in print technology. As Stephen Prickett and Norbert Schürer have shown, the French Revolution was "textually" determined in England in the sense that narrative accounts of the storming of the Bastille prison (and later, the storming of the Versailles palace), which often deviated from what really took place, were the primary medium through which English men and women encountered this event. Romantic writers engaging with the meaning of the term revolution were thus rarely encountering events in France firsthand (although first-generation writers like Wordsworth and Helen Maria Williams would travel to France during the 1790s), but were definitely embedded in a print culture that was saturated with news, images, debates and information about the event.

The French Revolution is thus an undisputable contemporaneous context for understanding writing emerging in the Romantic period in England. For our purposes here, to establish the way the French Revolution formed an important intellectual context, it is necessary to pay close attention to the modes of circulation of information about this event. We will thus focus on what is perhaps as important an event as the Revolution itself: the revolution in *writing* that was responsible for translating, interpreting and mediating what was essentially an external event, for a local or national audience. It is useful to separate the sociopolitical events that comprise what is now termed the Revolution in France and the diversity of writing that enabled a growing literate population to interpret these events. For the writers coming of age at various points between the 1790s and the early nineteenth century therefore, the events comprising the Revolution have to be understood as their intellectual inheritance via the *writing* about these events that they no doubt encountered. Not only was literary significance measured at this time in terms of the number of copies of one's work published and circulated, but also in terms of its capacity to influence readers – measured through the number of responses occasioned and, in some cases, the degree of government scrutiny invited by these works and their writers. The French Revolution is thus an important intellectual context for Romanticism in England not only because it brought about irreversible change in the sociopolitical order but also because it prompted a change in the way writers and writing itself was perceived. It is also important to note at this stage that the most influential writings in this period that responded to the events in France are little-explored forms in the Romantic canon. Rather than poetry or the novel, pamphlets and speeches were among the more widely circulated instances of the "literary" in England in the immediate aftermath of the Revolution. It is to these forms that we will now turn, to examine the first significant English response to the revolution in France. Often described as the "pamphlet war", these published exchanges between important figures of the age on the French Revolution set the tone for understanding this event and its significance for the English public in the Romantic age.

The Pamphlet War

This famed pamphlet war was inaugurated on 4 November 1789, with a sermon delivered by Richard Price, a dissenting minister who was well known for supporting the cause of American independence. The sermon was delivered to the London Revolution Society, constituted to celebrate England's Glorious Revolution of 1688. The Glorious Revolution, also called a "bloodless" revolution by supporters, saw the overthrow of the Catholic James II by the Protestant William and Mary, made possible largely through parliamentary decrees. This event, thus, was interpreted as England's liberal political inheritance.

Price's sermon, published under the title *A Discourse on the Love of Our Country, delivered on Nov 4, 1789, at the meeting-house in the Old Jewry, to the Society for commemorating the Revolution in Great Britain*, highlighted what he felt were the principles the Glorious Revolution in England stood for. These were, as stated by Price and the reports published by the Revolution Society, first, "the right to liberty of conscience in religious matters", second, the right to resist the abuse of power, and third, the right to choose one's governors, to "cashier them for misconduct" and to be able to elect a government of one's own choosing (30). It was these principles, Price argued, that enabled the Glorious Revolution to be termed as such, given that it restored England to its "true" state, where civil authority is invested by the people and the sovereign is their "servant" rather than their divinely ordained master. Price, like other supporters of parliamentary reform, used the Glorious Revolution as a way of both celebrating Englishmen's native prerogative of political and religious liberty, and critiquing contemporary inadequacies in legislative representation and religious tolerance. The more controversial note in his sermon, however, had to do with parallels he made between the Glorious Revolution and the events inaugurating the French Revolution. Price addressed the London Revolution Society about four months after the formation of the National Assembly and the storming of the Bastille in France, and about a month after thousands of women stormed Versailles and coerced the royal family to return with them to Paris. This most recent event signalled the complete collapse of monarchy and resulted in the royal family's imprisonment. These events were, however, alluded to by Price in terms that referred more abstractly to the triumph of liberty rather than to the evaluation of the modes through which this was achieved: expressing gratitude over being alive at such an eventful time he said, "I have lived to see thirty millions of people, indignant and resolute, spurning at slavery, and demanding liberty with an irresistible voice, their King led in triumph and an arbitrary monarch surrendering himself to his subjects" (40). The end of his speech explicitly referenced three revolutions as "glorious", referring to the events of 1688 in England, the toppling of the monarchy in France, and the American colonies' independence. For Price, this comparison allowed him to remark that the present was "auspicious" for the "ardour of liberty" to "catch and spread", thus inviting his audience to share in and contribute to the revolutionary cause, now seen as unstoppable and almost certainly destined for success.

Price is thus a good representative of those in England who sounded a jubilant note in response to the revolution unfolding in France. His sense of hope for protecting "English" values of liberty and freedom and insistence on the present need for reform would be echoed by others in this period, notably by abolitionists and those seeking recognition for the rights of women. If Price represents the inspirational mood that the events in France evoked, then the first and most famous published response to his sermon, Edmund Burke's *Reflections on the Revolution in France* (1790), illustrates the cautious, conservative view. *Reflections*, like Price's sermon, aimed to produce a way of interpreting and understanding events in France and by extension, English character, its history and political principles.

In Burke's *Reflections* we also see the beginnings of the association of the term revolution and the overthrow of the monarchy in France becoming conflated with mob rule, violence and anarchy. So, rather than viewing the storming of Versailles as Price did, as an instance of the common people throwing off the shackles of oppression, Burke recounts this event in sensational detail to underscore the savagery that commoners could display. Burke's account of the storming of Versailles focuses on the shock, humiliation and fear of the royal family at being overwhelmed by an unruly mob. It makes the case that "all the unutterable abominations of the furies of hell in the abused shape of the vilest of women" showed no mercy to the royal family and their aides when they forcibly marched them back to Paris, leaving "scattered limbs and mutilated carcasses" in their wake (88). This, for Burke, was not something to be seen as a triumph but was rather a deplorable act that went against the civilised mores of inhabitants of all of Europe, and indicated the end of an age of chivalry. His criticism of Price, thus, took the form of recasting how English readers viewed the events that led to the overthrow of the monarchy in France over the first few months of the Revolution. Burke advocated revulsion and fear at these events where Price preached a sense of hope and the dawn of an age of liberty. This also fed into Burke's larger attempt in *Reflections* to break the associations Price made between the Glorious Revolution in England and the French Revolution.

In addition, Burke also questions in *Reflections*, the credibility of the French National Assembly in taking charge of restructuring their country's political system and declaring a Constitution that sought to do away with all its feudal socioeconomic structures. He raises suspicion about the rank and learning of the French National Assembly members and seeks to unseat Price's claim that peoples' "rights" to choose and remove their own governors is a natural inheritance. Not only did Burke wish his readers to see recent events in France as anomalous and unnatural, he also wanted to underscore how they represented a new and dangerous order of things, founded on no credible political tradition. The "new conquering empire of light and reason", for Burke, sought to destroy the traditional, conventional order of determining governance through inheritance, patronage and learning, and was replacing "natural protectors and guardians" with a "swinish multitude".

Burke's arguments against Price played an important role in setting the tone for how meanings of the term revolution were discussed in this period. Price and other supporters of the French overthrow of monarchy were greatly influenced by Rousseau's social contract theory which argued for a political society being constituted only via a social pact that allowed its members to freely choose the mode of governance they would offer their allegiance to. Burke sought to revise this idea of a social contract in *Reflections* by stating that the partnership that exists between a state and its citizens cannot be seen as temporary but "becomes a partnership not only between those who are living, but between those who are living, those who are dead, and those who are to be born". He insists, thus, on an "eternal" contract that precedes and outlasts individuals. Burke clearly situates the individual as subordinate to this contract, further underscoring the events in France as an illustration of the "antagonist world of madness, discord, vice, confusion and unavailing sorrow" that will no doubt follow the breaking of submission to a pre-existing mode of governance. Burke's articulation of the individual as essentially evil and requiring inherited social safeguards is an important context for this period. Several of the responses to *Reflections* rallied against this definition of the individual and what was seen as a disregard for the oppressive and inhuman conditions created by the same long-standing modes of government Burke celebrated. Burke's description of the Parisian mobs as a "swinish multitude" struck the supporters of the French Revolution in England as wilful dehumanisation of the poor in order to elicit sympathy for their oppressors.

Among the most famous responses to Burke is Thomas Paine's *Rights of Man Part I* (1791), in part because of its considerably wide circulation (which provoked the English government to ban the work in 1792) and also for its clear articulation of the ideals of revolutionary reform.[3] Paine entered the English debate over the meaning and consequences of the French Revolution as an outsider, having migrated to America in 1774, then returning briefly to England in 1789, before fleeing to France to live there after he was charged with sedition and issued a death sentence by the English government in 1792. Paine's *Rights of Man* effectively broke the association built by Price and later by Burke between England's Glorious Revolution and the French Revolution by reforming the meaning so far associated with the idea of a revolution itself. For Paine, earlier revolutions in England and other revolutions around the world differed from the case of the American and French Revolutions because they were fought against tyrannical "individuals" who became an enemy to those that opposed them. These other revolutions were thus characterised by the removal only of one tyrannical *individual* but a return, nevertheless, to the earlier forms or *practices* of government. Paine here offers a distinction, one that he argues Burke did not understand, between a despotic person and a despotic form of government, which is how he characterises the state of France even prior to the tenure of the present king.

The people in France and America before this, according to Paine, revolted against the "despotic principles of the government" rather than against individuals, as Burke had argued about the French Revolution and Price had argued about the Glorious Revolution. Moreover, this kind of revolt was necessary since the despotic state apparatuses had become "too deeply rooted to be removed, and the Augean stable of parasites and plunderers too abominably filthy to be cleaned, by anything short of a complete and universal revolution" (97). Thus, over the course of this early English response to the French Revolution, the term revolution itself would undergo a transformation: now it no longer merely signified the gradual return to a fixed point but a sudden overturning and uprooting – a complete transformation or clean break from the past. This mode of thinking about revolution as achieving a completely "new" state and fully breaking from the past, perceiving that there is little to salvage in it, would have an enormous influence on the English Romantics.

Mary Wollstonecraft too, like Paine, would extend Price's argument that the revolution in France portended the necessity and imminence of political liberty, discussed so far in England's public sphere as being characterised by the right to choose and interrogate the mode of governance people were subjected to. In addition, the pamphlet war in England was by now establishing certain rhetorical cornerstones in the debate around personal and political liberty that was now an inevitable consequence of the ubiquitous presence of the events in France in various English media. The storming of the Bastille, for instance, was widely reported and visually illustrated in English periodicals at the time and dramatised many times, generally in a positive light, on the English stage (Schürer, 2005). The pamphlet war, along with the other mediations of this event in the English public sphere, would begin a discussion over people's rights that now characterised writing in this period but, in many ways, continues even today.

Some recurring topics in the discussion we have seen so far include, for instance, considerations about what liberty meant for Englishmen at a time when their neighbours had so recently rebelliously overthrown their government and how their own modes of governance and history of rebellions compared with those of France. Recent events in France and their destruction of traditional symbols of power like a palace and a state prison had repercussions on how individuals viewed their place in the world: did tradition hold any sanctity at all, and if not, how does any group set about building a radically new structure in the absence of a precedent? Did it follow from France's example that the individual, whether learned or not, hereditarily or professionally enabled or not, had a say in how he/she should be governed? England, at this time, was situated against the backdrop of nations being formed and restructured (America, France and even rebellious colonies like Haiti),[4] and the very basis of the creation of new political entities and the individual's place in it were now taking centre stage in the pamphlet war we are following. The writers of these texts questioned the very foundations of an individual's social status: were all men equal? Did they deserve an equal share in property, especially land? Did they have a right to participate in interpreting the political events of the time? Were those who governed them different from them (to be determined through heredity) or to be represented by and answerable to those that were like them? Burke, in his *Reflections* for instance, as a statesman and member of the landed gentry, repeatedly questioned Price's credibility and authority on matters of politics on account of his being a preacher.

Mary Wollstonecraft's *A Vindication of the Rights of Men* (1790) sought to bring back much of the inspired and hopeful mood of Price's sermon and vitiate Burke's alarmist response to the idea of revolution and change. She responds to Burke's critique of Price's discussion of political matters in the "pulpit" with the assertion that the occasion for delivering the sermon, the commemoration of England's own Glorious Revolution, was reason enough to invite deliberation on the nature and necessity of revolution in the present. *A Vindication* doesn't merely return to comparisons between England's past and France's present revolutions but draws attention to England's current sociopolitical problems, thereby questioning the efficacy and fruits of the established tradition that Burke celebrated. For instance, Wollstonecraft draws attention to the prevailing legal custom in England of awarding the death penalty for petty crimes like killing deer on the property of the rich. English law, Wollstonecraft suggests, sees poor men as being of lower value than the game and livestock owned by the rich. She returns repeatedly to the question of prevailing inequality in England in the ownership of land and distribution of wealth, privilege and education, to demonstrate the necessity of reform in tradition rather than its unquestioning celebration.

Another striking example of prevailing socioeconomic inequality and oppression explored in *A Vindication* is that of the family. Wollstonecraft critiques the prevailing violations of personal liberty carried out within the sanctified institution of the family: the imprisonment of children to ensure the perpetuation of noble lineage through marriage, the exiling and diverting of younger children to prevent their encroachment on the eldest's share of the estate. For Wollstonecraft, filial relationships ranked among the many publicly venerated traditions in England that were in serious need of reform. Other traditions critiqued in *A Vindication* that deserve mention are the slave trade and the case of caste oppression. In response to Burke's insistence that the ideals of liberty were eternal and could not and need not be interfered with by the individual, Wollstonecraft presented the case of the slave trade in Britain and caste-based occupations in India. The slave trade in England and the caste system in India, she argued, were long-standing traditions and legally protected but inhuman nevertheless. She terms the slave trade an "abominable mischief" that goes against the common principles of humanity and Christianity – several reformers over the course of this period would appeal for the abolition of slavery on the grounds that it was unchristian. Arguing for the emancipation of slaves by appealing to the Christian values of the English permitted slaves to be viewed as "men" who were very much privy to the tradition of political liberty and rights that Price and Burke had alluded to.

Having made the case that there are a class of individuals in England, like in France – comprising slaves, the urban poor and peasants – who are not viewed as human, or as possessing rights, Wollstonecraft further seeks to establish that it is precisely this class that stands to gain from revolution and reform. For Wollstonecraft, arguments like Burke's that appealed to a veneration of monarchical patronage and endowments, especially as they related to property, only stood to benefit the rich with little proof that things would change. "Health can only be secured by temperance"; she writes, "but is it easy to persuade a man to live on plain food even to recover his health, who has been accustomed to fare sumptuously every day? Can a man relish the simple food of friendship, who has been habitually pampered by flattery?" (42). And later, supporting the French Revolutionary goals of redistributing property, especially that amassed by the Church, she asks, "Can posterity be injured by individuals losing the chance of obtaining great wealth, without meriting it, by its being diverted from a narrow channel, and disembogued into the sea that affords clouds to water all the land?" (49). Wollstonecraft thus brings to this pamphlet war, following the start of the French Revolution, a stark portrayal of the necessity for reform not only abroad but at home in England too.

As is clear in the case of the pamphlet wars, the immediate English literary response to the events of the French Revolution, a new notion of what it meant to be an individual would emerge in the wake of an older form of governance losing support. Men" were now defined as having rights that were guaranteed to them at birth and the most significant of these was the right to "choose" their mode and agents of governance. We can now move on to other key themes in English Romantic literature that emerged in response to the sociopolitical upheaval characteristic of the revolutionary context, namely, anxieties about the future that manifested as the imagining of utopias or a Biblical Armageddon. In addition, revolution would become a master trope through which to evaluate social and political realities in the present in England. The French Revolution would also become a source of disillusionment for several Romantic writers as it would take an increasingly violent turn and the ideals it represented would appear to them as being far from achievable. The next section explores these and other themes more closely.

A Revolutionary Climate in England

English writing in the immediate context of the French Revolution, thus, not only engaged with the meaning and impact of the events of the Revolution but also renewed interest in issues of socioeconomic inequality and the need for reform in England. William Blake, in his *Songs of Innocence and Experience* (1794), paints a grim picture of London at the time. In his poem "The Chimney Sweeper", for instance, Blake responds to the cruel practice prevalent at the time in England, of employing children, sometimes as young as six years old, to clean soot from chimneys. These children were sold to the chimney sweeping trade by their families to escape extreme poverty and starvation. The conditions in which they worked and lived were deplorable and several of them would develop cancer from soot exposure. While efforts were made to regulate the trade in 1788 through a Chimney Sweepers Act, to fix the minimum age of apprenticeship at eight, to improve living conditions and limit working hours, it did not come to pass. Blake shows his awareness of the inhuman conditions under which the chimney sweep's child apprentices laboured in both versions of "The Chimney Sweeper".[5] In the first poem, from the *Songs of Innocence*, the child chimney sweep speaks directly to the reader to say that his father "sold me while yet my tongue could scarcely cry weep, weep, weep, weep" (Eaves et al., "Songs of Innocence and Experience [Composed 1789, 1794]"). Linda Freedman suggests that Blake employs a poetic strategy to show us that the words "weep" and "sweep" can barely be differentiated in terms of sound and the child too, is unable to differentiate between them. Thus, he is able to show how the child's limited language makes him accept great tragedy as a routine everyday circumstance.

This version of the poem goes on to employ irony to show how the young chimney sweeps believe in the Christian idea of heaven – a paradise they will attain upon their death as a reward for work done in this life, a place where they will be free from their earthly burdens. On the other hand, the child narrator in "The Chimney Sweeper" from *The Songs of Experience* uses language very consciously to refer to himself as a "little black thing", underscoring how society views him as a commodity. He recognises the word "weep" as one of "woe" and goes on to criticise his parents for being unable to see the truth of his material circumstances (his trade that he calls the "clothes of death") because he is smiling. However, they are committed, he says, to the truth of something they have no material proof of – the Church and its teachings. "God and his priest and King", he says, "make up a heaven of our misery" (Eaves et al.). The lens of "experience" has taught the child narrator of this version of "The Chimney Sweeper" that organised religion tells the lie of an equal share in paradise for all while ignoring the truth of injustices and inequalities of daily life. Blake's poem "London" similarly portrays the city as one in which man lives in a never-ending cycle of misery – the very streets and even the Thames are "chartered", or in other words, owned and curbed by institutions that oppress their subjects and breed misery.

Blake's *Marriage of Heaven and Hell* (1790) perhaps bears the most direct reference to the American and French Revolutions and sets out the impact of these for England. The work itself is a criticism of organised religion and seeks to show the importance of the individual rather than the institutions of the Church, the Pope and religious texts, specifically the Bible. In the final section of this work titled "A Song of Liberty", Blake symbolises revolution as an imminent birth that was heard "over all the Earth" in the form of the "Eternal Female's" groan. The other auguries of this event are the "rending" of the Bastille in France and a suggestion to Spain and Rome to also bring down the Roman Catholic Church and papal authority. What follows in "A Song of Liberty" is a mythical narrative that pits Urizen (Blake's creation who symbolises an oppressive ruler) against Orc (the character who is the spirit of revolution, born of the Eternal Female). Orc eventually triumphs by stamping Urizen's "stony law" (a reference to the ten commandments in the Bible that were inscribed on stone tablets and were thus seen as "set in stone" or unchanging) to dust, thus bringing about a new age where the Empire would end and rulers of the *ancien régime*, represented here as the lion and the wolf, would cease to be. Blake's many allusions to Biblical prophecies (in works like *The French Revolution* [1791] and *America: A Prophecy* [1793], for instance) and his use of these to represent American independence and the storming of the Bastille in France as preordained events meant to liberate humankind is another major theme in early Romantic writing in the context of the Revolution. Like Richard Price's sermon that viewed the events in France as preordained and unstoppable, Blake's vision of revolution in his *Marriage of Heaven and Hell* is also explicitly theological in its imagination of an apocalyptic event that would destroy the existing world order to usher in a new one.

In addition to the theological ideas attached to the French Revolution inaugurating a prophesied return to paradise, several writers would also turn to the imagining of social–political utopias, perhaps illustrated best by William Godwin's *Enquiry Concerning Political Justice* (1793). This text and its imagination of personal liberty and social equality would remain a source of inspiration for a subsequent generation of writers who would no longer see the French Revolution as holding immense promise, but rather as having been unable to live up to its ideals. In his *Enquiry*, Godwin presents man as "perfectible" or being inclined to "perpetual improvement" and most significantly, as needing to break free from norms and conventions that only serve to stifle reason. Such an ambitious notion of the individual, one for whom even the widely practised cooperation and cohabitation necessitated by marriage was seen as an unnecessary curtailing of individual liberty, has been identified as a characteristic trait of writing classified as Romantic. *Enquiry* imagines equal distribution of property, sound individual reason suited to the circumstance, and overcoming socially governed rules that were meant for all and were thus suitable for none as the culmination of the spirit of revolutionary times in which it was composed. For Godwin, the unequal distribution of wealth and socially sanctioned traditions like marriage were a cause for the individual's immense investment of time in accumulating property, titles and other external accomplishments, at the expense of cultivating personal judgement and confidence in one's own abilities. Godwin here makes an interesting separation, just like Blake, between the institution (often both writers speak of social institutions whose workings are evident in behaviour, beliefs and attitudes as much as laws and convention), that is universal and the individual, whose circumstances are at odds with the norms of the world he/she lives in.

It is interesting to note here that the writings that comprise the English response to the French and American Revolution were not always directly engaging with the widely publicised political events of the 1790s alone but were also interpreting and representing this event, investing it with a great richness of meaning that later writers would inherit. Godwin's espousal of shared property as a necessary social reform following the Revolution, for instance, would go on to inspire young Coleridge and Robert Southey to plan the setting up of a utopian community governed by egalitarian principles in America that they would call Pantisocracy. Describing the "idea" of the place in his sonnet "On the Prospect of Establishing a Pantisocracy in America" (1826), Coleridge writes that here,

> Where dawns, with hope serene, a brighter day
> Than e'er saw Albion in her happiest times,
> With mental eye exulting now explore,
> And soon with kindred minds shall haste to enjoy
> (Free from the ills which here our peace destroy)
> Content and Bliss on Transatlantic shore. (lines 9–14)

Coleridge clearly sees this utopian society as not belonging in England, but rather on "Transatlantic" shore. In addition, with the phrase "mental eye exulting", Coleridge signals at yet another representation of the revolutionary age that would be seen as characteristic of Romantic writing – the idea of a conscious human will that could lend shape to external events.

Coleridge and Southey's plans for their utopian community had to be abandoned, but William Wordsworth was able to join his countrymen on a tour of revolutionary France in 1790. Like Helen Maria Williams, Wordsworth was able to witness the anniversary of the fall of the Bastille prison. Both these poets record the joy and promise posed by this event for them and French citizens. Williams records in her *Letters from France*, for instance, a range of emotional responses to the memory of the start of the Revolution:

> How am I to paint the impetuous feelings of that immense, that exulting multitude? Half a million of people assembled at a spectacle, which furnished every image that can elevate the mind of man; which connected the enthusiasm of moral sentiment with the solemn pomp of religious ceremonies; which addressed itself at once to the imagination, the understanding and the heart. (6)

Williams repeatedly provides vivid details about her time in Paris in her *Letters*, with a record of the *effects* produced on her and other Parisians' minds and emotional states. Wordsworth records in Book IX of his autobiographical *The Prelude* that upon seeing a poor, hungry girl in his time in France he believed, together with his companion, that it was against this poverty that the Revolution was being waged. Speaking of a "spirit" that had now taken over "abroad", whose force could not have been curbed, Wordsworth seeks to counter the pain he feels at seeing the deprived girl with a vision of what the Revolution will soon achieve:

> All institutes for ever blotted out
> That legalized exclusion, empty pomp
> Abolish'd, sensual state and cruel power
> Whether by edict of the one or few,
> And finally, as sum and crown of all,
> Should see the People having a strong hand

In making their own Laws, whence better days
To all mankind. (Book IX, lines 525–32)

Here again, a powerful image of the revolutionary spirit is evoked, one that is almost biblical in the retribution it seeks to bring for the sins of traditional institutions like monarchy and feudalism.

Wordsworth also relies, like Coleridge, on the poetic form, to remind his readers that revolution as a complete transformation can also manifest in writing and expression. Thus, the revolutionary spirit, for Romantic writers, also demanded a new mode of expression. Wordsworth's often-quoted line about the emotions evoked by the Revolution is perhaps a very characteristic romantic mode of addressing or responding to one of the biggest events of the age: he says, "Bliss was it in that dawn to be alive, but to be young was very heaven" (Book XI, lines 108–09). Wordsworth's autobiographical poem, though published in a comprehensive version only posthumously in 1850, is a good contemporary account of the impression made on the Romantics by the revolutionary time of the late eighteenth century.[6] Wordsworth tells us about his most formative influences in this poem and this quote about the Revolution encapsulates ideas that later writers would return to: first, that the Revolution was synonymous with hope; and second, that when remembered in retrospect, the Revolution could be compared with youth, in the sense of innocence and idealism.

Counter-revolution in England

It is significant that Wordsworth associates the start of the Revolution with his youth – while it was an accurate record of his age when he visited France and was swayed by revolutionary fervour, it should also serve as a reminder that along with other young French and English citizens, he would not see this fervour last. The enthusiastic support of and the millennial hope associated with the early years of the French Revolution would soon wane when it turned increasingly violent. By 1790, one of the most radical groups from France's National Convention, the Jacobins, had risen to power and by 1791, the royal family had been imprisoned. Between 1792 and 1794, amid fears of counter-revolution from both within and outside the country, France would declare war on Britain, publicly execute their king and queen and thousands of prisoners suspected to be supporters of monarchy and counter-revolutionary measures, and declare themselves a republic. This period would come to earn the title of the Reign of Terror, symbolising the violent extremes to which the young republic would go to secure sociopolitical change.

For Romantic poets such as Coleridge, Wordsworth and Williams who encountered the promise of the Revolution in its early years, its more violent phase necessitated a more tempered response. The 1790s in England was also a time that witnessed a growing anti-revolutionary activism that made it dangerous for a writer to declare publicly their support towards the French cause. It would be useful here to offer a brief account of what constituted radicalism or revolutionary activity in England at this time. Religious dissenters like Richard Price, as we have seen in reference to the pamphlet war, supported the French Revolution as heralding the biblical prophecy of a soon-to-come paradise. In addition to dissenters, radical publishers and booksellers were instrumental in the printing and circulation of pro-revolutionary works like Paine's *Rights of Man*, both parts of which sold 200,000 copies within a year of their publication. Perhaps the most significant radical activity was carried out in what were called "corresponding societies", a term for organisations that were committed to parliamentary reforms, and to this end would correspond with other politically like-minded organisations both within and outside the country. Membership in these societies, the most well-known one being the London Corresponding Society,[7] was governed by modest fees, thus enabling participation from across the social strata, unlike the more elite Society for Constitutional Information. Price delivered his *A Discourse on the Love of Our Country* (1789), for instance, to the London Revolution Society, which chiefly comprised dissenters and was in active correspondence with members of the newly formed National Assembly in France in the early years of the Revolution. Debating societies, though not solely dedicated to the discussion of politics, were also an important forum where Englishmen, and later women, from across classes came together to discuss topics of contemporary relevance. These societies were an important mode through which key political ideas at the time could spread and be interpreted by a diverse array of people.

To add to this, the Romantic period saw a dramatic rise in the volume of cheap street literature, taking the form of chapbooks, broadsides and broadsheets, and cheap editions of works by radical authors that fed a growing literate lower-class readership with a critique of their social and political superiors.[8] Protestant dissenters who argued for religious and political reform in England, for instance, showed their support of the French by celebrating the anniversary of the fall of the Bastille prison. This sparked a protest by "Church and King" supporters who engaged in a violent three-day riot, which destroyed several dissenters' chapels and homes, including the home of the scientist Joseph Priestley. Anna Laetitia Barbauld would write in her poem "To Dr Priestley, Dec. 29, 1792",

> To thee, the slander of a passing age
> imports not. Scenes like these hold little space
> In his large mind, whose ample stretch of thought
> Grasps future periods. (lines 13–16)

Speaking of the turbulence of the times as momentary when compared with the ideals of the reformist that would last for posterity, Barbauld here articulates the need to keep up the commitment to reform even in the face of violent retaliation. In addition to the threat of violence from loyalist supporters, the English government too would act against growing radicalism and extra-parliamentary agitation for reform. A Royal Proclamation was passed against "seditious writings and publications", whose impact is best represented by the case of *Rights of Man*. Paine was charged with seditious libel and *Rights of Man* banned on the grounds that its cheap price and extensive circulation is what spoke to its dangerous quality. Marilyn Butler (1981), for instance, demonstrates how contemporary critics would compare Wordsworth and Coleridge's *Lyrical Ballads* to Paine's *Rights of Man* to illustrate the work's subversive potential. While the popular view held even today is that *Lyrical Ballads* inaugurated a new aesthetic (a simple style) and themes (rustic life and characters) that allowed Romantic literature to be set off from earlier eighteenth-century writing, Butler instead urges us to consider the longer history of the ballad form. Rather than credit the reanimation of this older form with revolutionary potential, Butler focuses her attention on its intended audience. Against the backdrop of the French Revolution, Wordsworth's claims in his Preface to these poems – to a simplicity of style and a focus on rural characters – is perceived by contemporary critics as a threatening transfer of sovereignty to the masses.

Wordsworth and Williams were among the English writers who were torn between complex affiliations they had built as citizens of the world: Williams would say of witnessing the Bastille Day celebrations in France, for instance, that "this was not a time in which the distinctions of country were remembered" (Letter II, 11). On his visit to France in 1791, Wordsworth would meet and fall in love with Annette Vallon, a French woman from a royalist family. Annette and Wordsworth's daughter Anne-Caroline was born in 1792, soon after Wordsworth left France for England to prepare for his family to live with him there. Louis XVI's execution and the declaration of war between both countries prevented Wordsworth from going back to his family. Williams on the other hand, would continue to live and report on events unfolding in France and was even imprisoned for six months during the Terror. Her commitment to the ideals established early in the Revolution would, however, remain strong. For English Romantic writers witnessing the many upheavals following the start of the revolution in France, support of revolutionary ideals meant a growing complexity of affiliations and loyalties. Coleridge, for instance, in his *Conciones ad Populum* (1795) describes the terror in France as a warning to Britain. "French freedom is the Beacon", he writes, "which while it guides to Equality, should shew us the Dangers that throng the road" (684).

Williams too, while recording her growing anguish at the bloody turn the Revolution had taken in France, nevertheless questions whether England's Glorious Revolution can be termed "bloodless" in contrast. She contends that the Jacobite uprisings of 1715 and 1745 against the overthrow of the Stuart dynasty by the British government were a product of the Glorious Revolution and says that "no people ever traveled to a temple of Liberty by a path strewed with roses; nor has established tyranny ever yielded to reason and justice, till after a severe struggle" (Mellor and Matlak, 527). In her letters documenting the bloody phase of the French Revolution, Williams thus implores her English readers to reconsider their country's perceived superiority over the French struggle to achieve revolutionary ideals. She was a harsh critic of the public executions and the lack of consideration for the human rights of those executed, including King Louis XVI. However, like Coleridge, she too upholds the *ideals* of the revolutionary cause and seeks to separate this from its *practice* at the time in France.

Similarly, in Book X of *The Prelude*, Wordsworth remembers that the early years of the French Revolution made the "stale" and "forbidding" modes of traditional governance take on the "attraction of a Country in Romance". "The whole earth" to him seemed to wear "promise" and persons of every temper would find this a source of happiness. He makes a further comparison between this time and "an inheritance new-fallen", which a man takes pleasure and entitlement in moulding to his liking. The feeling of hope in the early years of the Revolution, Wordsworth suggests, had to do with the possibilities associated with the new-fallen inheritance of rights and moulding it to one's needs. As documentation of Wordsworth's life, *The Prelude* is able to use the power of hindsight to analyse how the significance of the Revolution changes over the late eighteenth and early nineteenth centuries. In Book XI, Wordsworth frames the decline of political ideals in France (from the mass beheadings under the reign of Robespierre to the coronation of Napoleon as Emperor in 1804) as a turning point in his career as a poet. He says,

> But when events
> brought less encouragement, and unto these
> The immediate proof of principles no more
> Could be entrusted, while the events themselves,
> Worn out in greatness, stripped of novelty,
> Less occupied the mind, and sentiments
> Could through my understanding's natural growth
> No longer keep their ground, by faith maintained
> Of inward consciousness, and hope that laid
> Her hand upon her object–evidence
> Safer, of universal application, such
> As could not be impeached, was sought elsewhere. (lines 194–205)

The universal application of the political ideal symbolised by France throwing off monarchical rule was now no longer tenable and Wordsworth records losing faith in these "outward accidents" that turned him away from "Nature's way" (Book XI, lines 290–91). Towards the end of Book XI, Wordsworth credits his sister Dorothy with reminding him of his "office" as a "Poet" who is the "willing audience" of "Nature's self". Nature thus replaces the no longer useful (or universally applicable) ideals of the Revolution and upholds him "through the later sinkings of this cause" (line 354). The progress and decline of revolutionary ideals at the turn of the century, thus, offers a forceful and apt lens for Wordsworth to frame his own intellectual journey as a poet from youth to maturity. For English Romantic writers responding to the Revolution at this time, it was difficult to sacrifice the ideals of liberty and equality they had celebrated together with the French only a short while ago, as they witnessed first-hand the several abuses of the newly established powers in that country.

Following the execution of Louis XVI and the declaration of war with France, the English government began resorting to several repressive methods to control radicalism at home. This was a response to fears that a French invasion was imminent and would be supported by radicals and reformers in England. The most significant move made by the English government against a perceived threat of revolution was arrests of prominent radical leaders, including Thomas Hardy, John Horne Tooke and John Thelwall on suspicion of treason. Further, habeas corpus was suspended, allowing the government to detain those arrested on suspicion of seditious and revolutionary activity without trial. Proceedings against the arrested leaders, titled the Treason Trials sparked substantial public interest and thus served to highlight the government's tightening control over popular political debate. In 1795, the government would pass the Treasonable Practices Act, amending the conditions under which the Treason Act would apply, and the Seditious Meetings Act which sought to limit the numbers of people who could attend public meetings. Subsequent legislations would be passed in the early nineteenth century, imposing additional taxes on periodical publications and severe punishments for publishers convicted of libel twice.

Hannah More's *Village Politics* (1792) and her *Cheap Repository Tracts* which circulated between 1795 and 1798, are another mode through which radical thought was challenged in England. More's writings formed a part of loyalist propaganda which utilised popular forms of street literature like ballads to counter the revolutionary zeal preached by the cheap and widely circulating radical writing like Paine's *Rights of Man*. More's *Village Politics* is "addressed to all the mechanics, journeymen, and day labourers, in Great Britain" and takes the form of an imagined dialogue between Jack Anvil, a blacksmith, and Tom Hod, a mason. While Jack is in favour of maintaining the existing social structure, Tom has recently read Paine's *Rights of Man* and is strongly advocating constitutional reform, equality and following the way of the French in establishing a new social and political order. Through the dialogue, More illustrates what she perceives as gaps in the way Tom has interpreted Paine and his inability to understand the full implications of following in the manner of the French. Jack uses the analogy of an old English castle to convince Tom of the folly of destroying the old to bring in the new. The castle represents for Jack, tradition, foundation, and time invested by ancestors – to bring it down to erect something that would "go up in a day" is, for him, sheer folly. More, thus, makes the same argument as Burke in his *Reflections* but utilises a popular form and uses the voices of the working class to achieve a larger readership. Jack says of Tom's desire to see England follow France's example in seeking to liberate her people: "Why we've got it man! We've no race to run! We're there already! Our constitution is no more like what the French one was, than a mug of our Taunton beer is like a platter of their soup-maigre".

It is interesting to note here that More's text denies any similarities between France and England, while simultaneously inviting her readers to celebrate their own citizenship in a land that has already achieved liberty. The Revolution's violent turn in France as well as the declaration of war between the two countries resulted in the rise of patriotism and literature that roused nationalistic sentiment as another mode of repressing radicalism. More's *Tracts* would sell over two million copies within a year of their first circulation and espoused ideals similar to those found in *Village Politics*. Both texts encourage readers to be content with what they have, to participate industriously in their work, to view their individual needs and wants as subservient to the maintenance of law and order and the general good. Most importantly, these texts aim to convince readers that rioting is more likely to compound their difficulties (famine and food shortages as a result of war with France) rather than do them any good. In "The Riot; or Half a Loaf is Better Than No Bread" (1795), for instance, Tom Hod the mason returns to say, "A dinner of herbs, says the wise man, with quiet, Is better than beef amid discord and riot" (218).

James Gillray is another prominent figure of counter-revolution in England, known for his scathing cartoon caricatures of political figures and contemporary events. For instance, prints like *Bonaparte, 48 Hours After Landing* (1803) and *Maniac Raving's-or-Little Boney in a Strong Fit* (1803) use the form of the satiric political cartoon to mitigate the fear of a French invasion led by Napoleon. These prints explicitly reference the power of newspapers in widely disseminating an unflattering and almost comical image of Napoleon – he appears diminutive in stature (*Bonaparte, 48 Hours After Landing* features him in the form of a decapitated head carried at the end of a yeoman's pitchfork), agitated over his portrayal in English media and burdened by his imperial agenda. Gillray is also an interesting figure among the Romantic writers and artists of the revolutionary years because his political stance is difficult to determine. Compared to More and Burke's partisan affiliations, Gillray's satires spare neither the French nor the English and present a pessimistic vision of England emerging from the loss of revolutionary idealism, the threat of war and rising state repression. His *French Liberty/English Slavery* (1792), for instance, shows pronouncements describing the "milk and honey of liberty" in France and the "oppression by taxes" faced in England to be hollow by having the words spoken by an impoverished French republican and a wealthy, obese Englishman, respectively. His *The Plumb Pudding in Danger* (1805) similarly casts Napoleon and William Pitt as equally charged by the ambition for geopolitical control. In this famous print, both leaders' eyes hungrily appraise a globe in the form of a plum pudding that they are both carving. Revolution, war and ensuing violence and xenophobia, for Gillray, gave rise to base instincts in the leaders and citizens of both countries, and this inward ugliness in human temperament was revealed in many of his representations of contemporary events.

Wars and Nationalism

The English government's actions to curtail revolutionary ideas at home, together with growing fears of an imminent invasion following the declaration of war with France would contribute to a growing Francophobia over the latter half of the eighteenth century. It was now necessary to break the association built earlier between the two countries' pursuit of liberty and the ideals set up in the early years of the Revolution. English writers would now begin to distance themselves from France's example of liberating its people, all the while struggling to articulate how their own country should come to be identified. Several years of war with France would ensue following the execution of King Louis XVI, only to be briefly halted by the Treaty of Amiens in 1802. Resuming war in 1803, followed by the meteoric rise of Napoleon, his coronation as Emperor and his military takeover of almost all of Europe would give rise to periodic fears of invasion in England, until Napoleon's defeat in 1815. Given France's larger territory, greater population and superior military force, England's fears about France's capacity to invade were very real. In such a climate, addressing a universal, or even international audience in the style employed by Wordsworth in the *Lyrical Ballads* and writers earlier in the eighteenth century, was fraught and more partisan sentiments were favoured in literary works. England would also discover that the human and financial costs of such a sustained war effort were very high and would cause a major strain on the country's resources. The several years of war in the late eighteenth and early nineteenth centuries would thus provide the impetus for England to define and interpret what it meant to be a nation, especially at a time when one was at war with another newly formed republic with whom several Englishmen had belatedly felt a close kinship. Kinship ties to a single national entity had to be built among a diverse population and territory that still held strong commitments to local and regional politics at the time. These ties were also crucial to tackle the financial and recruitment challenges of the war. This period in Britain was thus characterised by writing which was patriotic but often also sceptical about war efforts.

Coleridge's "Fears in Solitude" (1798), composed to reflect the mood in the village of Stowey following news that the French planned to invade the English coast via a landing there, criticises the effects of war while petitioning readers to think of themselves as English in very specific ways. Following a detailed evocation of the Stowey landscape, Coleridge lists for the reader the many wrongs and injustices people from "east to west" battle over. The English, secure in their home, turn a blind eye to these. In the same way, he argues, those who support the war effort without actually seeing its material reality (several patriotic celebrations and commemorations of soldiers and victories were a prominent feature of rural England at the time), are blind to the long-term consequences of war. He writes,

> We, this whole people, have been clamorous
> For war and bloodshed; animating sports,
> The which we pay for as a thing to talk of,
> Spectators and not combatants! (lines 91–94)

At the same time, Coleridge hopes that the English will triumph over their "impious foe" and his description of English and

French opposition is interesting in the light of patriotism and difference:

> Father and God! O spare us yet a while!
> O let not English women drag their flight
> Fainting beneath the burden of their babes,
> Of the sweet infants, that but yesterday
> Laugh'd at the breast! Sons, brothers, husbands, all
> Who ever gaz'd with fondness on the forms,
> Which grew up with you round the same fire side,
> And all who ever heard the sabbath bells
> Without the infidel's scorn, make yourselves pure! (lines 129–37)

The emphasis on filial and local allegiances is interesting to note here, as they illustrate the reliance on these bonds during wartime. A strong local community was what would prove to be a good defence of Britain's island borders when a French invasion seemed imminent.

Moreover, Coleridge emphasises the national character of what needs to be protected at such a time by identifying English women and their children as being under threat. The "Sabbath bells" heard by the English in defiance of the "infidel's scorn" sets up the by now important distinction to be made between the English, associated now with having religious faith, and the French who had by 1793, abolished the worship of God. The concept of the "ideal" nation was thus defined and contested at a time of war between two countries who had also been competing in the realm of imperial expansion. Another well-known response to the war years following the Revolution is Anna Laetitia Barbauld's "Eighteen Hundred and Eleven" (1812), where Britain's position as an imperial power is evaluated in a global context. Barbauld also demonstrates, like Coleridge, a degree of anxiety about the human and material costs of war and its long-term consequences on the identities of the participants. For Barbauld, in addition to the immediate physical threat posed to the nation-as-home, the emotional consequences of families losing loved ones also looms large. She paints a picture of England at the time where newspapers and maps bring to the country's readers, introductions to faraway lands and events that double as unexpected obituaries for family members who have perished at war. At the time of the poem's publication, England had been at war with France for seventeen years and had entered a period of extremely hostile relations with America. This was, therefore, a time when three powerful nations with imperialist designs were fighting for dominance in the wake of a revolution that had promised liberty and equality to all. Barbauld's poem reflects this through its touches of patriotism, cynicism about the stability of power and anxiety about the future. The poem stages a fascinating apocalyptic future for Britain based on its present state of affairs. In Barbauld's imagination of Britain's future, America has risen as the dominant power but in an eerie imitation of what will soon be in the past for the English:

> Nations beyond the Apalachian hills
> Thy hand has planted and thy spirit fills:
> Soon as their gradual progress shall impart
> The finer sense of morals and of art,
> Thy stores of knowledge the new states shall know,
> And think thy thoughts, and with thy fancy glow; (lines 83–88)

Meanwhile, England, she imagines, would be reduced to "gray ruin" and "mouldering stone", meant only to be a past benchmark which others, aided by the rise of global and levelling powers like "Commerce", have now exceeded. Barbauld ends on a prophetic note to say, "Arts, arms and wealth destroy the fruits they bring; Commerce, like beauty, knows no second spring" (lines 315–16). The tussle for power, Barbauld concludes, can never be won, if the goal is to achieve endless expansion and future glory with little care for the concomitant growth of "misery" in the present.

As shown in Philip Shaw's *Waterloo and the Romantic Imagination* (2002), the topic of war is a neglected area in

Romantic studies. Romantic writers would play a significant role in concretising images and ideas about war for their country and their works record a rich diversity of opinion. Shaw notes, for example, that Coleridge and several other writers were more ambivalent in framing the cost of lives and violence in the context of war, when compared with Byron. Byron's representation of battle scenes in his "Childe Harold's Pilgrimage" (1812–18), a point discussed in the chapter on Empire, uses vivid detail to evoke bodily pain and suffering as a consequence of war – something that was elided from the many patriotic poems produced at the time.

Citizenship and Rights

As support for the French Revolution waxed and waned in England, it nevertheless inspired a consistent engagement with questions of rights and political reform throughout this period. Among the prominent debates over rights that writers engaged with, following the early example of the French Revolution's own declaration of the Rights of Man, were those pertaining to the poor, to slavery and the status of women in England. For the writers who consistently spoke out publicly regarding these issues, the dismantling of feudal oppression in France served as an impetus to raise questions about what was considered the "necessary" subjugation of various people at the time in England – the racial subjugation of African slaves by their owners, women's inferior status in every sphere of life when compared with men and the oppression of the poor by the unequal distribution of wealth and property. The wars with France during Napoleon's reign would put great economic and social pressure on Britain and this was manifest in the use of labour-saving technology to increase productivity in industries. Automated looms were brought into the textile industries at Yorkshire, Nottinghamshire, Derbyshire and Leicestershire, thereby intimidating the local weavers residing there into thinking that their livelihoods were now at risk. These workers would soon resort to breaking machinery at their mills to protest these sudden shifts in the trade that would put them out of work at a time of great scarcity. The government, pressured by the dual wars with France and America, felt a rising anxiety about labour unrest and passed special acts to ensure the maintenance of peace in these districts. The Frame Work Bill is a good example of such government measures to curb Luddism, as this worker protest would come to be called, and Byron would respond to it in a Parliamentary Speech at the House of Lords in 1812.

Byron, along with others who opposed such stringent measures of punishment, would emphasise the great adversity that resulted in the taking up of arms against mill owners and equipment. Criticising the definition of "criminal activity" that allowed the protestors to be arrested, Byron stated that the police found men to be guilty of "the capital crime of Poverty" (885). Byron's illustrations of the workers' rights in his speech are truly characteristic of an age shaped by revolutions. Referring to them as a "mob", a reference most likely to the idea entertained by the parliament that these rioting workers were revolutionaries in the making, Byron challenges the understanding of this very contentious word. "Are we aware of our obligations to a mob?", he says, "It is the mob that labour in your fields and serve in your houses,—that man your navy, and recruit your army,—that have enabled you to defy all the world" (886). The "mob" is thus humanised first by emphasising their English character and then by highlighting how they provide sustenance to defend this Englishness. Byron also contrasts the value of governing the life of a man and that of a machine in his speech, thus harking back to debates about law and individual liberty early in this period. Other famous responses to the government's repressive anti-revolutionary measures in this period include William Hone's *The Political House That Jack Built* (1819) and Percy Shelley's "England in 1819" and "The Masque of Anarchy", both published posthumously in 1849. The radical publisher William Hone uses the format of a popular children's rhyme to mount his criticism on an authoritarian government in his *The Political House*. The pamphlet carried illustrations by George Cruikshank, the most notable of which was a frontispiece showing the pen (a quill in the illustration) outweighing scrolls of paper signifying legislations passed by the government to curb the powers of the radical press. The printing press becomes another important symbol in the pamphlet, shown as being too powerful to be restrained by the government's combined forces of increased taxes and military might. Like Hone's pamphlet, Shelley's "England in 1819" expresses rage and discontent with nearly all institutions of the day: the monarchy, the parliament, the army and religion. The people in turn, Shelley writes, are "starv'd and stabb'd in the untill'd field", referencing the Peterloo Massacre of August 1819 in which the military violently dispersed a peaceful protest for parliamentary reform. Shelley's poems of dissent remained unpublished in his lifetime for fear of governmental backlash but are, nevertheless, an important record of how writers perceived their role in a politically tumultuous time. The closing lines of "England in 1819" – "a glorious Phantom may/Burst, to illumine our tempestuous day" – make an interesting return to the theme of millennial hope articulated in Romantic writing at the start of the French Revolution (xx, 13–14).

The declaration of the Rights of Man in the early years of the French Revolution would allow writers of the Romantic period to reflect very differently on how man and the individual was understood in relation to society. The very public (widely disseminated) debate over foundational principles regarding the right to rule, the method of governance and constitution of citizenship would pave the way for several writers to make a case for how they understood personhood in the context of civil and political rights. For Byron, the personhood of the Luddite rioters was rooted in their necessary emancipation from economic strife. Mary Wollstonecraft would make a case in 1792 in her *Vindication of the Rights of Woman: With Strictures on Political and Moral Subjects*, that women are no different from men in their capacity for reason and moral action, and thus ought to be brought under the purview of the Rights of Man. *Vindication of the Rights of Woman* was a response to the newly elected French Constituent Assembly's decision to provide state-supported education to women students primarily to enhance their preparedness for marriage. Wollstonecraft argues instead for the cultivation and development of women's capacity to reason by removing their focus from matters of domesticity alone. Her appeal to educate women differently refers to the contribution women are likely to make to matters of national significance – teaching patriotism and humanistic values to their children, the next generation of English citizens. This gives us some insight into the political climate and readership that Wollstonecraft addresses: patriotism or the consciousness of a shared national identity would usually accompany every case made for individual rights.

Wollstonecraft, along with her close friend, the writer Mary Hays, should also be seen in the context of their contributions to the debate over women's rights that continues to this day. One important link between these writers and feminist movements of the present day for example is their insistence on the equality of both genders and their common human aspirations. Wollstonecraft would state in her *Vindication*, for instance,

> Dismissing then those pretty feminine phrases, which the men condescendingly use to soften our slavish dependence, and despising that weak elegancy of mind, exquisite sensibility, and sweet docility of manners, supposed to be the sexual characteristics of the weaker vessel, I wish to shew that elegance is inferior to virtue, that the first object of laudable ambition is to obtain a character as a human being, regardless of the distinction of sex; and that secondary views should be brought to this simple touchstone. (73)

In her *Appeal to the Men of Great Britain in Behalf of Women* (1798), Mary Hays would similarly attempt to quell fears about the "sexual transgressions" of women – or women's behaviour and aspirations running contrary to those established by social conventions and conduct books of the time. For Hays, like Wollstonecraft, the exercise of reason and acquisition of knowledge and learning was not exclusively a masculine domain. Women with these aspirations, she would argue, should therefore not be branded as having pretensions to masculinity. "If therefore", she says, "we are to understand by a masculine woman, one who emulates those virtues and accomplishments, which as common to human nature, are common to both sexes, the attempt is natural, amiable, and highly honorable to that woman, under whatever name her conduct may be disguised or censured" (41). Hays and Wollstonecraft reflect the concerns of their age when they express interest in understanding and defining "human nature", while simultaneously speaking to modern readers' concerns with the unequal distribution of the benefits of education and employment across genders.

Several women writers in this period would respond to the question of rights for women and would consistently address women's education – what they should study and what their education should prepare them to do. In addition, writing about the rights of women in England would also engage with questions about the "nature of women" – how to understand who women are in society and whether they are only to be made sense of in relation with men. Writing in this period that argued for women's rights, whether to vote, for equitable education and employment or even to delineate their duties, was addressed to both men and women and like other writing in the aftermath of the Revolution, was committed to reform. In England at this time, women lived in what was termed "coverture": by law, their bodies and whatever they possessed, including their children, was the property of their husbands or fathers. They were seen as inferior with respect to their capacity to reason and were held up by prevailing medical and religious beliefs as innately different in their "sex", a point I will return to in detail in the chapter on gender. Writers arguing for women's rights, thus, faced the challenge of changing the attitudes and beliefs of a society that viewed women with ambitions to equal men in education and profession as "masculine" and needed to develop a careful stance. Not all writing about women's rights is homogenous: some writings, like *On Needle-Work* by Mary Lamb (1814) focused on respectable and better-paid employment for women, all the while presenting sewing as work that is innately feminine. Thus, Lamb suggests better conditions for a job that was a primary occupation for several lower-class women but, at the same time, diverges from Wollstonecraft's view that women and men can be employed for the same kind of work.

Writing produced by women about their rights permits us to observe how the French Revolution would give rise to a host of new "subjects" in England and other countries. In other words, new voices would emerge to recast the image of man, as he was constituted by the revolutionary struggles of the time. This man, emerging as he did in France as a new political subject, would be found wanting and unfamiliar to England's poor, to the country's women and especially to African slaves, several of whom now inhabited London. The "guarantee" of rights and entitlement to personal liberty espoused by the debates surrounding the early years of the French Revolution would come to strike English citizens as hollow unless they applied to the vastly diverse categories of individuals contained within the term "human". The progress of the revolution in France and the long war years were not the only sources of disillusionment in this age. The aims set at the start of the French Revolution would continue to serve as targets for writers in this period who either saw them, like Burke and Hannah More, as hasty and without the experience of tradition, or like Wollstonecraft, Lamb and Mary Hays, as requiring continuous amendment to reflect the truth of the society in which they purported to be executed.

Women writers would also feature prominently in the abolitionist movement in eighteenth-century England, arguably the most popular campaign for reform mobilised in this period. Public outcry against the slave trade and slavery was present in Britain well before the start of the French Revolution. Abolitionists' petitions for the rights of enslaved Africans were not a consequence of events in France alone. The Romantic period is unique for witnessing the flourishing British transatlantic slave trade as well as its legal demise. I will offer a brief context to the nature of this trade and its impact on public consciousness before discussing the impact of the Revolution on the campaign for abolition.

Europeans in the British Americas would import African slaves to work on their fields, primarily for their muscle power. With the discovery of immense commercial success in certain export crops, notably sugarcane, indigo, coffee, cotton, chocolate and tobacco, the demand for slaves to work for British "planters" in American colonies would rise exponentially. A complex network of trade would emerge in this period, where the steady import of Africans into America would contribute to fuelling the growing demand for sugar, cotton cloth and tobacco in Britain. Consuming these slave-produced commodities in Britain would curiously attain associations of upward social mobility, genteel tastes and exoticism rather than the horrors and misery that characterised the lives of the enslaved African workers. After the first generations of African slaves failed to reproduce naturally, owing no doubt to the harsh conditions under which they had travelled to and worked in the Americas, the slave trade opened to allow various interested investors to participate in what promised to be the most lucrative trade at the time by ensuring a steady supply. The prevalent legal status of these slaves was that they were the "property" of their masters and were bought and sold like any other commodity in the economy, thereby stripping them of any human attributes. Abolitionist writing at this time had to thus contend with the less-than-human status of slaves as well as the associations built in public consciousness by those with commercial interests, that the British Empire would collapse if it were not for the slave trade.

The term abolition broadly encompasses activities that aimed to organise groups of people in Britain to join a movement against the slave trade and this hugely popular campaign would culminate in the passage of the Abolition Act of 1807. In countering the views of tradesmen lobbying for the continuation of a very prosperous enterprise, abolitionists would appeal to the sentiments and conscience of an increasingly literate English public. In his "The Negro's Complaint" and "Pity for Poor Africans", both published in 1788, William Cowper would make an appeal to English readers to consider the human costs at which they continued to consume slave-produced goods. "The Negro's Complaint" gives voice to a slave who asks the reader to "think how many backs have smarted, for the sweets your cane affords" (Mellor and Matlak, 62, line 23). In "Pity for Poor Africans" Cowper illustrates sardonically the personality of the white Englishman who argues that the slave trade ought to continue, if only to compete with other imperial powers who would themselves never back down. In the same year, Hannah More published her "Slavery, A Poem" in which Britain's notions of liberty are contrasted with those of others and found to be similarly wanting so long as her participation in the slave trade continued. Englishmen and women who signed abolitionists' petitions and read the widely circulating anti-slavery propaganda would grow increasingly conscious, in the period between the 1780s till the end of the century, of their commitment to the ideals of liberty especially in as far as it discerned their Englishness and contrasted it with the tyranny of other nations.

In 1787, the Society for Effecting the Abolition of the Slave Trade was established in England and would mark the start of serious campaigning in the country against the slave trade as well as the institution of slavery itself. The Society's members, the most prominent being Thomas Clarkson, were well known for their novel reform campaigns against slavery – signature petitions, gathering witness testimonies about the conditions aboard slave ships, sugar boycotts and writing and publishing abolitionist material. William Wilberforce, a subsequent and influential entrant in the Society, would use the petitions and evidence gathered by Clarkson as part of his speech to the parliament in 1789, where he would put forward twelve propositions for the abolition of the slave trade. The year 1787 also saw the publication of Ottobah Cugoano's *Thoughts and Sentiments on the Evil and Wicked Traffic of Slavery* and would add to the abolitionists' cause a new kind of voice – that of the former slave. Cugoano's account of his own capture, like a few other slave narratives published in England at the time, would serve to "authenticate" the horrors experienced by slaves in their travel to work in European plantations. Cugoano argues in *Thoughts and Sentiments* that slavery is unchristian and to that end appeals to Britain to demonstrate its true Christian nature through abolition. By quoting the Bible extensively, Cugoano also appeals to his readers as a fellow Christian, thus forcing them to see him as human and a fellow countryman.

A home-grown movement for reform with respect to slavery was clearly well underway in England even prior to the start of the French Revolution. By the time of the abolitionists' success with the crown assenting to the abolition of the slave trade in 1807 and the abolition of slavery itself in 1833, however, events in France would have a significant impact on the way in which English writers responded to the rights of slaves. Inspired by the Declaration of the Rights of Man by the French National Assembly, free men of colour in the French colony of Saint-Domingue also sought recognition as French citizens. In March 1790, civic rights were granted to free men of colour, but the National Assembly set the bar at a certain socioeconomic class and gave the local colonial government the power to put this decree into practice. Saint-Domingue boasted a Black population much larger than that of the resident white Europeans and slave labour was the backbone of the island's economic prosperity. The colonial authorities, seeking to further their prosperity and not viewing the local population as human in the light of the decree of liberty proclaimed by France, would refuse civic rights to their residents of colour. This would prove to be a trigger for several violent clashes between the Black and white populations on the island eventually resulting in the formation of the first independent Black republic in 1804. Led by several militarily astute former slaves, most notably, Toussaint Louverture, Saint-Domingue, now rechristened Haiti, would come to represent irrepressible violence against domination by colonial powers who now had to reconsider the status of their enslaved colonies. In England, the violent uprisings in Haiti, seen as a direct consequence of the French Revolution, would prove to be a setback in the abolitionists' campaign to see slaves as human. Abolitionists themselves would now have to be wary of explicitly supporting the French Revolution, for fear that their efforts to emancipate slaves would be viewed as revolutionary incitement.

The Haitian Revolution is a good context in which to situate several of the abolitionist writings produced after 1790, when the first slave rebellion occurred. It is interesting to note, for example, that several prominent responses to the slave trade and slavery, like Southey's "The Sailor Who Had Served in the Slave Trade", published in 1798, and Amelia Alderson Opie's "The Negro Boy's Tale" and "The Black Man's Lament" published in 1824 and 1826, respectively, continued to feature persons of colour in an unchanging way. The slave characters in these poems are often alone, meek, timid and afraid, and appeal to the paternalistic love and protection of their presumed white readers. They bear no relation at all to the slaves that systematically destroyed all vestiges of colonial rule in Haiti or even to those conscripted and given arms to fight for Britain in the war years against France. The abolitionist response to the slave trade and slavery was thus resolutely rooted in a sense of English superiority over their colonial subjects as well as other imperial powers. It can even be argued that the eventual success of the abolitionists' campaign was dependant on English citizens identifying themselves as the most well-suited to award liberty to their enslaved populations. It was through Christian teaching – it was popularly argued – that slaves could be truly emancipated and finally seen as human. Freedom from slavery, thus, did not imply the recognition of rights alone but, as with the rights of women, gave rise to questions about the nature of racial selfhood and who would have the power to define it.

The French Revolution's impact on English Romantic literature was thus complex and far-reaching, with consequences felt in Britain and throughout the British Empire.

Works Cited

Barbauld, Anna Letitia. "Eighteen Hundred and Eleven." *British Literature 1780–1830*, edited by Anne K. Mellor and Richard E. Matlak, Harcourt Brace, 1996, p. 182.

———. "To Dr. Priestley. Dec. 29, 1792." *The Poems of Anna Letitia Barbauld.* edited by William McCarthy and Elizabeth Kraft, U of Georgia, 1994.

Burke, Edmund, and George Sampson. *Reflections on the Revolution in France With an Introduction by George Sampson*, W. Scott, 1790, http://archive.org/details/revolutionfran00burkuoft.

Butler, Marilyn. *Romantics, Rebels and Reactionaries: English Literature and its Background 1760–1830.* Oxford UP, 1981.

Byron, George Gordon. "Parliamentary Speeches in the House of Lords, Debate on the Frame-Work Bill, February 27, 1812." *British Literature 1780–1830*, edited by Anne K. Mellor and Richard E. Matlak, Harcourt Brace, 1996, pp. 885–87.

Coleridge, Samuel Taylor. "Conciones ad Populum; or Addresses to the People." *British Literature 1780–1830*, edited by Anne K. Mellor and Richard E. Matlak, Harcourt Brace, 1996, p. 684.

———. "Fears in Solitude." *British Literature 1780–1830*, edited by Anne K. Mellor and Richard E. Matlak, Harcourt Brace, 1996, pp. 694–97.

———. "On the Prospect of Establishing a Pantisocracy in America." *Samuel Taylor Coleridge: The Complete Poems*, edited by William Keach, Penguin, 1997, p. 58.

Cowper, William. "Pity for Poor Africans." *British Literature 1780–1830*, edited by Anne K. Mellor and Richard E. Matlak, Harcourt Brace, 1996, pp. 62–63.

———. "The Negro's Complaint". *British Literature 1780–1830*, edited by Anne K. Mellor and Richard E. Matlak, Harcourt Brace, 1996, pp. 62–63.

Cugoano, Ottobah. *Thoughts and sentiments on the evil and wicked traffic of the slavery: and commerce of the human species, humbly submitted to the inhabitants of Great-Britain, by Ottobah Cugoano*, 1787. *Eighteenth Century Collections Online Text Creation Partnership*, 2011, http://name.umdl.umich.edu/K046227.0001.001. Accessed 17 Dec 2019.

Doyle, William. *The French Revolution: A Very Short Introduction.* Oxford UP, 2001.

Duff, David. "From Revolution to Romanticism: The Historical Context to 1800." *A Companion to Romanticism*, edited by Duncan Wu, Blackwell, 1999, pp. 25–38.

Eaves, Morris, Robert Essick, and Joseph Viscomi, editors. *America a Prophecy* (Composed 1793). *The William Blake Archive*, 1996–2019, http://www.blakearchive.org/. Accessed 09 September 2022.

———. *Songs of Innocence and Experience* (Composed 1789, 1794). *The William Blake Archive*, 1996–2019, http://www.blakearchive.org/. Accessed 09 September 2022.

———. *The French Revolution* (Composed 1791). *The William Blake Archive*, 1996–2019, http://www.blakearchive.org/. Accessed 09 September 2022.

———. *The Marriage of Heaven and Hell* (Composed 1790). *The William Blake Archive*, 1996–2019, http://www.blakearchive.org/. Accessed 09 September 2022.

Freedman, Linda. "Looking at the manuscript of William Blake's 'London'." *British Library*, 2014, https://www.bl.uk/romantics-

and-victorians/articles/looking-at-the-manuscript-of-william-blakes-london. Accessed 11 December 2019.

Gillray, James. *Buonaparte, 48 Hours After Landing. BritishMuseum.org*, 1803, https://www.britishmuseum.org/collection/object/P_J-3-30. Accessed 13 January 2021.

———. *French Liberty/English Slavery. BritishMuseum.org*, 1792, https://www.britishmuseum.org/collection/object/P_1868-0808-6253. Accessed 13 January 2021.

———. *Maniac Raving's–or–Little Boney in a Strong Fit. BritishMuseum.org*, 1803, https://www.britishmuseum.org/collection/object/P_1868-0808-7120. Accessed 13 January 2021.

———. *The plumb-pudding in danger: -or- state epicures taking un petit souper. BritishMuseum.org*, https://www.britishmuseum.org/collection/object/P_1851-0901-1164. Accessed 13 January 2021.

Godwin, William. *An Enquiry Concerning Political Justice*, edited by Mark Philp, Oxford UP, 2013.

Hays, Mary. "Appeal to the Men of Great Britain in Behalf of Women." *British Literature 1780–1830*, edited by Anne K. Mellor and Richard E. Matlak, Harcourt Brace, 1996, pp. 38–41.

Hobsbawm, Eric. *The Age of Revolution 1789–1848*. Abacus, 1977.

Lamb, Mary. "On Needle-Work." *British Literature 1780–1830*, edited by Anne K. Mellor and Richard E. Matlak, Harcourt Brace, 1996, pp. 50–52.

Mee, Jon. "Popular Radical Culture." *The Cambridge Companion to British Literature of the French Revolution in the 1790s*, edited by Pamela Clemit, Cambridge UP, 2011, pp. 117–28.

Mellor, Anne K., and Richard E. Matlak, editors. *British Literature 1780–1830.* Harcourt Brace, 1996.

More, Hannah. "Slavery, A Poem." *British Literature 1780–1830*, edited by Anne K. Mellor and Richard E. Matlak, Harcourt Brace, 1996, pp. 206–10.

———. "The Riot; or Half a Loaf is Better Than No Bread." *British Literature 1780–1830*, edited by Anne K. Mellor and Richard E. Matlak, Harcourt Brace, 1996, p. 218.

———. *Village politics: Addressed to all the mechanics, journeymen, and day labourers, in Great Britain. By Will Chip, a country carpenter*. J. Harrop, 1793. *Eighteenth Century Collections Online Text Creation Partnership*, 2011, http://name.umdl.umich.edu/004847021.0001.000>. Accessed 17 Dec 2019.

Opie, Amelia Alderson. "The Black Man's Lament." *British Literature 1780–1830*, edited by Anne K. Mellor and Richard E. Matlak, Harcourt Brace, 1996, pp. 82–84.

Paine, Thomas. *Rights of Man, Common Sense and Other Political Writings*, edited by Mark Philp, Oxford UP, 1995.

Philp, Mark. "Revolution." *An Oxford Companion to the Romantic Age: British Culture 1776–1832*, edited by Iain McCalman, Oxford UP, 1999, pp. 17–26.

Price, Richard. *A Discourse on the Love of Our Country, Delivered on Nov. 4, 1789, at the Meeting-House in the Old Jewry, to the Society for Commmemorating the Revolution in Great Britain*. London: Revolution Society, 1790. *Evans Early American Imprint Collection Text Creation Partnership*, 2011, http://name.umdl.umich.edu/N17608.0001.001. Accessed 10 December 2019.

Prickett, Stephen. *England and the French Revolution*. Macmillan Education, 1989.

Shelley, Percy Bysshe. "Sonnet: England in 1819." *British Literature 1780–1830*, edited by Anne K. Mellor and Richard E. Matlak, Harcourt Brace, 1996, pp. 1166.

Schürer, Norbert. "The Storming of the Bastille in English Newspapers." *Eighteenth-Century Life*, vol. 29, no. 1, 2005, pp. 50–81.

Shaw, Philip. *Waterloo and the Romantic Imagination*. Palgrave, 2002.

Southey, Robert. "The Sailor, Who Had Served in the Slave Trade." *British Literature 1780–1830*, edited by Anne K. Mellor and Richard E. Matlak, Harcourt Brace, 1996, pp. 68–70.

Wheale, Nigel. *Writing and Society: Literacy, Print and Politics in Britain 1590–1660*. Routledge, 2005.

Williams, Helen Maria. *Letters From France, Volume IV*, edited by Anne K. Mellor and Richard E. Matlak, Harcourt Brace, 1996, p. 527.

———. *Letters on the French Revolution, written in France, in the summer of 1790, to a friend in England; containing, various anecdotes relative to that interesting event, and memoirs of Mons. and Madame Du F--*. Boston: J Belknap and A Young, 1791–92. *Evans Early American Imprint Collection Text Creation Partnership*, 2011, https://quod.lib.umich.edu/cgi/t/text/text-idx?c=evans;idno=N18502.0001.001. Accessed 10 December 2019.

Wollstonecraft, Mary. *A Vindication of the Rights of Men and A Vindication of the Rights of Woman*, edited by Janet Todd, Oxford, 1993.

Wordsworth, William. *The Prelude 1799, 1805, 1850* edited by Jonathan Wordsworth, M.H Abrams and Stephen Gill, Norton, 1979.

Notes

1. See Hobsbawm's chapter titled "The French Revolution" in his *The Age of Revolution* for a list of other eighteenth-century rebellions against existing political and economic systems (74).
2. For a more detailed analysis of the conditions leading to the French Revolution and its influence outside England and the Romantic period, see William Doyle's *The French Revolution: A Very Short Introduction.*
3. Moreover, Paine had been an important voice in the American Revolution, having published *Common Sense* in 1776, which sold 120,000 copies within the first three months of its publication.
4. Previously called San Domingo, Haiti was an important French colony and run almost entirely through the work of African slaves. With the declaration of the Rights of Men by the French National Assembly in 1789, the ongoing slave resistance in the colony would achieve the impetus needed to push for their own liberation and demand suffrage for all men, including Blacks. The enslaved Black population would organise a successful rebellion against their white rulers and achieve independence from France in 1803, but after great bloodshed and loss of life on both sides. The case of Haiti, thus, struck fear in the hearts of those still supporting monarchical rule at the time.
5. Blake's *Songs of Innocence and Experience* is well known for attempting to examine a duality in perspective about a set of topics. He first published a number of poems, including "The Chimney Sweeper", in a collection titled *The Songs of Innocence* in 1789. Later, in 1794, he published *The Songs of Innocence and Experience: Shewing the Two Contrary States of the Human Soul*, which included more poems and illustrations in addition to those in the earlier *Songs of Innocence*. There are, thus, two chimney

sweeper poems, one each in the *Songs of Innocence* and the *Songs of Experience*, both permitting the reader to dwell on the issue of child labour through the lens of "innocence" and "experience".

6. These lines from *The Prelude* were composed in 1805 as part of a poem titled "The French Revolution".
7. See John Mee's "Popular Radical Culture" for an account of the role played by societies like the London Corresponding Society (LCS) in publishing and disseminating radical writing.
8. See Nigel Wheale's *Writing and Society: Literacy, Print and Politics in Britain 1590–1660* for a longer history of the growth of literacy and the expansion of the literary sphere to include writers and readers from diverse socioeconomic backgrounds in Elizabethan England.

TWO

Gendering Romanticism

One of the most prominent ways in which studies of Romanticism seek to revisit its traditional categories of analysis is through the lens of gender. Gender in this case is understood as the extent to which literary writing and cultures (reading, leisure activities and meaning-making) influenced and were influenced by ideas relating to what it meant to be men and women in eighteenth-century society. Recent studies focusing on gender and English Romantic literature move beyond an analysis of writing that produces certain notions about men and women and focus more on the study of biases inherent in how we read male and female writers and identify with qualities of masculinity and femininity. Anne Mellor in her *Romanticism and Gender* (1993), the first book-length study of the subject, would identify the gendered biases inherent in critics, and consequently in generations of students who studied the period identified as "Romantic" in England. She points out for instance, how our understanding of this period of rich literary production – whether through courses studying works of authors in this period or through anthologies that compile their writings – is limited to six male poets: William Blake, William Wordsworth, Samuel Coleridge, George Byron, Percy Shelley and John Keats. Through this succinct critique of nearly a couple of centuries of scholarship regarding the English Romantic writers, Mellor identifies an interesting mode through which Romanticism is *gendered*. Focusing on six male poets as the most significant figures of this time leads to associations about genre, authorship and gender. For instance, this formulation somehow suggests that male writers were the most productive and celebrated at the time and that poetry was the dominant genre that was practised and consumed. Moreover, it suggests that poetry is a craft in which male writers excelled and any of their women contemporaries (of whom there is often a brief mention in textbooks and course syllabi as a *separate* category) are viewed as a novel inclusion or a coincidental exception.[1] In other words, gender is not explicitly invoked as a consideration for reading English Romantic writing but is nevertheless *implied* in the way academic courses are designed, in the way that anthologies are planned and in the content of academic literature about the period. Our access to this period, especially in the present, is heavily mediated by these projects of canonisation or institutionalisation of writing considered significant to be studied and preserved. Hence, we ought to be vigilant about the ways in which associations are formed over several years of writing about a period far removed from us between writers and the contexts in which their writings emerge. This chapter will thus aim to illustrate that gender is a significant aspect of reading and writing not only in scholarship about any period of literary output but also the sociopolitical landscape of the period itself.

The writing of this period allows the student to explore the range of responses to what were thought to be "ideal" men and women in English society. In many ways, English Romantic literature is a rich resource for understanding how individuals made sense of what it meant to be identified as male and masculine or as female and feminine. As in any period, including our own, the stories we read and share are a significant learning tool for making sense of why we are differentiated from others with respect to our biology, behaviour, likes and dislikes and even professional choices. Before moving on to a broad picture of ideas informing femininity and masculinity (the *qualities* of being seen, both by oneself and others, as being "like a woman" or "like a man" rather than the biological differentiation between the sexes or the sociocultural meanings attached to belonging to a particular gender), a brief caveat about the term writing. Writing here will be tested as a category that is not only confined to the traditional forms of poetry, novels and drama alone but can include more diverse cultures of producing and consuming meaning like the media (magazines, journals, newspapers and advertisements) and visual arts. This is an important redefinition of what constitutes literary production for this period since it witnesses a change in how writing and writers are viewed. I will return to this idea in the chapter on Romantic literary cultures but for the present it is important to keep in mind that writers and their works were being forced to contend with a new social order in this period. Royal or aristocratic patrons and their familiar whimsies were a known commodity for writers in the eighteenth century. In the late eighteenth and early nineteenth century however, a growing public of literate (but anonymous and belonging to the middle and lower classes) readers (many of them women) would participate in literary cultures (of reading and making sense of writing of various kinds) in new and unanticipated ways that would change how writers and writing itself was understood. This chapter will consider both the thematic and formal content of English Romantic literature to demonstrate how its emergence and subsequent interpretation can be seen as gendered. We can begin with a discussion of several of the well-known female novelists of the time and what they understood to be codes of conduct that typified men and women.

Romantic Literature and Social Conduct

In this section, I will offer an overview of the established social codes of conduct prevalent in England in the eighteenth century as a way of distinguishing between what can be seen as the masculine and feminine strands of Romanticism. The popular literary form of the novel, perhaps the most prominent in the eighteenth century, will be used as a test case to demonstrate what literature can tell us about the way men and women made sense of their social roles. As argued in the previous chapter, the French Revolution's idea of a new social order and liberty for all was found to be applicable only to men and that too of a certain race and social background. Mary Wollstonecraft in her *A Vindication of the Rights of Woman* would argue against equating the category "human" with that of "man" and would supply instead, the means for reforming education such that women too could aspire to qualities that were believed to biologically inhere only in men. We can turn to *A Vindication* again to make observations that will be of relevance to the question of how gender and Romanticism are linked. While the previous chapter focused on the clues that this text's rhetoric offers us to understand the political climate of the revolution in France, here I want to focus on the picture of family life and social roles that it draws for the contemporary reader.

Domesticity and ideas related to gender are intricately linked in this period, as it is in our own, and we shall see this via Wollstonecraft's reasoning in her appeal for women's rights. "If children are to be educated to understand the true principle of patriotism, their mother must be a patriot", Wollstonecraft asserts, thus demonstrating the changing role of women in the family in this period (66). The mother was now someone whose *duty* it was to educate her children and her own education was thus seen to be a direct determiner of the quality of England's future citizens' preparedness. We can also observe here a redefinition of the family itself, now seen as a space for education and for cultivating civic and moral rootedness. *A Vindication* returns repeatedly to the issue of marriage to assert how a rethinking of this institution can become a viable educational resource. Wollstonecraft argues that in this time where "equitable laws" are shaping citizens,

> marriage may become more sacred: your young men may choose wives from motives of affection, and your maidens allow love to

> root out vanity. The father of a family will not then weaken his constitution and debase his sentiments, by visiting the harlot, nor forget, in obeying the call of appetite, the purpose for which it was implanted. And, the mother will not neglect her children to practice the arts of coquetry, when sense and modesty secure her the friendship of her husband. (68)

A changed educational curriculum that allows reason to replace coercion in teaching the duties to be maintained by both sexes is for Wollstonecraft a successful model for the family and by extension, the nation. But what is significant for us here is Wollstonecraft's delineation of duties in the home that tells us a great deal about prevailing ideas with respect to men and women.

As is clear from the above description of how marriage "ought" to be, women were seen to be responsible for child rearing and men for stability in the household. Both sexes were meant to be responsible for reigning in their passions with reason and sensibility in order to work together to sustain a more egalitarian marriage. The family was being rethought to bring about a transformation of certain qualities that were believed to inhere in each of the sexes. Wollstonecraft here aligns coquetry with women and an excessive sexual appetite with men and attempts to rethink the institution of marriage in such a way that these sex-based predilections can be curbed. The "friendship" alluded to here, albeit within a marriage, is another illustration of a transformation in meanings attached to the relationship between the sexes at this time. Heterosocial interactions or interactions between men and women would become, in eighteenth-century England, a mark of what was termed "sensibility". This was a feature that distinguished a rising middle class, whose fortunes were built through emerging trade opportunities in this period. There would be an increasing insistence in English literature produced in the eighteenth century and early nineteenth century (this is especially true of the genre called the literature of sensibility or novel of education) that the man of sensibility was one who could set aside rough homosocial activities like animal-baiting or dueling to participate in heterosocial "scenes" where men and women together consumed objects produced for social pleasure alone. Eighteenth-century manufacturers of social objects like decorative items for the home or tea-serving crockery thus also fostered a civilising mission that aimed to reform gendered behaviour that was at odds with a newly defined sense of inhabiting public spaces. While certain kinds of behaviours and attitudes seemed to writers of the time to be typical of men and women, these were also constantly questioned in the context of social and political changes.

The importance of a specific kind of education for women, following Wollstonecraft's lead, was an important theme in the novels written by women in this period. These women novelists, in exploring their female protagonists' gaining of a particular kind of education, were also illustrating certain dominant views about women and men at the time. Maria Edgeworth for instance, describes the eponymous protagonist in *Belinda* (1801) and the young women of her time as seen through the eyes of her aunt thus:

> But nothing to my mind can be more miserable than the situation of a poor girl, who, after spending not only the interest, but the solid capital of her small fortune in dress, and frivolous extravagance, fails in her matrimonial expectations (as many do merely from not beginning to speculate in time). She finds herself at five or six and thirty a burden to her friends, destitute of the means of rendering herself independent (for the girls I speak of never think of *learning* to play cards), *de trop* in society, yet obliged to hang upon all her acquaintance, who wish her in Heaven, because she is unqualified to make the *expected* return for civilities, having no home, I mean no establishment, no house, &c. fit for the reception of company of a certain rank. (4–5)

This passage is illuminating for the vivid picture it offers of the way in which women's access to social status is perceived at this time. If a young woman does not possess the privilege of wealth and connections at birth, Edgeworth suggests a well-chosen husband as the only means available for social advancement. Moreover, a person who receives social favours is *expected* to return them, thus illustrating the class and gender barriers inherent in the kind of social mobility an individual could aspire to at this time.

Edgeworth also illustrates the prevalent disadvantages that existed even for women of a higher social class, through characters seen lacking in particular aspects of intellectual and social preparedness. Lady Delacour, for instance, is a rich heiress whose lack of understanding about her finances leads directly to her being swindled out of her fortune by male bankers and financiers. She is thus forced to be dependent on a husband she despises only to avoid destitution. Moreover, Lady Delacour finds that following marriage, a woman's actions are only ever viewed in relation to the man. When she becomes engaged in a duel with a rival candidate during local elections for instance, voters reject this candidate's husband in favour of one whose wife was "a proper behaved woman" (54). Edgeworth also illustrates how women were seen as commodities traded via the institution of marriage as evident by the way in which Belinda and her aunt are discussed at a masquerade party. Mistaken for Lady Delacour, Belinda is privy to a conversation where a young gentleman at the party describes his knowledge of her thus, after an account of the many nieces Mrs Stanhope has married off advantageously:

> As for this Belinda Portman, 'twas a good hit to send her to Lady Delacour's; but I take it, she hangs upon hands; for last winter, when I was at Bath, she was hawked about every where, and the aunt was puffing her with might and main. You heard of nothing, wherever you went, but of Belinda Portman, and Belinda Portman's accomplishments—Belinda Portman, and her accomplishments, I'll swear, were as well advertised, as Packwood's razor strops. (20)

The use of the term "hawked" is significant here, making clear that women were not viewed as possessing sexual subjectivity; partners were chosen for them by parents or parent-like figures and they had, if at all, only the authority to refuse but never to make a marriage proposal. Much like a commodity that is created to match market-specific needs that are created in turn by manufacturers, like Packwood's razor strops, Belinda too, it is suggested, is made more attractive through advertisement than any innate qualities of practical value. It is interesting that Belinda is here being made sense of in the language of newly emerging capitalism where products like consumer goods (here likened to women in search of husbands) were so ubiquitous and varied that only an additional investment of capital in advertisement and building familiarity with a "brand" could guarantee sales and profit. Moreover, the term hawked connoted a very different class of trader in eighteenth-century England. As Mathew White and The Gentle Author have shown, itinerant traders like hawkers and peddlers who sold a variety of items door-to-door and on city and town streets were perceived as threatening specialised consumer-goods shops in London and Bath. Advertisements for some baked goods sold by traders who owned shops for instance, carried warnings about "fakes" being distributed by hawkers who misrepresented where their products were made. Government-issued licenses criminalised hawkers who were not officially recognised and deepened a sense of suspicion towards these nomadic traders. Belinda as commodity and her aunt as trader are thus likened to a class that were seen as illicit and of a lower social status. In the age of growing consumerism, social status was linked more with visiting a trader's shop (with an established pedigree in terms of a local reputation) rather than with hawkers, who, if they were women, were also commonly believed to be selling their bodies.

Anne Mellor has argued that *A Vindication* had a significant impact on female novelists in the Romantic period. She calls attention to the novels of Jane Austen and Maria Edgeworth among others to illustrate how certain kinds of social behaviour were gendered and critiqued in the light of the rational marriage espoused in *A Vindication*. Austen and Edgeworth for instance, both critique maternal neglect, coded in their novels in the form of women characters who cause domestic conflict because of an incorrect execution of their duties in this sphere. Both these novelists also explore the social role of mothering by focusing not only on biological mothers but on various female mentor figures who care for, educate and eventually work towards the social integration of the main female protagonists. Thus, while Lady Bertram's competence as a mother and lady of the household is questioned in *Mansfield Park* (1814), Austen also critiques her sister (who has no children) Mrs Norris's attitude towards guiding her nieces and nephews. Similarly, the eponymous heroine of Maria Edgeworth's novel *Belinda* is educated primarily by female authority figures who are not her mother – her aunt Mrs Stanhope and the Lady Delacour. Both are found wanting in the execution of their duties. Mrs Stanhope's reputation of working tirelessly to settle her many nieces advantageously tarnishes Belinda's social reputation, as she is the last of the nieces to be married. Lady Delacour, chosen by Belinda's aunt to be her tutor in all matters regarding fashion and social success, is seen to be hiding social, emotional and physical ruin and only putting up the appearance of success and beauty.

Lady Bertram as biological mother in Austen's *Mansfield Park* is contrasted with Sir Thomas Bertram regarding her participation in the moral education of their children, especially their two young daughters. Lady Bertram's financial and social circumstances are the best among the three sisters as the lady of Mansfield Park and she is thus called upon to take the responsibility of education and development of one of her nieces, Fanny. Fanny's own family is very large (she is one of nine children) and seen as unfit in providing the close attention required for a young person to thrive. Austen describes Lady Bertram's disposition at the time of Fanny's arrival and acclimatisation at her new home thus:

> To the education of her daughters, Lady Bertram paid not the smallest attention. She had not the time for such cares. She spent her days in sitting nicely dressed on a sofa, doing some long piece of needlework, of little use and no beauty, thinking more of her pug than her children, but very indulgent to the latter, when it did not put herself to inconvenience, guided in every thing important by Sir Thomas, and in smaller concerns by her sister. (18)

Reflecting on her role in Fanny's education subsequently, Lady Bertram

> could only say it was very unlucky, but some people *were* stupid, and Fanny must take more pains; she did not know what else was to be done; and except her being so dull, she must add, she saw no harm in the poor little thing—and always found her very handy and quick in carrying messages, and fetching what she wanted. (18)

Fanny's development into an individual with a sound sense of moral duty towards her adoptive family is seen to be made possible *despite* the neglect of Lady Bertram and specifically *because* of the guidance of Sir Thomas Bertram and his younger son, Edmund. The irony in the description of Lady Bertram's attitude to Fanny's difficulty with learning is evident when contrasted with the individualised attention and care with which Thomas Bertram facilitates someone of Fanny's social background to achieve the status his own children possessed at birth.

Lady Bertram's daily activities described above represent a disposition that is at odds with the requirements posed by any family expecting to retain a social standing during a transitional time in England. The children of the Bertram household, including Fanny, are expected to participate in the heterosocial activities of the day (card playing, dining outside the home, ballroom dancing and horse riding, among others) but at the same time exercise reason and moral judgement since these very activities leave them vulnerable to corruption and likely social disgrace. Lady Bertram's disposition (along with her sister's), made stark by Sir Thomas's long period of absence, is almost directly linked to the moment in the novel when a heterosocial activity is seen to threaten order at Mansfield Park. The young Bertram children, including the eldest daughter who is engaged to be married, are influenced by their close acquaintances (a brother–sister pair visiting the parsonage adjoining Mansfield Park) to put up a play while Sir Thomas is away at his plantation in the West Indies. With no responsible parent supervising rehearsals, all members in the household give free reign to their desires, ultimately exposing the Bertram children to individuals who would bring ruin to their lives.

Wollstonecraft's insistence on the friendship between the sexes necessary to inculcate a more equitable marriage is also explored in Austen's novels in her analysis of the different types of marital relationships of her time.[2] While she is well-known for her portrayal of marriage as the only means through which women could attain financial security, she also focuses on the means through which women could negotiate this constraining circumstance. Developing their reason and moral sense was the means through which women could choose partners with whom they could also aspire to a degree of liberty and friendship, *earned* from the man in the sense in which Wollstonecraft describes the ideal marriage for both sexes. Through the exercise of reason, modesty and a careful judgement of her own and others' actions, Austen's female protagonists *earn* the affections of their partners rather than enticing them through coquetry or deception that furthers their own selfish ambitions to become wealthy and powerful. While her female characters discern themselves through the exercise of reason, the men in her novels are also shown as wanting in the performance of their duties as fathers, brothers and companions to women. Successful marriages in her novels result not from unchecked passions and feelings but from a patient preparation of the mind and the self that sets aside immediate (individual) gratification in favour of following a larger moral code. The eldest Bertram daughter, Julia, is seduced by Henry Crawford in *Mansfield Park* while she is engaged to Mr Rushworth during the staging of the play in Sir Thomas's absence. Julia's lack of proper education (resulting from parental neglect) and the overzealousness of friends and acquaintances in matchmaking merely to further social advantages contribute to her poor judgement regarding marriage in the novel. She assesses Henry Crawford and Mr Rushworth's potential candidatures as future husbands driven only by sexual desire in the first instance and by social standing in the second. Thus, when Henry Crawford's attentions suddenly cease, Julia reacts petulantly and seeks revenge rather than judge his character for pursuing an engaged woman. Moreover, for Julia,

> Independence was more needful than ever; the want of it at Mansfield more sensibly felt. She was less and less able to endure the restraint which her father imposed. The liberty which his absence had given was now become absolutely necessary. She must escape from him and Mansfield as soon as possible, and find consolation in fortune and consequence, bustle and the world, for a wounded spirit. (198)

And once her mind is made up, Austen ironically remarks "In all the important preparations of the mind she was complete; being prepared for matrimony by an hatred of home, restraint, and tranquility; by the misery of disappointed affection, and contempt of the man she was to marry" (199). It is through the exploration of this line of reasoning in the novel that the eventual failure of Julia's marriage and a resulting life of scandal and isolation is prefaced. Julia, unlike Fanny, does not see her home and family as a resource. She also enters marriage determined to assert her individual needs and desires and is thus doomed never to be happy.

Henry Crawford's affections would soon turn to Fanny and her responses to his overtures and eventual proposal of marriage are significant in their contrast to Julia's. Fanny refuses his proposal even in the face of criticism from everyone at Mansfield. On being pressed for a reason by Edmund (conversations with whom are often an extended social commentary on one's choice of partner and career) she says,

> that every woman must have felt the possibility of a man's not being approved, not being loved by some one of her sex, at least, let him be ever so generally agreeable. Let him have all the perfections in the world, I think it ought not to be set down as certain, that a man must be acceptable to every woman he may happen to like himself. (349–50)

Speaking of the character of Crawford's sisters for their insistence that Fanny should accept, she says, "And, and—we think very differently of the nature of women, if they can imagine a woman so very soon capable of returning an affection as this seems to imply" (350). Fanny is proven right in her judgement of Henry Crawford as an unsuitable partner for he would, even as he professed commitment to her, elope with the married Julia, bringing scandal and ruin to both their families. Even more significant is Austen's characterisation of how a young woman ought to respond to the attentions of a man. For her, through Fanny, even when one's social security depends entirely on marriage, reason and moral sense above all is what should guide the choice of partner. It is also important to note here that both Wollstonecraft and Austen advocate an equality of both genders, and Austen is even careful in *Mansfield Park* to attribute Fanny's improved temperament as an adult largely to Edmund Bertram who goes on to marry her. Edmund too, like Henry Crawford, has a change of heart to love Fanny since he is seen to desire Henry's sister Mary through most of the novel. Austen however sees the sudden awakening of love for Fanny as "natural" since,

> Loving, guiding, protecting her, as he had been doing ever since her being ten years old, her mind in so great a degree formed by

> his care, and her comfort depending on his interest, dearer by all his own importance with her than any one else at Mansfield, what was there now to add, but that he should learn to prefer soft light eyes to sparkling dark ones. (469)

Even as Fanny is seen to possess the power to refuse Henry Crawford's unsuitable proposal, she still must wait for Edmund to realise the choice that is most "natural" for him, illustrating again, the limits placed on women's autonomy with respect to marriage at this time. Moreover, Edmund's care and the opportunities afforded by Mansfield Park for educational and social advancement are precisely what make Fanny a suitable partner, illustrating subtly the vestiges of hierarchy that will remain even in a carefully planned marriage. Austen draws attention here to the limited access that middle-class women had at the time to social resources like education and cultural refinement that were necessary to secure an advantageous marriage. Education and marriage were thus important themes that were explored at this time in the context of gender. Men and women were seen by writers like Wollstonecraft, Austen and Edgeworth to be prepared differently by their social circumstances to enter important institutions like marriage and professional trades. While Wollstonecraft advocated for a change in women's educational curriculum at school and within the family as a means of better preparing them for equality in marriage, writers like Austen and Edgeworth would explore in their novels, the various modes through which the cultivation of one's mind and the operation of reason could protect young men and women even when endangered by parental neglect and the faulty judgement of siblings and peers.

Gender and Romantic Aesthetics

Among the well-known modes of writing that emerge in the period designated as Romanticism in English literature is writing focused on writing itself – the effects produced by a piece of writing, the process of composition, the relationship between the one who writes and the object he/she produces. Often grouped as "aesthetics" and "literary criticism", writing of this kind assesses the merits and demerits of various literary forms while also attempting to situate them in a larger framework of understanding. For instance, writers in this period would return repeatedly to questions about the roles played by the dominant forms of literary writing – the novel, poetry and drama – and the effects produced by either following or breaking with the long-standing conventions they each followed.

Several writers, most notably Wordsworth and Coleridge in their *Lyrical Ballads* (1798), aimed to set their poetic endeavours apart from the conventions that had governed this form thus far. Wordsworth would add a preface to this collection of poems that sought to clarify not only his and Coleridge's aims to reimagine poetry but would also comment on the role of the poet and his audience. Several other writers too, like William Hazlitt, Percy Shelley, Anna Barbauld, Clara Reeve and Joanna Baillie, would write and reflect on the nature of their role as poets, critics, dramatists and novelists. What is significant for our purposes in this chapter is to examine how the profession of writing at this time was in fact gendered. In other words, the form one chose or sometimes, even the subjects one wrote about, were associated with one's gender. Poetry, as we shall see, was made sense of as a male domain and given values that can be seen as masculine. Similarly, writers and publishers viewed their markets in a gendered way as well – it was well documented for instance that novels, especially romances, were largely read by women. In its extensive focus on the social role of writers, English Romantic literature offers us plenty of evidence to study the social values attached to different kinds of writing by men and women, some of which persist even today.

As we have seen already via discussions of men and women's participation in domestic and civic life, English romantic writers like Wollstonecraft, Jane Austen and Maria Edgeworth would reflect on the ideals of masculinity and femininity prevalent at the time. The sexes were also distinguished during this time based on how they approached and made sense of the world. Burke's *A Philosophical Enquiry into the Origin of our Ideas of the Sublime and Beautiful* (1757), was an early and influential text in the tradition of those that explored sex-based differences in perception and feeling. Burke studies in this work, human responses or "passions" that arise in response to various external stimuli. Among these passions he focuses on the sublime and the beautiful as two important and extreme responses that can be evoked by nature and works of art that seek to convey the external world to their audiences. Burke is responding here to the classical ideal of "clarity" which he challenges through an exploration of human understanding premised instead on incomprehension, unknowability and obscurity. Burke is interested in the passions he describes as sublime and beautiful since they arise through a mixture of pain and pleasure, thus demonstrating an intermingling of states of feeling generally thought to be distinct.

A Philosophical Enquiry is interesting here for the ways in which it characterises differences between the sexes. In discussing the relationship between utility and beauty, Burke says that "if beauty in our own species, was annexed to use, men would be much more lovely than women; and strength and agility would be considered as the only beauties" (85). It is evident here that physical attributes like strength and agility are seen to inhere only in men, just as weakness and passivity are a defining feature of women. "The beauty of women", Burke says for instance, "is considerably owing to their weakness, or delicacy, and is even enhanced by their timidity, a quality of mind analogous to it" (101–02). Throughout *A Philosophical Enquiry* Burke returns to the idea that the passions of the sublime and the beautiful and the many states of being and objects that evoke them are distinct. However, Burke also clearly outlines a hierarchy between the two, thus reflecting the greater social authority enjoyed by men and masculine values at the time. One of Burke's illustrations for impressing upon his readers the inherent differences between the sublime and beautiful for instance, is the responses he believes the mother and father elicit in a child. The father's "authority", Burke states, while "being useful to our well-being" and "justly venerable" does not elicit love in the way that the mother does where the "authority is almost melted down" into "fondness and indulgence" (93–94). Authority is thus invested in the father, necessitating the child's submission while the mother's "melted down" authority *submits to* the child through indulgence. This encoding of male power as active and terrifying and female care and love as submissive illustrates a tacit privileging of one over the other. In addition, qualities associated with men and women, seemingly arising in biology, would have an effect, as evident in Burke, on social and cultural aspects of life as well.

The sublime would also become an important category for figuring a self in Romantic writing, especially poetry. I will return to this idea in the chapter on the self but it would be useful at this point to illustrate how the sublime as portrayed in poetry also has implications for gender. For instance, the sublime is often evoked in Romantic poets' descriptions of states that give rise to conflicting emotions or when faced with objects of immense scale. Shelley's "Mont Blanc" is a classic instance of the sublime in poetry, staging as it does a moment of mental "blockage" when faced with the awe-inspiring sight of the Alpine mountain. Rather than "submitting" to the terrifying sight of the mountain however, Shelley uses the contrary emotions it evokes to make concrete another entity – the poet's imagination and his capacity for creation. The poet's capacity to receive and comprehend the complex (and sublime) emotions evoked by a remote and expansive landscape enhances his significance in this place rather than diminishing it. Contemporary psychoanalytic readings of the poem and by extension, the category of the sublime in Romantic literature, argue that this illustrates an index of masculinity. Patricia Yaeger (1989) for instance, in developing a theory of the "female" sublime, argues that male Romantic poets' expression of moments of blockage as in the case of "Mont Blanc" is an enactment of a pre-Oedipal desire to merge once again with the maternal. This desire for a feminine other, however, needs to be masked to preserve the unity of the poet's male self. The "masculinisation" of the mountain in "Mont Blanc" occurs precisely to ensure the "unity" of the male self – it is only through the appropriation of this seemingly distant and masculine force that the poet–subject is able to assert himself. Yaeger distinguishes this from the "feminine sublime", using examples from women poets in the twentieth century, that returns to the masculine sublime of the Romantics to reclaim it as a way of expressing female identity. This feminine sublime, for Yaeger, attempts to be intersubjective (exploring connections between the subject and the perceived sublime object/experience) and confronts difference without feeling a threat to the self.

Tim Fulford too has shown that Burke's formulation of paternal authority as sublime and terrifying illustrates a dominant model of masculinity in the Romantic period and one specifically associated with the English aristocracy. In the revolutionary climate of the late 1790s, England sought to distinguish itself from France in many ways. Gender roles and the sexual practices of the ruling class became, Fulford argues, one of the primary lenses through which revolutionary politics was fuelled in the Romantic period. England thus establishes a particular "chivalric" code of masculinity or male ideal to distinguish its perceived superiority from France at the time. The French monarchy, specifically Marie Antoinette, would come to be regarded by revolutionaries as excessive in their appetite for consumption especially when situated against the severe economic distress the country was in at the time. Antoinette was viewed as sexually promiscuous and was targeted by France's revolutionary citizens as representing everything that was wrong with a monarchical form of rule. Burke would famously state in his *Reflections* that the "age of chivalry" can be considered as having passed if a queen (Marie Antoinette) could not find protection in the (sublime) power of the monarchy. Burke's critique of the early events of the French Revolution are based in the idea that in monarchy there resides a masculine power whose chivalric code includes the protection of the weak (especially and including women). This chivalric code, according to Burke, is destroyed by the acts of revolutionaries who attempt to unseat the present social order.

While the public denouncing of a queen's immorality led to a rearticulating of how politics was gendered in France (Robespierre and Napoleon both represented different modes of being a male leader that separated them from the excessive frivolities of the aristocratic regime), sexual scandal involving the children of George III led to a similar reorientation of gender norms in England. The Duke of York, son to George III and the British army's commander-in-chief, became implicated in a scandal in 1808 involving his mistress, a well-known courtesan named Mary Anne Clarke, who was believed to be offering promotions to men in the army in return for bribes. For many members of the British public, this was indicative of corruption and sexual impropriety on the part of the aristocracy and a weakening of military strength at a time when it was most needed in the ongoing war against France. Clarke managed to garner a great deal of public support in the aftermath of the scandal while the Duke was censured in Parliament and temporarily even relieved of his post. George IV, who ascended the throne in 1820, would similarly face public censure over the long trial faced by his wife, Queen Caroline, over allegations of adultery.

The public support shown for Caroline and Clarke can be interpreted as the desire to appropriate them within a chivalric code of masculinity that was distinctly English and to be distinguished from the weakening of this code in France where Antoinette was instead reviled through the lenses of sexual misconduct and impropriety. Moreover, as Fulford has shown, the Regency-era princes would fail to rise up to the masculine code of military valour necessitated in the time of war with France and were compared unfavourably with Lord Nelson, the naval commander who led the British to victory in the Battle of Trafalgar in 1805. In an England anxious to avoid revolution and extend the people's support for their monarchs (at a time when they were being publicly sentenced to death in France), the chivalric masculine code of duty and honour was personified in popular war heroes like Lord Nelson and typified in the fictional world by the male protagonists of Walter Scott's novels.

Poetry in the Romantic period was imagined in very masculine terms resulting in it being privileged over other dominant forms like the novel. Anna Barbauld records in *On the Origin and Progress of Novel-Writing* (1810) that while poets are practitioners of only one kind of fictional writing, they still receive undue admiration when compared to the writers of other popular fictional forms like romance novels. Poetry is also gendered as masculine with respect to the language used to describe its process of creation – several theories of authorship at this time would describe the poetic profession as male while comparing the act of poetic creation itself to giving birth thereby appropriating/controlling female powers of creation. Speaking of the manner in which the poems in *Lyrical Ballads* differ from the poetic traditions that precede them, Wordsworth says in his preface of 1802 that even as they exclude him, they nevertheless "from father to son have long been regarded as the common inheritance of Poets" (101). Poets and poetry are thus tellingly visualised here as property that passes via a male lineage.

Several other works in the period, including those by women, cite Milton and Shakespeare as the primary norm against which all subsequent works are compared, thereby establishing a strong association between poetry (especially poetry of a good quality) and men. Writing about the capacity that distinguishes a poet, Wordsworth says that he

> rejoices more than other men in the spirit of life that is in him; delighting to contemplate similar volitions and passions as manifested in the goings-on of the Universe, and habitually impelled to create them where he does not find them. To these qualities he has added a disposition to be affected more than other men by absent things as if they were present; (104)

Creating in the absence of immediate external stimuli is thus viewed here as essential to poetic practice. The poet is distinguished by the capacity to recognise the "spirit of life" he carries within him and can direct the "creation" of that which he finds absent. While the capacity to create life may be exclusively feminine, Wordsworth here appropriates this life-generating capacity for poetry and also designates it as being directed via a conscious exertion of will. The male poet can create "from the structure of his own mind" alone, without even the need for "immediate external excitement" (104). Coleridge in his *Biographia Literaria* (1817) similarly describes imagination as being "essentially *vital*, even as all objects (as objects) are essentially fixed and dead" (712). Moreover, for Coleridge, imagination is the "synthetic and magical power" which the poet is able to "put in action by the will and understanding" (714). Here again, poetry is viewed as "vital" or life-giving while at the same time being directed by the poet's "will and understanding" alone rather than through external stimuli.

William Hazlitt in his *Lectures on the English Poets* (1818) describes poetry as that which "puts a spirit of life and motion into the universe. It describes the flowing, not the fixed" (149). In his *A Defence of Poetry* (1821), Shelley too would speak of the life-force of poetry that is inherent in the poet when he speaks of the inability to translate what the poet "creates" into another language. "The plant must spring again from its seed", he says, "or it will bear no flower" (1236). Comparing the "poetical faculty" to painting and sculpture, Shelley says, "a great statue or picture grows under the power of the artist as a child in the mother's womb, and the very mind which directs the hands in formation is incapable of accounting to itself for the origin, the gradation, or the media of the process" (1244). Poetry would thus continue to be characterised in this period in *active* terms while poets themselves were largely associated with and claimed affiliation to men. In addition, associating poetry with men and likening the act of creating poetry with giving birth essentially excludes women from activities that necessitated both men and women at this time. Citing the case of *Frankenstein* (1818), where a man is literally able to give birth with no need for a woman, Barbara Caine has argued that women's role and significance were diminished in eighteenth-century England by the reimagining of masculinity at this time (43). The man of sensibility was one who would now increasingly appropriate qualities that were considered feminine like childbirth and care. In addition, the qualities of rationality, genius and humaneness would come to be seen as exclusively male. As we shall see, this would have important implications for female authorship in this period.

A distinct strand from this kind of "masculine" theorising about poetry in the Romantic period can be seen among writers like Clara Reeve, Anna Barbauld, Hannah More and Joanna Baillie. These women writers focus on vastly different aspects of the writing process when compared with their male counterparts. Rather than visualising the poet's or writer's self as embodying a vital, life-giving capacity, they focus on his/her moral responsibility. Writing is viewed as a process in which the reader is an equal participant and whose needs are determined by gender. Interestingly, these writers characterise forms of writing, whether poetry, novels or drama, based on their *effects* on the reader, thus moving away from arguments made by Wordsworth, Coleridge and Hazlitt that seek to separate poetic skill from external stimuli. This can be seen in Clara Reeve's *The Progress of Romance* (1785), where she traces the history of romances from ancient Greece to her time in order to illustrate what this genre lends to the modern novel while remaining distinct from it. By writing the piece as a series of evening conversations between three characters, Hortensius, Euphrasia and Sophronia, Reeve is able to explore the gender implications of reading romances and novels. Speaking of the ills of circulating libraries – institutions set up in the late eighteenth century that offered middle-class women an unprecedented access to books – Hortensius remarks that women now expected their suitors to treat them in the manner of a hero from a romance. The effects of reading romances for Hortensius are an increasing gap between the material reality of women of the time and the adventure, intrigue and adoration they are accustomed to in the world of the romance. The selection of a suitable partner, Hortensius fears, would be impossible for a woman who would find every gentleman suitor "plain" in comparison to the heroes of the romance. Tellingly, Hortensius states that it is women who read romances and novels and are thus in greater danger than men. Euphrasia counters this by stating that men too, aided by their educational syllabi, encounter the classic romances and in being taught to revere these, also imbibe the morals, vices, idolatry and follies they espouse. This conversation ends with all three friends agreeing that a careful selection is necessary to protect young readers of both sexes from those works in any genre that are "vicious and immoral" (156). Reeve here makes a clear connection between the modern novel and the impact it has on ideas of romantic love and young men and women's sense of self.

Perhaps the most extensive exploration of this moral responsibility that imagines the Romantic writer's self as emerging in relation to another rather than in isolation, is in Joanna Baillie's "Introductory Discourse" to her *A Series of Plays, In Which It Is Attempted to Delineate the Stronger Passions of the Mind, Each Passion Being the Subject of a Tragedy and A Comedy* (1798). Contrary to the idea of the poetic self as developed by Wordsworth, Coleridge and commented on by Hazlitt, Baillie describes what she calls a "sympathetick curiosity" that is activated by the dramatist. For Baillie, we are all inherently curious about human nature and as a result, even from our childhood, always keenly observe others. Building on this idea of an "instinct" for an interest in others, Baillie argues that we are moved and entertained but also learn a great deal from viewing (at a safe distance) actors who simulate situations of great calamity or distress. Speaking of "sympathetick curiosity", Baillie says, "from it we are taught the proprieties and decencies of ordinary life, and are prepared for distressing and difficult situations. In examining others we know ourselves" (442). For Ballie, it is those writers who have successfully activated this part of their nature both in themselves and their readers that are successful and "instructive". Speaking specifically of poetry, Baillie suggests that even if the poet were to present readers with the "grandest scenes" that entered his imagination but with all reference to man removed, then there could be no resulting pleasure for we seek always to see and understand those like us. Anna Barbauld in *On the Origin* similarly argues for the celebration of that aspect of a writer's talent that activates a particular kind of pleasure in the reader. She says, "above all, the power exercised over the reader's heart by filling it with the successive emotions of love, pity, joy, anguish, transport or indignation, together with the grave impressive moral resulting from the whole, imply talents of the highest order and ought to be appretiated accordingly" (172). Barbauld too, like Reeve and Baillie, is interested in the execution of the writer's moral responsibility rather than his/her embodied talents alone.

Moreover, these writers are especially interested in the role played by reading and writing for women. They argue for a gendered aspect to the appreciation and creation of writing that gives us a sense of differential access to education and social interaction. Speaking of the differences in audiences for poetry, plays and novels, Barbauld argues for novel-reading being a "domestic pleasure". Drama and poetry for Barbauld carry class connotations as well; drama requires "expense" while poetry a "certain elevation of mind and a practised ear" (176). In addition to being cheap, the novel exposes the female reader to characters whom she "in the retired scenes of life hardly meets with at all, and many whom it is safer to read of than to meet" (177). The novel for Barbauld thus has a distinct moral responsibility to each of the sexes and given women's poor access to education, functions as their primary mode of instruction about the larger world. Barbauld echoes Hannah More's ideas in her *Strictures on the Modern System of Female Education* (1799) that women read so they can improve their minds and conduct. For More, a lady "is to read the best books, not so much to enable her to talk of them, as to bring the improvement which they furnish, to the rectification of her principles and the formation of her habits" (222). More here argues for a "practical approach" to reading, where women only accumulate knowledge and learning that will prove useful for the profession they are to enter –marriage and motherhood.

While contemporary readers may note that More conflates women's biology with only one kind of usefulness, in the context of the Romantic period it is interesting to observe that even one's relationship with reading and writing was thought to be determined by gender. It is important to note here that there were multiple strands of making sense of what it meant to be a man or woman, especially in the context of the literary sphere. While the widely studied male authors describe a certain model of being an author or a public literary figure, the female writers considered here significantly differ in their approach. Women writers like Reeve, Barbauld and Baillie can be seen to focus on the didactic value of literary texts, especially as they pertained to women's education and the development of their judgement. Also notable is their focus on both genders and an insistence on equality rather than the marking of the literary and aesthetic terrain as exclusive.

For instance, Baillie and Barbauld both demonstrate an awareness of the role played by gender in writing a play and a novel. Baillie notes in her "Introductory Discourse" that with "some degree of softening and refinement, each class of the tragic heroes I have mentioned has its corresponding one amongst the heroines" (448, n. 11). For Baillie, the norm is clearly not masculinity in the context of characters representing certain passions (she lists the tender and "pathetick", the great and magnanimous, the passionate and impetuous as being equally typified by men and women) in a tragic play. Baillie asserts that a dramatist can show the presence of a "corresponding" spirit in both male and female characters when portraying responses to a tragic event thus illustrating her belief in behaviour not being rooted in biology. Barbauld, while arguing for separate spheres in novel reading and writing nevertheless seeks to explore the structural circumstances that lead to this division. Speaking of the expression of "melancholy" in novels, she reflects in *On the Origin* that this is very often a feature of women's writing. She attempts to find an explanation for this in something outside biology however when she says "Is it that they suffer more, and have fewer resources against melancholy? Is it that men, mixing at large in society, have a brisker flow of ideas, and, seeking a greater variety of characters, introduce more of the business and pleasures of life into their productions?" (176). Barbauld thus identifies something typical about men and women writing but also seeks a sociocultural explanation for this difference. In stating that women have "fewer resources against melancholy" and men "mix at large in society", Barbauld hints at social factors that work alongside biological traits to determine difference.

Dorothy Wordsworth's journals and poems can also be seen as presenting a very different kind of self when compared with other male Romantic poets and especially her brother, William Wordsworth. For instance, Dorothy's sense of experiencing the place where she lived with her brother – the Lake District –

is markedly different in how it evokes a sense of community. While several of Wordsworth's poems – the famous "Daffodils", "Resolution and Independence", "The Discharged Soldier" – present the poet-narrator's solitude, Dorothy's journal entries detailing her life with her brother capture a much more "embedded" sense of self. Her record of their life together captures many people and voices – the Wordsworths' many visitors, the rural community surrounding their cottage and their almost daily interactions with them – rather than sharpen and concretise her perspective alone. Moreover, Dorothy's recording of the minutiae in her surroundings were expressly intended as a source of detail for several of Wordsworth's poems. She often performed the role of his scribe and editor as he wrote and revised several of his poems for publication. Dorothy's stance as a poet and writer is thus different from Wordsworth in tone as well since she writes (very often) in her journal *for him* and he writes for a *public* that, while comprising strangers, is much larger in scope.

It may be useful at this point to consider the Wordsworths' account of an event they witness together to observe differences in how they see others and their relationship with them and most importantly, their role as writers. The event is their meeting with a leech-gatherer, recounted by Dorothy in *The Grasmere Journals* (1800–03) and by Wordsworth in his "Resolution and Independence" (1807). Dorothy's entry is dated Friday, 3 October 1800 and reads:

> When William and I returned from accompanying Jones, we met an old man almost double. He had on a coat thrown over his shoulders above his waistcoat and coat. Under this he carried a bundle and had an apron on and a nightcap. His face was interesting. He had dark eyes and a long nose (John, who afterwards met him at Wythburn, took him for a Jew). He was of Scotch parents but had been born in the army. He had had a wife, 'and a good woman, and it pleased God to bless us with ten children'; all these were dead but one of whom he had not heard for many years, a sailor. His trade was to gather leeches, but now leeches

> are scarce and he had not strength for it. He lived by begging and was making his way to Carlisle where he should buy a few godly books to sell. (664)

Dorothy continues this entry to detail the man's analysis of why leeches were now a scarce commodity and his memory of having been wounded when it was "late in the evening, when the light was just going away" (664). Wordsworth's "Resolution and Independence", published in 1807, recalls the meeting with the leech-gatherer following a lengthy prefatory musing on his own state of mind that day:

> To me that morning did it happen so,
> And fears and fancies thick upon me came,
> Dim sadness, and blind thoughts I knew not nor could name (lines 26–28)

Wordsworth attempts to clarify these "fears and fancies" and "dim sadness" by invoking the figures of Thomas Chatterton and Robert Burns, both of whom, in his mind, are representative of the fate that awaits all poets—"We poets in our youth begin in gladness, / But thereof comes in the end despondency and madness" (lines 48–49). Wordsworth's sorrow in being reminded of poets whose work no longer makes them happy (or rather, ceases to have vocational utility) is what precedes his encounter with the leech-gatherer in his narration. The moment in which he sees the man is dramatised as much as the details regarding his appearance and demeanour which follow -

> Now whether it were by peculiar grace,
> A leading from above, a something given,
> Yet it befell that, in this lonely place,
> When up and down my fancy thus was driven,
> And I with these untoward thoughts had striven,
> I saw a man before me unawares—
> The oldest man he seemed that ever wore grey hairs. (lines 50–56)

Wordsworth would then use Dorothy's description of the man as "bent double" before comparing him to a huge stone on top of a cliff, a sea-beast that emerges from the water to sun itself and finally as someone who seemed "not all alive nor dead, / nor all asleep, in his extreme old age" (lines 71–72).

Several differences are immediately apparent when we see the Wordsworths' descriptions of the same event side-by-side. What is of interest is the kind of relationship they establish between themselves and the old man they meet. Both writers clearly see their role as one that must mediate the story of this poor rural-dweller for a genteel audience, while also expressing awareness of a socioeconomic superiority. Dorothy takes pains to reproduce the old man's account in his own words and recalls John's observations about him, while Wordsworth very much stages the encounter as taking place when he is alone. "I saw a man before me" establishes the poetic presence in a landscape very differently from Dorothy's "William and I" and "we met an old man". Moreover, both writers perceive the object in the landscape, in this case the old man, very differently. Dorothy clothes him (even while observing some eccentricity) in the attire of other common people (a coat, waistcoat, apron, nightcap), describes his parents and wife, his trade, opinions and memories. In short, she contextualises his presence in the land in very local and individualised ways. In contrast, Wordsworth's comparisons of the old man with a huge stone, a sea-creature, and extreme and ambiguous states of being ("not all alive nor dead", "extreme old age") strive to take him out of the place where he is into an abstract plane.

The old man is rendered more familiar and rooted (while being conscious of the resemblance with a Jew) in Dorothy's account than in Wordsworth's where he appears unfamiliar enough to be similar in nature to clouds and other things which are motionless. Wordsworth's presence is also very consciously marked as poet in his account while Dorothy disappears in hers after the initial statement about meeting an old man. The repetition of "he" in Dorothy's account, along with the rich detailing of the old man's side of their conversation (one assumes that he responds to questions asked but her account makes no mention of this) is what serves as characterisation. Wordsworth's account on the other hand creates a dramatic setting for the transference of the old man from corporeal entity to poetic memory:

> And the whole body of the man did seem
> Like one whom I had met with in a dream,
> Or like a man from some far region sent
> To give me human strength, and strong admonishment.
> (lines 116–19)

And later,

> While he was talking thus, the lonely place,
> The old man's shape and speech, all troubled me;
> In my mind's eye I seemed to see him pace
> About the weary moors continually,
> Wandering about alone and silently. (lines 134–38)

Like in the case of the poet-ego in Mont Blanc, in Wordsworth too, the object's effects on the poet's sense of self, integrity and unity are of primary importance. In Wordsworth's account, the old man's presence begins to fade almost exactly at the point when he begins to speak – Wordsworth is even forced to repeat questions because his mind is so occupied by creating an image of the old man "within himself". Dorothy awards primacy to the old man and a thick detailing of his life's circumstances while characterising the meeting itself as routine and very much a part of everyday occurrence in the communal life of the district where she resided at the time. The novelty of Wordsworth's encounter and its significance for his poetic identity (and capacity) occupies more of his poem than a description of the old man's local/filial contexts.

Dorothy Wordsworth's own encounters with mysteries in nature do not serve the function of repairing or resolving a conflict within. They also are not utilised, as in the case of Wordsworth, to illustrate the poet's capacity to create without external stimuli.

Instead, there is a mode of seeing that appears to be unique, especially when viewed against the literary community (including Wordsworth, Coleridge and Charles Lamb among others) in which Dorothy was embedded. For instance, in her "Floating Island at Hawkshead, An Incident in the Schemes of Nature" (1842), she refuses to imaginatively reconstruct the mystery of "how" a "slip of earth" was "loosed from its hold". She also does not view the floating island as a spectacle that serves as an index of her imaginative prowess and instead describes it through a keen ecological sensibility: birds find shelter on it, fruits and flowers bloom in it and "there insects live their lives-and die: / A peopled *world* it is; in size a tiny room" (Dorothy Wordsworth, lines 15–16). She also does not mourn the eventual disappearance of the island because to her "the lost fragments shall remain, / To fertilize some other ground" (lines 27–28). The object in nature, in her poetry and writing, does not pose a threat to the unity of self or overwhelm the capacity for comprehension. Instead, as in the case of the floating island teeming with life and guaranteed infinite existence in some form, she confronts this difference with a sense of wonder and curiosity rather than anxiety.

The case of the Wordsworths offers the student of Romantic literature a unique insight into the intersection of gender and writing – two writers who lived and documented their life together, produced nearly comparable quantity of writing and yet received such different contemporary and historical attention and recognition. There were several structural factors that allowed gender to map the Wordsworths in the way that it has. As an unmarried woman for instance, Dorothy's role in her brother's household was that of a caretaker, and the time and opportunity available for composing and publishing verse was vastly different for both of them. As the next section explores, a woman's entry into public life as a writer in the eighteenth century was made sense of and negotiated in very specific ways. The Wordsworths' very different writerly postures are thus also a reflection of these structural differences – Dorothy would write of a "bashfulness, a struggling shame" about writing poetry in her posthumously published "Irregular Verses" (1978) –rather than an intrinsic difference in writing as a man or woman in the Romantic period. Jill Ehnnen, for instance, is cautious in imposing too rigid a separation between "masculine" and "feminine" modes of writing such that these categories appear impermeable and literary works by women are consequently seen as existing entirely outside the canon of male, "high" Romantic literature. Ehnnen instead urges us to look at the interdependent nature of the Wordsworths' authorship – their use of Dorothy's journals as a common source, their invocation of each other in their writing and their negotiation of a writerly stance – rather than focus on their contribution to exclusive modes of writing. In this manner of revisiting the Wordsworths, masculine and feminine modes of being in the world through writing are viewed as being equally available to and negotiated by both writers.

In the next section of this chapter we will explore a larger context for what we have been describing as masculine and feminine strands of English Romanticism. Ideas about men and women were influenced, this section will show, both by the literary accomplishments of the previous generation as well as the changing circumstances under which the generation that came to be known as Romantic was writing.

Gender and Romantic Theories of Authorship

As detailed earlier in this chapter, gender is one of the most prominent modes through which the study of English Romanticism has been revisited. A significant intervention made by gender studies of Romantic literature is in theories of authorship or, in the ways in which certain notions about writers and writing developed in this period. Detailed attention will be paid to the emergence and understanding of the individual in a subsequent chapter on the self in Romantic writing, but at this point I would like to briefly illustrate how gender relates to ideas of authorship at this time. Romantic writers were, as Andrew Bennett has shown, very interested in theories about literary creativity and production. Studying these theories can thus tell us a great deal about Romantic attitudes towards gender and literary creation. The very widely studied theories of authorship from this time have been detailed earlier in this chapter – Wordsworth's *Preface*, Colerdidge's *Biographia Literaria,* Shelley's *Defence* and Hazlitt's essays make up what is considered typical of Romantic-era thinking about who or what an author is. As argued earlier however, not only did these writers imagine authorship (with respect to poetry) as exclusive to men but also overtook typically female roles like reproduction in the visualising of poetic skill as being rooted in the male poet's body.

Several women writers, however, imagined their role as authors very differently – the author in their works is tasked with the responsibility of instructing his/her readers in developing the right attitude and judgement to navigate life in a rapidly transforming England. For instance, Diane Hoelver argues that the genre of the Gothic novel, known for its popularity among women readers and writers, created a heroine who was "professionally feminine" even as she worked to dismantle the various institutional structures that oppressed her. Against the backdrop of a rapidly industrialising England and a bourgeoisie middle class emerging in the wake of the French Revolution, the heroines and (female) authors of Gothic novels created narrative worlds in which they, along with their readers, could reimagine the existing social order. Hoelver posits that the heroines in these novels adopt a role of "studied femininity" that veils the threat of their ultimate takeover of filial inheritance or the creation of matriarchal family structures in the novels. A specialised genre within the popular form of the novel is thus utilised by female authors to express desire for covert rebellion against institutionally sanctioned codes of feminine conduct and women's role in the family and home.

Another way to understand how female creativity and literary production by women was seen in the period is by paying attention to public discourse about women writing. Anne Mellor, for instance, traces a history of the use of the term "bluestocking" to demonstrate the anxiety over female authorship that was on the rise in the Romantic period. Bluestocking referred, in mid-eighteenth-century Britain, to any member of an informal intellectual group that came together to discuss arts, politics and literature. Members of this group included artists, writers, translators and publishers, and belonged largely to the gentry and the professional middle classes. Meetings were organised and facilitated by a leader, typically elite women, who hosted these gatherings at their home and thus controlled the agenda and membership of this circle. The prominent early bluestocking leaders included Elizabeth Montagu, Elizabeth Vesey and Frances Boscawen, all representative of the kind of high-profile woman the term was initially associated with.

Montagu, Vesey and Boscawen had access to wealth and learning (they were also able, by virtue of belonging to the gentry, to thrive in social life especially after and notwithstanding the deaths of their husbands) and used this to patronise the writers and artists in need in their circles, in addition to performing philanthropic activities. Even though the term bluestocking originated from the worsted wool stockings (a choice which separated the working classes from the gentry and aristocracy) worn by a man (the bishop Stillingfleet) to gatherings hosted by Vesey, it would increasingly refer to women alone by the late eighteenth century. A second generation of bluestockings expanded the scope of meetings from London to provincial towns like Bath, Batheaston and Lichfield but continued to feature female hostesses or organisers of meetings. This second generation features several writers of the Romantic period, notably Anna Barbauld, Hannah More and Anna Seward, who were influenced by the bluestocking circles and would carry their values and traditions forward in the late eighteenth and early nineteenth century.

As Mellor, Eger and Pohl and Schellenberg have shown, studying historical contexts and scholarship about the bluestockings can reveal prevailing (and enduring) ideas about women writers. These works study public perceptions about women writers in order to demonstrate the processes through which gender becomes linked with intellect, literary production and entry into social and public life. They observe, rather significantly, that the term bluestocking would come to suddenly attach itself to a woman writer in the Romantic period without connoting the respect and admiration it did in an earlier part of the century.

In 1779, for instance, the painter Richard Samuel would hail nine of the prominent bluestocking women, including Montagu, Barbauld and More, as "The Nine Living Muses of Great Britain". But by the late eighteenth century, especially in the wake of the French Revolution, the bluestockings would become subjects of satire and ridicule and a female writer or a woman of intellect started to connote a danger to social stability. Richard Polwhele would publish *The Unsexed Females* in 1798 where he alleges that women writers go against nature and abandon their biological disposition towards softer sensibilities by looking "sternly" upon the violent outcomes of revolution in France. He mentions the bluestocking writers celebrated in Samuel's painting, but divides them into two categories. Barbauld and Kauffman (among other women writers like Mary Robinson, Charlotte Smith and Helen Maria Williams) belong to his first category as examples of "unsexed" women who defy nature and biology to embrace a life of the mind (by pursuing reason and intellect) in the "democratic storm" unleashed by the French Revolution. For Polwhele, these writers have emerged as unsexed on account of being influenced by Wollstonecraft's works, especially *A Vindication*. Speaking of the transgressions occasioned by women entering the sphere of politics, reason and philosophy, he writes,

Nor the quick flutter, nor the coy reserve,
But nobly boast the firm gymnastic nerve;
Nor more affect with Delicacy's fan
To hide the emotion from congenial man;
To the bold heights where glory beams, aspire,
Blend mental energy with Passion's fire,
Surpass their rivals in the powers of mind
And vindicate the Rights of womankind. (lines 83–90)

Polwhele thus recognises that vindicating the rights of women in the context of debates surrounding the rights of man following the French Revolution necessitates the "power of mind" or in other words, participating in the public sphere and writing in a literary genre dominated by men until then: the political pamphlet.

Women writers like Wollstonecraft and those she inspired, Polwhele suggests, transgress the biological traits of womanhood like the "quick flutter" and "coy reserve". Moreover, by making several references to Wollstonecraft's much publicised private life in his poem (Wollstonecraft would die at childbirth in 1798 and an account of her life, including two affairs, an illegitimate child and multiple suicide attempts, was detailed by her husband, William Godwin, in a memoir following her death), Polwhele draws attention to her unsuitability as a public figure. He contrasts the unsexed female writers who ride the wave of radicalism occasioned by the Revolution with female writers who address "listening girls" with "grave advice" and names Hannah More, Frances Burney and Ann Radcliffe as belonging to this category. These writers, for Polwhele, exert a more favourable influence on society through moral instruction and by assuming their natural (biological) role of engaging the realm of feeling and emotions rather than reason. Hannah More, as noted earlier, takes a more conservative approach to women's education when compared with Wollstonecraft. For More, as set out in her *Strictures on the Modern System of Female Education*, women are to be educated to improve their capacity to care within the context of the household and family and not for the sake of "literary vanity" or pretensions to "genius". These female writers, whose public role Polwhele approves, also notably remain within the genres traditionally associated with women: novels and conduct books. Clara Reeve's *The Progress of Romance* was reviewed favourably in *Town and Country Magazine* in 1785 for instance since it was "elaborate" on a subject that "is so peculiarly the province of the fair sex" (Robinson 428).

Byron's *The Blues: A Literary Eclogue* (1821) similarly illustrates a shift in the way female authorship is perceived in its satirising of bluestocking gatherings. The bluestocking is described here as a learned and wealthy woman who is unsuited for marriage and whose literary competence is questionable. Lady Bluebottle, the bluestocking hostess of Byron's play organises gatherings at her home that her husband describes thus:

> No pleasure! no leisure! no thought of my pains,
> But to hear a vile jargon which addles my brains;
> A smatter and chatter, glean'd out of reviews,
> By the rag, tag, and bobtail, of those they call 'BLUES;'
> A rabble who know not—But soft, here they come!
> Would to God I were deaf! as I'm not, I'll be dumb. (Eclogue the Second, lines 20–25)

Two men at the start of the play when discussing whether to attend Lady Bluebottle's gathering, decide that seeing Miss Lilac, Lady Bluebottle's yet unmarried daughter, would make their attendance worthwhile. When one of the men professes to wanting to marry Miss Lilac, the other cautions him thus: "You wed with Miss Lilac! 'twould be your perdition: She's a poet, a chymist, a mathematician" (lines 64–65). The intellectual woman is clearly viewed here as transgressive – she is seen as being unable to conform to the social categories of wife and mother in the private and domestic sphere while her entry into public life is viewed as contributing nothing but a "vile jargon" comprising a "smatter and chatter".

Women's presence in public life, as authors and as intellectuals, had to thus be carefully negotiated as this could have an impact on one's literary reputation. As the case of Wollstonecraft makes clear, the boundaries of literary genres and the evaluation of literary accomplishment was carefully policed in the Romantic period such that the author's gender played a big role in determining his/her "authority" and sphere of influence. Polwhele's listing of the more "acceptable" models of femininity in public life via figures like Hannah More suggests the conflating in this period of biology with artistic ambition and capability. To belong to one's sex, that is the female sex for example, meant the restriction of one's literary ambition to more feminine spheres – comprising, as discussed earlier in this chapter, the genre of the novel, and topics relating to domestic life and the development of moral judgement. Mellor (2013) has argued that a marked shift can be traced in the way that women writers presented themselves in public from the start of the Romantic period in the 1790s to the early nineteenth century to confront the growing anxiety about female literary success. She notes that the satirising of female authorship by male writers in this period stems from the anxiety over the entry of several women readers, writers and publishers into the literary market in this period. For her, Hannah More typifies the figure of the "virtuous" female intellectual who negotiates public life by aligning with issues important for women – practical education and employment – while at the same time distancing herself from the more glamorous image of an earlier generation of bluestockings. In this way, More and other women writers who followed her example would create a more acceptable model for a woman as a public intellectual by foregrounding in their writing, the importance of motherhood and skills for governing the household. By the early nineteenth century, successful female authors would no longer pose a threat to their male counterparts so long as they disavowed the radical politics of the period following the French Revolution and argued against excesses of any kind.

As detailed in the previous chapter, women writers played a prominent and public role in the abolitionist movement in England. Here too, a feminine aesthetic can be discerned in women's participation in this widespread reform movement. Male writers' participation in this enterprise was from a social position that allowed them to speak in recognisable institutional spaces like parliament and through the polemical style of pamphlets, histories and reports. Women's role in the abolitionist movement, especially as it pertained to writing, utilised sentimental modes to allow white readers to identify with the condition of slaves. Hannah More for instance establishes this mode in her "Slavery, A Poem" that inaugurated a new kind of aesthetic for women abolitionist writers. Moreover, More's social authority as a popular writer who is sanctioned by the Abolitionist society situated her style of representing slaves and the institution of slavery as the standard for the age. This standard comprised a focus (in addition to appealing to Christian sentiments and seeing slaves as fellow-Christians) on the domestic and filial attachments of the slave.

Following More, other writers like Ann Yearsley ("A Poem on the Inhumanity of the Slave Trade", 1788) and Amelia Alderson Opie ("The Black Man's Lament", 1826) would criticise the impact of slavery on filial relationships like siblings, partners and children. These poems feature extended scenes in which families are separated when slaves are transported and sold. For instance, Yearsley challenges the slave merchant's hypocrisy in breaking apart slaves' families thus:

> Away, thou seller of mankind! Bring on
> Thy daughter to this market! Bring thy wife!
> Thine aged mother, though of little worth,
> With all thy ruddy boys! (lines 83–86)

Opie presents an imagined Negro voice in her "The Black Man's Lament", an anti-slavery poem written for children, who prefaces his account of being transported by saying,

From parents, brethren's fond embrace;
From tender wife, and child to tear;
Then in a darksome ship to place,
Packed close, like bales of cotton there. (lines 21–24)

Women abolitionists thus urged their readers to situate slaves within their families while recreating sentimentalised scenes of separation. Moira Ferguson argues that this sentimental mode within abolitionist literature would even result in the public labelling of such themes in writers like William Cowper as "feminine". The abolitionist movement is thus another important context for studying the intersection of gender and authorship in the Romantic period. Abolitionist writing by women (in women-dominated forms like children's literature as well as the "masculine" forms like poetry) allowed for the creation of a specialised and publicly legitimised feminine rhetoric for rights at a time when women did not have political representation. Women abolitionist writers also saw parallels between their own status (inferior to men in a variety of social, political and economic arena) and those of African slaves. While this abolition-enabled political participation would contribute significantly to the cause of female emancipation in England, it would also simultaneously perpetuate a stereotypical lens through which slaves would come to be viewed even in the subsequent century. Ferguson argues for instance, that British women writers producing abolitionist poetry, especially in the eighteenth century, tended to homogenise the figure of the slave such that he/she was seen as a passive victim in need of uplifting by social and cultural betters – the English.[3] As demonstrated in the chapter on revolutions, the figure of the slave also needed tempering in the light of successful slave revolts in England's colonies following the example of the French.

English Romantic writing thus offers insights into the various social roles prescribed for men and women in the late eighteenth and early nineteenth century. In addition, to see writing in this period as gendered is to pay attention to the ways in which writers made sense of what qualities comprise femininity and masculinity. As this chapter has demonstrated, the lens of gender allows us to re-evaluate writing from this period and see a greater diversity in what we have come to view as English Romantic literature.

Works Cited

Austen, Jane. *Mansfield Park*. Wordsworth Classics, 1992.

Baillie, Joanna. "Introductory Discourse." *A Series of Plays. British Literature 1780–1830*, edited by Anne K. Mellor and Richard E. Matlak, Harcourt Brace, 1996, pp. 439–58.

Barbauld, Anna Letitia. "On the Origin and Progress of Novel-Writing." *British Literature 1780–1830*, edited by Anne K. Mellor and Richard E. Matlak, Harcourt Brace, 1996, pp. 171–80.

Bennett, Andrew. "Expressivity: The Romantic Theory of Authorship." *Literary Theory and Criticism*, edited by Patricia Waugh, Oxford UP, 2006, pp. 48–58.

Burke, Edmund. *A Philosophical Enquiry into the Origin of Our Ideas of the Sublime and Beautiful*. R and J Dodsley, 1757, *Eighteenth Century Collections Online Text Creation Partnership*, 2011, http://name.umdl.umich.edu/004807802.0001.000. Accessed 23 Dec 2019.

Byron, George Gordon. "The Blues: A Literary Eclogue." *The Works of Lord Byron, Poetry, Volume IV*, edited by Ernest Hartley Coleridge, 1901, *Project Gutenberg*, https://www.gutenberg.org/files/20158/20158-h/20158-h.htm. Accessed 24 Dec 2019.

Caine, Barbara. "Women". *An Oxford Companion to the Romantic Age: British Culture 1776– 1832*, edited by Iain McCalman, Oxford UP, 1999, pp. 42–51.

Coleridge, Samuel Taylor. "Biographia Literaria." *Romanticism: An Anthology*, 4th ed., edited by Duncan Wu, Wiley-Blackwell, 2012, pp. 711–14.

Edgeworth, Maria. *Belinda*. 1801, Hachette, 2010.

Eger, Elizabeth. "Introduction." *Bluestockings Displayed: Portraiture, Performance and Patronage 1730–1830*, edited by Elizabeth Eger, Cambridge UP, 2013, pp. 1–12.

Ehnnen, Jill. "Writing against, Writing through: Subjectivity, Vocation, and Authorship in the Work of Dorothy Wordsworth." *South Atlantic Review*, vol. 64, no. 1, 1999, pp. 72–90.

Ferguson, Moira. *Subject to Others (Routledge Revivals): British Women Writers and Colonial Slavery, 1670–1834*. 1992, Taylor & Francis, 2014.

Fulford, Tim. *Romanticism and Masculinity: Gender, Politics and Poetics in the Writings of Burke, Coleridge, Cobbett, Wordsworth, De Quincey and Hazlitt*. Macmillan, 1999.

Hazlitt, William. "Lectures on the English Poets." *British Literature 1780–1830*, edited by Anne K. Mellor and Richard E. Matlak, Harcourt Brace, 1996, pp. 149–51.

Hoeveler, Diane Long. *Gothic Feminism: The Professionalization of Gender from Charlotte Smith to the Brontes*. Penn State UP, 1998.

Mandell, Laura. "Canons Die Hard: A Review of the New Romantic Anthologies." *Romanticism on the Net*, no. 7, 1997, https://doi.org/10.7202/005755ar. Accessed 11 Feb 2021.

Mellor, Anne K. *Romanticism and Gender*. Routledge, 1993.

———. "Mary Wollstonecraft and the women writers of Wollstonecraft's day." *The Cambridge Companion to Mary Wollstonecraft*, edited by Claudia L. Johnson, Cambridge UP, 2002, pp. 141–59.

———. "Romantic Bluestockings: From Muses to Matrons." *Bluestockings Displayed: Portraiture, Performance and Patronage 1730–1830*, edited by Elizabeth Eger, Cambridge UP, 2013, pp. 15–38.

More, Hannah. "Slavery, A Poem." *British Literature 1780–1830*, edited by Anne K. Mellor and Richard E. Matlak, Harcourt Brace, 1996, pp. 206–10.

———. "Strictures on the Modern System of Female Education." *British Literature 1780–1830*, edited by Anne K. Mellor and Richard E. Matlak, Harcourt Brace, 1996, pp. 220–24.

Opie, Amelia Alderson. "The Black Man's Lament." *British Literature 1780–1830*, edited by Anne K. Mellor and Richard E. Matlak, Harcourt Brace, 1996, pp. 82–84.

Polwhele, Richard. *The Unsexed Females*. Cadell and Davies, 1798, *University of Virginia Library Electronic Text Center*, 1994, http://etext.lib.virginia.edu/toc/modeng/public/PolUnse.html. Accessed 24 Dec 2019.

Prince, Mary. "The History of Mary Prince, A West Indian Slave." *British Literature 1780–1830*, edited by Anne K. Mellor and Richard E. Matlak, Harcourt Brace, 1996, pp. 869–80.

Reeve, Clara. "The Progress of Romance." *British Literature 1780–1830*, edited by Anne K. Mellor and Richard E. Matlak, Harcourt Brace, 1996, pp. 152–56.

Robinson. "The Progress of Romance, through Times, Countries, and Manners". *The Town and Country Magazine, Or, Universal Repository of Knowledge, Instruction, And Entertainment 1769–1796*, vol. 17, 1785, pp. 428–29, *Hathi Trust Digital Library*, https://hdl.handle.net/2027/hvd.hw28y4. Accessed 24 Dec 2019.

Shelley, Percy Bysshe. "A Defence of Poetry." *Romanticism: An Anthology*, 4th ed., edited by Duncan Wu, Wiley-Blackwell, 2012, pp. 1233–247.

The Gentle Author. "The Cries of London". 15 May 2014, *British Library*, https://www.bl.uk/romantics-and-victorians/articles/the-cries-of-london. Accessed 11 Feb 2021.

Thomason, Laura E. "The Dilemma of Friendship in Austen's 'Emma.'" *The Eighteenth Century*, vol. 56, no. 2, 2015, pp. 227–41.

Todd, Janet M. *Women's Friendship in Literature*. Columbia UP, 1980.

White, Mathew. "The Rise of Consumerism". 14 October 2009, *British Library*, https://www.bl.uk/georgian-britain/articles/the-rise-of-consumerism. Accessed 11 Feb 2021.

Wollstonecraft, Mary. *A Vindication of the Rights of Men and A Vindication of the Rights of Woman*, edited by Janet Todd, Oxford, 1993.

Wordsworth, Dorothy. "The Grasmere Journals." *British Literature 1780–1830*, edited by Anne K. Mellor and Richard E. Matlak, Harcourt Brace, 1996, p. 664.

———. "Floating Island at Hawkshead, An Incident in the Schemes of Nature." *British Literature 1780–1830*, edited by Anne K. Mellor and Richard E. Matlak, Harcourt Brace, 1996, p. 659.

———. "Irregular Verses." *British Literature 1780–1830*, edited by Anne K. Mellor and Richard E. Matlak, Harcourt Brace, 1996, pp. 667–69.

Wordsworth, William. "Resolution and Independence." *British Literature 1780–1830*, edited by Anne K. Mellor and Richard E. Matlak, Harcourt Brace, 1996, pp. 593–95.

Wordsworth, William and Samuel Taylor Coleridge. *Lyrical Ballads 1798 and 1802*. Oxford UP, 2013.

Yaeger, Patricia. "Toward a Female Sublime." *Gender and Theory: Dialogues on Feminist Criticism*, edited by Linda Kauffman, Basil Blackwell, 1989, pp. 191–12.

Yearsley, Ann Cromarty. "A Poem on the Inhumanity of the Slave Trade." *British Literature 1780–1830*, edited by Anne K. Mellor and Richard E. Matlak, Harcourt Brace, 1996, pp. 263–68.

Notes

1. See for example, the prefatory remarks about changes made in *The Norton Anthology of English Literature* and Duncan Wu's *Romanticism: An Anthology*. The Norton Anthology's eighth edition introduces changes to its volume on the Romantic period entirely through references to the expansion of women writers and their works. See also Laura Mandell's "Canons Die Hard: A Review of the New Romantic Anthologies" for a detailed analysis of how gender can guide the language of anthologising. Mandell notes gender biases even in inclusive attempts at anthologising which continue to favour male authors in the period in parameters relating to the number and length of works included.
2. The theme of friendship in Austen's novels and female friendships particularly, has received a lot of scholarly attention. See for instance, Janet Todd's *Women's Friendship in Literature* for a focus on representations of homosocial bonds between women in eighteenth-century novels. See also Laura Thomason's "The Dilemma of Friendship in Austen's *Emma*" for an overview of philosophical debates about friendship known to authors in the Romantic period. Thomason contends that eighteenth-century thinking about the goals of friendship – comprising egalitarianism, power hierarchy and autonomy to choose one's friend – were seen to be outside the purview of women who lacked the means and circumstances for such relationships. *Emma* suggests, in Thomason's view, that a woman could strive to fulfil some of these friendship goals through marriage.
3. Ferguson argues that the slave in women's abolitionist literature exists in a kind of non-place and is homogenised in his/her

victimhood. Outside of scenes of auction in Hannah More and sugar plantations in Amelia Opie, individualised details about the slave's family, cultural and social beliefs or perspective are not provided. For some variation in this trend of representing slaves and the institution of slavery see Yearsley's "A Poem on the Inhumanity of the Slave Trade" that visualises a relationship between the slave and other members of his family rather than just between him and his masters. Yearsley's slave, titled Luco, is also a rebel although brutally punished for it. See also Mary Prince's account of her years as a slave in *The History of Mary Prince, a West Indian Slave*. One of the earliest published narratives authored by a slave, albeit with extensive English publishing and editing support, *The History* is important for rejecting the existing conventions within which Africans and their experience of slavery was discussed in English poetry. Prince details the hardships of slave labour and her ill-treatment by white masters not via a sentimentalised lens alone but by making explicit her awareness that she is "subject" to a denial of rights that English citizens, even servants, are not.

THREE

Literary Cultures: Media and the Romantics

The loaded Press beneath her labour groans,
And Printers' devils shake their weary bones;
While Southey's Epics cram the creaking shelves,
And Little's Lyrics shine in hot-pressed twelves.
Thus saith the *Preacher*: "Nought beneath the sun
Is new," yet still from change to change we run:

(Byron, *English Bards and Scotch Reviewers: A Satire*, lines 125–30)

Nineteenth-century English media would give rise to the first modern literary celebrities, promote new authorial voices and shape cultural attitudes and tastes in reading and writing in the Romantic era. As seen in the case of the French Revolution in Chapter One, the 1790s was a crucial moment in the history of English literature as far as – what modern-day readers would describe as – the media is concerned. The early events of the French Revolution could only make the kind of impact they did on English men and women on account of the existence of a publishing and printing industry as well as the emergence of a new class of readers (middle and working class) that would continue to expand well into the Romantic period. The pamphlet war following the publication of Burke's *Reflections* as well as the unprecedented sales of Paine's *Rights of Man* (Part 1 is believed to have sold 150000 copies and Part 2 sold as many as 200000) also show that print media was becoming a dominant feature of life in eighteenth-century Britain. Most importantly, the growth of print media signalled the existence and creation of a reading audience over whom, in the politically volatile climate of the 1790s, both conservative and revolutionary writers would compete.

Looking closely at various aspects of the print media industry in the Romantic period will allow us to trace the beginnings of several modern notions about literature. Some of these are the idea of the professional literary career, the figure of the author as one that ought to be opposed to commercial values, the social dimension of literature and its audiences (moral instruction and propaganda) and the consequent need for regulation and censorship. To begin with, this chapter will explore periodicals and periodical culture as a prominent aspect of print media in the late eighteenth and early nineteenth centuries in Britain. The Romantic-era periodical is now itself an object of study, in addition to contributing valuable insights into the shifting attitudes towards reading and writing during this time.

The Romantic-era Print Economy

To fully understand why the study of media in the Romantic period contributes to our understanding of its literature, it is necessary to outline what constituted the media at the time. Eighteenth-century media was primarily composed of books and periodicals and sustained by a variety of factors.[1] However, no study of the media is complete without also considering its modes of circulation and readership. At the start of the Romantic period, in the late eighteenth century, book publishing continued to be very expensive and was thus largely the domain of the elite. Producing books, purchasing and storing them required resources, and the diffusion of this kind of media was thus limited to the upper classes. Technological improvements in the form of Earl Stanhope's Iron Hand Press in the early nineteenth century and later, the steam-driven printing presses acquired by *The Times* newspaper in 1814, led to a significant increase in the rate of production of printed materials. The number of books entering the market thus increased, allowing for the sale of second-hand books and reprints that supplied a larger and more diverse audience than before. Stephen Behrendt notes for example that in 1798, when the *Lyrical Ballads* first appeared, it was only one of 150 books published in that year dedicated to poetry alone. He further estimates the total number of separate volumes of poetry published between the years of 1770 and 1830 at 10000 (101).

Periodicals of various kinds were the other significant representative of print media in the eighteenth century. Periodical is a term that encompasses a broad range of dailies, weeklies, quarterlies and monthlies being published and circulated in Britain at this time. Periodicals, as Richard Altick, Jon Klancher and Marilyn Butler have shown, are a significant but generally ignored mode of writing that shaped eighteenth-century literature, in addition to the well-studied forms of the novel and poetry. Butler traces a history of the periodical in Britain to show how the predecessors of famous magazines like *The Gentleman's Magazine* and *The Monthly Review* were dedicated to specialised topics and were not meant for the general reader. With the publication of these periodicals the idea of the "general interest" magazine was born where eventually, reviews of literary works and the demand for developing original content would result in the commodification and professionalisation of writing itself. A discernible shift occurs in periodical publishing in the late eighteenth and early nineteenth centuries, where along with an increase in their numbers (over 80 literary journals appeared during the Romantic period), their tone and attitude towards readers too underwent a change. Where the eighteenth-century general interest as well as literary magazine aimed at informing what was assumed to be the newly forming middle classes, the nineteenth-century periodical would begin to diversify an already existing public into smaller groups along the lines of politics, profession and gender, among others.[2] The eighteenth-century periodical for instance, routinely featured letters from readers thereby establishing a nearly equal relationship between magazine/magazine-editor and the public it addressed.[3] From the start of the nineteenth century however, this kind of participation from readers would increasingly diminish and be replaced by the commissioned professional writer who, together with the periodical, assumed an editorial "voice" that talked directly to a pre-determined audience. The professional writer grew to occupy the space provided by an unprecedented demand for print. As this chapter will go on to discuss, this professionalisation reorganised writing and the writing persona by showcasing experimentation, providing publishing opportunities without bias to one's class or gender and taking an active role in commenting on literary and cultural standards. To complete our picture of print media in the Romantic period, let us now turn to a discussion of who these print materials were addressed to and how.

In the previous century, literary and artistic creations were only possible through patronage and were thus addressed to and circulated in a very small network of elite readers. The eighteenth-century "print marketplace", where literary works were mediated via various periodicals and publishers to specialised audiences, came to replace this earlier system of patronage. The expanding market for print media was further fuelled by documented knowledge of distribution networks both in the cities and provinces which led to the consolidation of a "national" public. Where the patronage system suffered from the inconsistencies and huge financial risks borne by a single investor, the eighteenth-century print trade was able, through models like subscription financing, to level the financial risk and provide a more equal footing for authors and their readers. Moreover, publication opportunities increased with the rise in the number of periodicals and English men and women from all ranks of society were able to find their way to a certain reading public. Editors of periodicals would routinely receive anonymous submissions in addition to several pieces sent in by members of the aristocratic and professional classes with literary ambition. A certain notional equality thus began to emerge with the rise of periodical publishing where anybody who wanted to could be published and read. Stiff competition between periodicals raised the demand for printed content, allowing writing to become a paid profession – periodical editors now solicited writing for a fee. However, sustaining oneself purely through money earned from writing was only possible at this time by taking over editorship or a particular column. Writing for the media would thus change what it meant to be a writer. Compared to the idea of the artist prevalent in the earlier system of patronage, the Romantic writer as contributor to periodicals had to contend with criticisms of being a slave to the market rather than achieving independent influence. The Romantic-era writer who earned a living from contributing to the growing print and publishing trade seemed to be losing autonomy in a sphere now increasingly shaped by a rapidly growing reading public. This new category of the public comprised an abstract ideal of a group of readers who were now empowered to select or reject one's work. With the power to make or break literary careers, this group was not always celebrated but seen as dangerous too.

Studies of periodical literature and publishing point to an emerging class of readers that were created by a set of economic, social and political factors in the eighteenth and nineteenth centuries. The circulating library for example, increasingly came to subsidise the rising cost of books and allowed the growth of a middle-class readership. While fiction was one of the main attractions of the circulating library, this institution in the late eighteenth century would also feature titles in many other categories. The classically-educated elite would however express anxiety over the effects of reading fanciful tales (like romances and sentimental novels) on the newest entrants from different classes into the realm of literacy and learning. The establishment and expansion of Sunday schools similarly contributed to higher literacy levels among the working classes and those with aspirations to gentility now had a sense of the immense value placed in this period on learning. This very same class of readers were also the target of much of the radical writing in the aftermath of the French Revolution. Moreover, the reader who comprised the audience or public for various print media need not necessarily be imagined only as an English man or woman who had come into contact with a circulating library, bookseller or had access to education. Altick has noted for instance that there is evidence of all classes of readers – even those who were illiterate – getting acquainted with the major English novelists of the Romantic period and later nineteenth century (like Walter Scott and Charles Dickens) through the common practice of reading aloud. Pubs and coffeehouses were common locations for reading aloud and as institutional subscribers, they were able to reach out to a larger audience (comprising their patrons) than the average household subscriber. Scholars studying the history and social background of reading thus consider factors like the cost of printed materials, educational efforts as well as practices of reading to make sense of the expanding market for print media in eighteenth- and nineteenth-century England.[4]

Studying the Romantic-era publishing industry as a whole allows us to form a picture of how readers encountered writers and their works, what factors influenced the production of various printed materials and what, if any, were the linkages in this network. In a more recent study of the Romantic publishing industry and reading practices, William St Clair offers some pertinent observations on the methods of literary history and their impact on how we understand literary works. St Clair's attempt is to widen what counts as evidence while interrogating the cycle of book publication and consumption in the past. While print sources about the discourses governing reading practices (generally studied as they appear in conduct books, periodical reviews and edition prefaces, for instance) are important for a history, so too are the numbers representing the functioning of the publishing industry – print runs, the cost of book editions and data about reading habits from circulating libraries. Moreover, to fully understand the impact of books on readers, one has to take into account when and in what manner authors and their works were read. For example, works from the Enlightenment and the seventeenth century were very much alive in the Romantic period through readers who had access to print editions of these in addition to contemporary works. Similarly, several contemporary authors and their works, notably Mary Wollstonecraft's *A Vindication of the Rights of Woman* or Jane Austen's novels, did not have quite as many readers in their lifetime. For St Clair, literary histories generally tend to follow a parade or parliament model – the first assumes that a parade of "great" works follow one another in the presence of passive reader-spectators and the second models the publishing-reading relationship of the past as a parliament-style debate between works. This notion of the reading practices of an earlier time do not take into account several other factors that influence a print economy while also perpetuating (often incorrectly deduced) ideas about the importance or marginality of select literary works.[5]

The successful proliferation of print media at this time would also not have been possible without the contribution of religious and political societies. Corresponding societies or parliamentary reform societies played a key role in disseminating radical literature in the 1790s, following the French Revolution. The London Corresponding Society for example, via its network of urban and provincial radical publishers and booksellers played an important role in ensuring a wide readership for the first edition of Paine's *Rights of Man.* Paine was quoted at every corresponding society meeting, enabling even those who could not afford the first edition to become acquainted with the work. He would eventually make the second part of *Rights of Man* as well as the first available in a much cheaper edition, resulting in the remarkable sales figures recorded even in his own lifetime. Altick suggests that if the circulation figures for

Rights of Man, Part 2, estimated to be 1500000 copies, are true then that would mean that there was approximately one copy of the book for every ten people in the United Kingdom at the time (70). Even before radical publications like *Rights of Man* reached the English working-class reader, there existed a street literature market for print media that was catering to the very same audience. Street vendors would hawk a variety of popular print media, often printed and sold very cheap, that comprised broadsides, broadsheets and chapbooks. The content of these was often topical, such as the immediate account of a recent public event of note or even a printed record of traditions that had so far been oral, for instance – ballads, myths and legends. Accounts of crimes committed and even what were purported to be "dying confessions" of those convicted were distributed in the form of broadsides at public executions.

Worried over unexpected consequences of their Sunday school system in the form of a newly literate working-class reader who could now read writing that incited him/her to revolution, the Anglicans responded with Hannah More's *Cheap Repository Tracts*. Modelled on the format of existing street literature like ballads and fables, these tracts preached patriotism and censured revolt. The *Cheap Repository Tracts* aimed to undo the effects of radical and popular print media, believed at the time to be primary agents of potential revolution in England. The Romantic period thus witnessed not only an unprecedented growth in the production of print media but also the emergence of a new kind of reader. There were now systems in place through which classes of Englishmen other than the aristocracy and nobility could access the printed word and this had an impact on reading and writing itself. Wordsworth's Preface to the *Lyrical Ballads* and Coleridge's *Biographia Literaria*, for example, can be meaningfully contextualised alongside the emergence of a new reading public. These texts sought to describe the poet's specialised social function while simultaneously offering guidance with traversing existing styles of writing. Romantic writers offering these instructions targeted emerging modes of print consumption – the circulating library, female and young readers and genres that addressed them – thus demonstrating awareness as well as anxiety about a transforming reading public. The diverse and growing English reading public would serve as yet another location of vulnerability in this age of revolutions and print industry. Print could now circulate with a logic of its own, posing challenges to regulation in important areas of national discourse: political and religious beliefs and literary and cultural tastes.

Writing for the Media: The Periodical Review

Writing in the Romantic era thus ought to be situated against this backdrop of a complex print culture that was responsible for crystallising modern notions of what it meant to be a reader and author and what constituted literary taste. We can now examine contemporary reviews of major Romantic writers to illustrate the key ideas discussed so far – the rise of a professional literary critic, the transition from eighteenth- to nineteenth-century periodical culture and the formation of a public that would replace an earlier patronage system in evaluating works of literature. An early review of Wordsworth and Coleridge's *Lyrical Ballads* in the *Analytical Review* in 1798 reads thus:

> There is something sensible, in these remarks, and they certainly serve as a very pertinent introduction to the studied simplicity, which pervades many of the poems. The 'Rime of the ancyent Marinere,' a ballad in seven parts, is written professedly in imitation of the style as well as of the spirit of the ancient poets. We are not pleased with it; in our opinion it has more of the extravagance of a mad german poet, than of the simplicity of our ancient ballad writers. Some of our young rhymesters and blank-verse-men, highly delighted with the delicacy of their own moral feelings, affect to look down on every thing human with an eye of pity. To them the face of nature is eternally shaded with a funereal gloom, and they are never happy but when their affections, to use the words

> of Sterne, are fixed upon some melancholy cypress. We are happy to conjecture, from some passages in these poems, that the author of them classes not with these fable songsters; (*Analytical Review*, XXVIII, Dec 1798, 583)

The "sensible" remarks alluded to at the start of this review are an extended quote from the "Advertisement" that accompanied the 1798 edition of *Lyrical Ballads* where Wordsworth speaks of the "experimental" nature of the poetry contained within. The quote chosen by the review is also interesting since it mentions in full, his statement that defining poetry should be left to poets rather than critics. Other than an unfavourable comment about Coleridge's famous contribution to this volume, this overall positive review goes on to quote his conversation poem, "The Nightingale" to illustrate how Wordsworth and Coleridge should not be classed with other poets of their time.

Another 1798 review from the *Critical Review* also echoes the idea that Wordsworth should be set apart in some way. Attributed to Southey, this review states that "the 'experiment', we think, has failed, not because the language of conversation is little adapted to 'the purposes of poetic pleasure' but because it has been tried upon uninteresting subjects. Yet every piece discovers genius; and, ill as the author has frequently employed his talents, they certainly rank him with the best of living poets" (*Critical Review* XXIV, Oct 1798, 204). A review in *The British Critic* in 1799 similarly endorses the poet's sole authority in judging what constitutes poetry. Wordsworth, for this reviewer, can thus be taken at his word when he says, "if poetry be a subject on which much time has not been bestowed, the judgement may be erroneous, and that in many cases it necessarily will be so" (qtd. in *The British Critic* xiv, Oct 1799, 365). The review in *The British Critic* also goes on to distinguish and approve of the simplicity of the poems in *Lyrical Ballads* against the "meretricious frippery" of those written by Erasmus Darwin. While these contemporary reviews are not homogenous in tone, there are certain common elements that emerge on scrutiny. The reviews certainly establish as convention, the evaluation of the author against his stated purpose *in his own words*. In fact, to ensure fidelity to the author's own arguments for his work, all the reviews cited above provide readers with extensive excerpts from the work to enable them to see for themselves rather than take the review's word. They seem, in other words, to be aiming for a certain neutral measure of "standards" and are anxious to avoid any indication of a bias or what was known at the time as "puffing" – talking up a work with the view to increasing its sales rather than evaluating its intrinsic merit. These reviews also address the reader assuming he/she is conversant with references to "early english poets", "elder poets" and "Spenser". At the same time, references made to popular forms like the ballad and reminders that Wordsworth's "Goody Blake and Harry Gill" in *Lyrical Ballads* is a well-known tale tell us that these reviews were addressing readers across the social spectrum. Overall, the reviews speak to the reader's literary sensibility, something they assume their readers already possess or aim to develop. The author, meanwhile, is viewed as existing in a professional domain where his standards of evaluation are the domain of his (past and present) professional peers alone. These reviews would also impact writers as evidenced by Wordsworth changing the order in which the contents of *Lyrical Ballads* were arranged in later editions. In the reviews cited above, Coleridge's "The Rime of the Ancient Mariner" was singled out for criticism, prompting Wordsworth to move the poem in later editions of *Lyrical Ballads* such that it was not the first thing readers encountered. He would even state, in a note appended to the poem in the 1800 edition of *Lyrical Ballads*, that it had "great defects".

The treatment of Wordsworth and Coleridge's poetry in the early nineteenth century in the periodical review can illustrate some further transformations that would occur in the relationship between literature and print media at this time.

The Edinburgh Review, or Critical Journal would announce in their inaugural issue that they meant

> to decline any attempt at exhibiting a complete view of modern literature; and to confine their notice, in a great degree, to works that either have attained, or deserve, a certain portion of celebrity. As the value of a publication, conducted upon this principle, will not depend very materially upon the earliness of its intelligence, they have been induced to prefer a quarterly, to a monthly period of publication, that they may always have before them a greater variety for selection, and be occasionally guided in their choice by the tendencies of public opinion. (Advertisement, *The Edinburgh Review*, I, October 1802)

The Edinburgh Review would come to occupy a significant place among nineteenth-century English periodicals of the Romantic period. Donald H. Reiman would note for example, that its influence on reviewing periodicals at this time is comparable to Christopher Marlowe's role in the growth of English drama (831). The advertisement above makes clear that *The Edinburgh Review* chose to separate itself from monthlies like the *Analytical Review* and *Critical Review* and sought to offer a more specialised commentary on works of literature. More significantly, it sees the review not as offering a summary and sample content of works published as in the case of the monthly but as presenting the "tendencies of public opinion" to readers. The tone of the advertisement indicates that the journal is discerning rather than comprehensive in its attention to works published and suggests thus that the reader too be aware that guidance is necessary for the evolution of literary taste in a time when printed matter is abundant.

Reviews published in this periodical are also noticeably different in tone especially with respect to author evaluations. *The Edinburgh Review* would launch for example, a series of attacks on Wordsworth, Coleridge and Southey, whom they referred to derogatorily as the "Lake School". Francis Jeffrey, the editor of the magazine, was responsible for the term and wrote several highly critical reviews of these three poets. His style can be seen in the extract below, in the first issue of *The Edinburgh Review,* from a review of Southey's *Thalaba the Destroyer:*

> The authors, of whom we are now speaking, have, among them, unquestionably, a very considerable portion of poetical talent, and have, consequently, been enabled to seduce many into an admiration of the false taste (as it appears to us) in which most of their productions are composed. They constitute, at present, the most formidable conspiracy that has lately been formed against sound judgment in matters poetical; and are entitled to a larger share of our censorial notice, than could be spared for an individual delinquent. We shall hope for the indulgence of our readers, therefore, in taking this opportunity to inquire a little more particularly into their merits, and to make a few remarks upon those peculiarities which seem to be regarded by their admirers as the surest proofs of their excellence. (*The Edinburgh Review*, I, Oct 1802, 64)

Jeffrey's tone is clearly different from that employed by earlier monthlies when he speaks about varieties of audiences that read the poets of their day. The "many" who are "seduced" into an appreciation of "false taste" are, for Jeffrey, a group that takes the author at his word.

Moreover, he identifies that there is such a thing as "sound judgment" and the current review itself serves as a way of making clear to the reader, how he/she can avoid erroneous judgment. Clearly then, *The Edinburgh Review*, as stated in its advertisement, not only presents "tendencies" of public opinion but also seeks to shape and reform it. Jeffrey would come to see Wordsworth's Preface (1800) to *Lyrical Ballads* as a heretical overturning of English poetic conventions established in the eighteenth century. Wordsworth's Preface was a more detailed version of the Advertisement that accompanied the previous edition of *Lyrical Ballads* and set out a new poetic theory that evaluated the contents of his and Coleridge's experimental volume. Rather than aiming to familiarise readers with the content of this new publication however, as earlier monthlies did, *The Edinburgh Review* instead sought to guard against the admiration of false taste and false claims to novelty. Quoting Wordsworth's famous claim from his Preface later in this review, that he sought to "adapt" and use in poetry, "ordinary language of conversation among the middling and lower orders of the people", Jeffrey challenges its viability. For Jeffrey, the language of the "lower orders" would deprave the beauty of English poetry since it had never been suitable for the form. In 1814, Jeffrey would again remark in a review of Wordsworth's *The Excursion*, that the poet writes with a sense of egoism that leaves the reader (especially the common reader) out entirely. "Long habits of seclusion", he would write, "and an excessive ambition of originality, can alone account for the disproportion which seems to exist between this author's taste and his genius" (*The Edinburgh Review*, XXIV, November 1814, 3). He goes on to suggest that the great poets have always lived in "the full current of society" and Wordsworth's self-imposed seclusion in the Lake District is responsible for his indulgence and lack of restraint in matters of poetic convention.

Barbara Benedict has noted that *The Edinburgh Review* reflected a change in eighteenth-century periodical culture through a focus on an elite and academic discussion of literature. Additionally, *The Edinburgh Review* displayed an overt political allegiance (Whig) while condemning writers like Wordsworth, thus equating one's stand on contemporary issues and the evaluation of literature. *The Edinburgh Review* would also largely focus on topics and writers of Scottish importance – philosophy and science rather than imaginative works with the notable exception of authors like Walter Scott. For Benedict, the periodical did not just create specialised audiences but was responsible for readers treating a discussion of literary works with the same importance as everyday news reports or national and international policy. Nineteenth-century periodical culture would differ in many respects from an extant culture of reading and writing in eighteenth-century Britain.

A coalition of copyright-owning publishers and booksellers, known as congers, would come into being in the eighteenth century and ensure the continued proliferation of classic works from the Graeco-Roman past as well as contemporary works by writers like Alexander Pope. This coalition of booksellers was responsible for early trends of commodifying literature, especially poetry collections, in the eighteenth century.

Since the congers owned copyrights, they were able to shape modes of book consumption and practices of reading by manipulating the presentation of the book itself – different kinds of editions, advertisements for other titles, fonts, book sizes and book catalogues. Many of these modes of paratextual advertising would be familiar to contemporary readers as well; think of the many different sizes, prices and editions (travel-size, pocket-size, hardback, paperback, first editions, revised editions) of already existing books that publishers continue to produce. Poetry collections or anthologies were very valued commodities and featured works by authors of recognisable quality along with a few contemporary works commissioned especially for the collection. Robert Dodsley's *A Collection of Poems in Six Volumes* (1763) for instance was not only popular but responsible for consolidating an index of literary achievement.[6] With an expanding market of readers and the (still) high costs of book production, the nineteenth-century periodical review transformed publishers' abilities to shape literary tastes. Not only did the periodical review's serious focus on discussing literary works come at a significantly lower cost than producing newer versions of older books but it also allowed for several categories of individuals outside the author to enter a public discussion about the value of writing and learning. The writer, critic, publisher as well as the reader were now a part of frequent discussions, in print, over the value of literary works. More significantly perhaps, political affiliations of those involved in periodical production also influenced the range of individuals who would now be considered authors and readers. The elite anthology featuring a pre-fixed standard of literary production or the fine editions of Greek classics were no longer the only modes of curating and negotiating value. The nineteenth-century periodical significantly expanded the class-categories of writers and readers, themes and forms of literary works and the extent of their role in the leading sociopolitical debates of the time.

There are several other notable instances of the nineteenth-century periodical directing readers' attentions towards trends in the production and consumption of print media but with a view to influence and create certain ideas with respect to literature and its evaluation. Coleridge's *Christabel*, for instance, would receive plenty of negative criticism at the time of its publication. *The Antijacobin Review* would state in 1816 that *Christabel* never ought to have made it to a second edition and that the popularity of the first edition was owing to women readers who could not resist Lord Byron's endorsement of the poem (*The Antijacobin Review*, L, 632). Just as there is a very clear bias here towards women's taste in reading, the well-known "Cockney School Attacks" in *Blackwood's Edinburgh Magazine* would characterise the writing of Leigh Hunt, William Hazlitt and John Keats as being vulgar and arising from low social stations. In a review of Keats' *Endymion* in 1818, John Gibson Lockhart (who led the charge against the "Cockney Poets" with his satirical reviews in *Blackwood's Edinburgh Magazine*) would write that composing verse in England has taken on the character of an epidemic which he calls "metromanie" or meter-mania. Lockhart points out the rising popularity of authors from unusual backgrounds (he mentions a female playwright, Joanna Baillie, and the Scottish labourer-poet, Robert Burns) at the time and states that now "farm-servants and unmarried ladies; our very footmen compose tragedies, and there is scarcely a superannuated governess in the island that does not leave a roll of lyrics behind her in her band-box" (*Blackwood's Edinburgh Magazine*, 3, 519). In Lockhart's comments there is evidence for the widespread nature of print media and the swelling of readers' ranks with those from lower social orders. However, Lockhart is also disturbed by the idea that like an epidemic, literary talent or genius too could be blind to one's social and economic circumstance. He is instead arguing for literary merit as only accruing from good breeding and education; he would state later in the review that it was clear that neither Hunt nor Keats were very knowledgeable in classical Greek learning, something that was only accessible at the time to a particular class of Englishmen. Thus, like other nineteenth-century periodicals, Lockhart's reviews sought to shape public opinion about what constitutes "good" English literature while purportedly reporting on public trends regarding reading, writing and publishing.

Lockhart's attacks on the Cockney School were themselves a response to an essay by Hunt in his radical weekly *The Examiner* titled "Young Poets" (1816) which praised Keats' poetic talents. "Young Poets" applauded the efforts of Shelley, John Reynolds and Keats in reviving a new school of poetry that showed a character distinct from the neoclassical styles prevalent at the time. Hunt suggests, echoing the rhetoric surrounding the early years of the French Revolution, that this style is perhaps new only in a revolutionary sense – a return to aesthetic principles and subject matter for poetry upheld since the Restoration in 1660. Keats' "On First Looking into Chapman's Homer" is the illustrative example Hunt uses to describe this return to earlier literary conventions in his *Examiner* essay. This was only Keats' second published poem during his life, and as John Kandl suggests, "On First Looking into Chapman's Homer" invites an additional layer of interpretation when viewed in the context of its publication in a weekly like *The Examiner*. Although the poem is generally studied for its fidelity to the formal sonnet conventions of an autobiographical and private tone, Kandl suggests that this kind of reading masks the very public and political nature of its publication. For Kandl, *The Examiner*'s radical leanings, together with Hunt's invocation of a revolution in poetry and Keats' sonnet celebrating an Elizabethan-era translation of a classical epic, can be taken together as evidence of a stance against interest-groups guarding literary conventions. Periodicals like *Blackwood's* for instance, represented the interests (political, social and literary) of the landed elite to the exclusion – as seen in Lockhart's response to Hunt and Keats – of writers from upwardly mobile (but not yet politically powerful) classes.

The periodical would thus play an important role in crystallising approaches to evaluating literature in the Romantic period. As illustrated by the case of reviews of major literary works of the time, periodicals aimed at reporting on prevailing trends in publishing while also contributing to existing ideas about reading and writing. Reviews were clearly taking a stand on issues regarding the suitability of men, women and certain classes to writing. Similarly, readers' identities were being pre-imagined in a sense and guiding the tone of reviews. For instance, the editors of *Blackwood's*, John Wilson and John Gibson Lockhart, sought a Scottish identity for their periodical in its early years during a politically transitional time for Scotland. Following political union with England in 1707, several of the Scottish elite worried that a distinct culture would be lost through integration with a wealthier and more militaristically powerful nation. Periodicals with Scottish interests like *Blackwood's* would seek to retrieve a unique Scottish identity within English public culture through a critique of ideas they perceived as arid intellectualism, typified in leading figures of the Scottish Enlightenment like Adam Smith and David Hume. They would celebrate instead, Robert Burns, Walter Scott, the simplicity of rustic life and the importance of classical learning in a bid to evoke a feelings-centred nationalism. Literary works like those of Burns and Scott lent an affective dimension to imagining Scotland's past (as distinct from England) and its unique character that was missing in the Scottish Enlightenment thinkers' more abstract theorising of human nature. *Blackwood's* would thus create literary conventions that permitted the existence of distinct cultures within the newly-integrated nations of Scotland and England, even as they politically supported union, integration and English monarchical rule.

Audiences of these periodicals were being asked to imagine that they were part of a highly diversified community where it was important to mark one's allegiance to a certain kind of politics, literary taste and social position. While reading a particular review, like those in the specialised nineteenth-century journal, the reader would immediately become aware that being swayed by an author or critic's opinion meant to not have an opinion of one's own. Characterising women as being seduced by Lord Byron's recommendations of *Christabel* is a clear instance of making readers contend with either aligning or differentiating themselves to a group that is too weak-willed to resist an individual opinion. As Klancher has shown, the periodical played the contradictory role of creating specialised audiences while bifurcating a larger reading public. For instance, several periodicals discussed thus far can be seen performing this contradictory role of both creating and breaking up reading communities. *The Analytical Review* for instance was a known supporter of parliamentary reform and revolutionary ideals, and critical of the government. Meanwhile, *The Antijacobin Review*, which published the critical review of *Christabel* in 1816, was against reform measures like abolition and criticised the growing pro-revolutionary sentiments that arose in England in the wake of the French Revolution. *Blackwood's Edinburgh Magazine* and *The Edinburgh Review* were distinguished by their aggressive and satirical review styles but divided in their political affiliations of Tory and Whig respectively. *The Lady's Magazine: Or Entertaining Companion for the Fair Sex, Appropriated Solely to their Use and Amusement* and *The British Lady's Magazine* were addressed exclusively to women and moved out of the sphere of fashion, needlework and domestic economy (like the *La Belle Assemblee* published from 1806 to 1832) to focus on literary and political writings too. Religious periodicals like *The Methodist Magazine* and *The Evangelical Magazine* catered to audiences very different from those targeted by radical publications like *The Black Dwarf* and *Political Register* but achieved large circulation numbers owing to their cheap prices. Audiences for periodicals were thus very aware that they came together and stood apart not only in their political and religious beliefs but in their socio-economic status as well.

The Romantic periodical is also significant because it provided a platform for several new forms of writing. Praise or admonishment of a literary work and political signalling were not the periodical's only role in shaping literary tastes. As Morrison and Roberts have noted in their study of *Blackwood's Magazine*, the periodical offered a space for experimentation to writers, critics and editors alike. Among the notable new forms inaugurated by *Blackwood's* is the short story, especially tales of terror, which influenced several famous practitioners like Edgar Allan Poe and Nathaniel Hawthorne in subsequent decades. The magazine also promoted original fiction by paying authors of these pieces as much as essayists and reviewers. *Blackwood's* featured the famously innovative *Noctes Ambrosianae* – a series of dialogues among fictionalised versions of the magazine's editors reflecting on their production process. This substantially complicates our understanding of the notion of authorship and its links with creativity in the Romantic period. Lockhart, for instance, during his stint at *Blackwood's* would not only contribute the controversial Cockney School reviews but would write, anonymously and embedded as part of the *Noctes*, several verse and prose compositions that reveal his range as a writer. Interestingly, Lockhart's oeuvre records views on contemporary writers and radicalism in Scotland that reveal a degree of ambivalence in the Tory views typically ascribed to *Blackwood's* writers.[7] Most importantly perhaps, *Blackwood's* would contribute to critical scholarship about emerging forms like the novel and the leading novelists of the day, thus consolidating the role of the critic in the Romantic public sphere.

Media and Romantic Authorship

A favourable or particularly vicious mention in the periodical press was sure to have an impact on the Romantic writer. *The Edinburgh Review* for example, would reach circulation numbers of 12000 copies by 1818. Several Romantic writers would thus come to adopt a persona that was closely linked to the new literary marketplace they found themselves in. Writers' responses to a newly formed public which consumed their works alongside the praise and criticisms of these in the periodical press would take several forms. Coleridge would ponder in his *Biographia Literaria* over the disproportionate criticism he earned over works he believed neither matched the literary standards of his peers like Southey and Wordsworth nor made a mark in the marketplace through large circulation numbers or frequent publications. He notes ironically that he owes his fame, such as it was, almost entirely to criticisms of his work. In the third chapter of *Biographia Literaria* he would say,

> But in promiscuous company no prudent man will oppugn the merits of a contemporary in his own supposed department; contenting himself with praising in his turn those whom he deems excellent. If I should ever deem it my duty at all to oppose the pretensions of individuals, I would oppose them in books which could be weighed and answered, in which I could evolve the whole of my reasons and feelings, with their requisite limits and modifications; not in irrecoverable conversation, where however strong the reasons might be, the feelings that prompted them would assuredly be attributed by some one or other to envy and discontent.

What is important to note about Coleridge's response is the anxiety regarding an unknown public that can judge his work for its merits. The "promiscuous company" being referred to here are the faceless readers of the periodical review whose opinions are influenced by "imprudent" reviewers who thus wield more power than the author himself. More importantly, promiscuity also refers to the unpredictable nature of literary tastes and trends – Coleridge here seems unable to predict the basis for favouring or rejecting an author's works. The periodical review is also compared here to "irrecoverable" conversation where Coleridge aligns "periodicity" with diminished quality. The regularity with which works were produced in the periodical press leads Coleridge to surmise that the passions/opinions giving rise to them ought necessarily to be fleeting and topical and hence of little enduring value.

He would also characterise the English "reading public" as degenerating on account of their patronage of circulating libraries where, he believed, they indulged in a "beggarly day-dreaming". While they were in this passive dream-state,

> the whole materiel and imagery of the doze is supplied ab extra by a sort of mental camera obscura manufactured at the printing office, which pro tempore fixes, reflects, and transmits the moving phantasms of one man's delirium, so as to people the barrenness of a hundred other brains afflicted with the same trance or suspension of all common sense and all definite purpose. (Coleridge)

Coleridge's description of the popular print media of his time as well as the literary periodical is fascinating for the similarities it shares with our present-day worries over the media's hegemonic influence on our literary and cultural tastes. For Coleridge, the print media appears as a powerful institution that seeks to replace the author through its professed aims of securing the best literary and cultural output for the audience it claims to serve. Additionally, Coleridge also appears to be responding to the rise of the critic as a category of writer whose reputation was inextricable from the print and periodical industry. Thus, while the author's professional merits and code of conduct is questioned, the periodical itself appears to operate via "imprudent" and petty vested interests.

In his *Adonais* (1821) for instance, an elegy published following Keats' death from tuberculosis, Shelley would famously blame the periodical reviewers for Keats' early demise. In the preface appended to the poem, Shelley would write,

> The savage criticism on his Endymion which appeared in The Quarterly Review, produced the most violent effect on his susceptible mind; the agitation thus originated ended in the rupture of a blood-vessel in the lungs; a rapid consumption ensued, and the succeeding acknowledgements from more candid critics, of the true greatness of his powers, were ineffectual to heal the wound thus wantonly inflicted. (1249)

The author is here characterised as powerless in the face of the periodical review's arbitrary powers of judgment. The poet's body and his social persona are seen here as one and the same and an attack on one's literary standing seemingly leads to not only a social but a physical death. Other notable responses to the periodical review and the print media include Byron's *English Bards and Scotch Reviewers* (1809) written in response to *The Edinburgh Review's* harsh criticism of his work, *Hours of Idleness* (1807). Rather than blame critics alone, Byron also attacks the nature of the literary marketplace of his time where

> new schools of Poetry arise,
> Where dull pretenders grapple for the prize:
> O'er Taste awhile these Pseudo-bards prevail;
> Each country Book-club bows the knee to Baal,
> And, hurling lawful Genius from the throne,
> Erects a shrine and idol of its own (*English Bards and Scotch Reviewers: A Satire*, lines 135–140)

For Byron, the orderly governing of taste is where a "lawful" (implying also rightful) genius who is deserving of praise rules as monarch without having his authority questioned by pretenders.

In the aftermath of the French Revolution and amidst fears of uprisings against the monarch in England, Byron's metaphor imagining a revolution in print is a particularly revealing one.

The print media had made a kind of mob rule possible, where the means of publishing, networks of distribution as well as the evaluation of standards (new schools of poetry, book clubs and their erection of idols and shrines) could now be the domain of classes and social ranks who were new entrants in the land of taste. The anxieties surrounding the Romantic-era print trade have been studied by Raymond Williams for what they reveal about current attitudes towards poetry, the arts and their ability to impart a sense of being civilised. Williams is interested in how the term "culture", in the sense of a repository of values or the ideal modes of thinking and behaving in a particular time, historically starts to become equated with works of literature. He argues that it was precisely at a time when the burgeoning print trade and a growing reading public constituted the external forces of demand and supply (that drove artistic production) that the idea of the "Romantic Artist" was born. Familiar to us even today as the image of an individual whose concerns with eternal notions of truth and beauty take him away from immediate social and political pressures, the Romantic Artist was an ideal that developed in response to the industrialising tendencies of the late eighteenth and early nineteenth century in England. This artist would take on, in other words, the social burden of maintaining standards of perfection in an age where they perceived their role as degrading in a market dominated by institutions like the print media.

Such a sense of historical individualism or a way of designating a set of individuals as unique and yet representative of their time would not have been possible without the existence of eighteenth-century media. As James Chandler notes, the many social upheavals caused by the revolutions in this period would invite individuals to begin a consideration of their age as being very different from what came before. It was newspapers and periodicals, however, which permitted the representation (the recording, in words and images) of this change in the way history itself was viewed. Daily newspapers would (as they did with the French Revolution) create an experience of simultaneity in accounts of revolts and their repression like the Peterloo Massacre in 1819. Accounts of these events, together with publications consolidating contemporary views by year – parliamentary proceedings, literary works, historical and political works – changed the significance attached to that specific date. Frequent journalistic discussions on the "spirit of the age" by writers like William Hazlitt and J. S. Mill were unprecedented in terms of their focus on contemporary times and shaped how individuals viewed themselves. Rather than look to the past for moral instruction, it was now possible to use one's own lifetime (together with attendant events, social and cultural norms and way of life) as an index of progress and development. This index would also take on a cultural dimension as in the case of Anna Barbauld's *Eighteen Hundred and Eleven* where the state in which a country (England) existed at a particular time could become an index to evaluate other nations. The historical novels of Scott were especially crucial in establishing this individualised sense of history where a comparison between two time periods as well as two states of being became possible. Scott's novels, set in a historically distant time (medieval England), sought to present a context for cultural norms, belief systems and situations that were different from his readers' present. Moreover, as Harold Orel demonstrates, Scott's extensive commentary on the conventions of the historical novel in his own time – the extent of fidelity to real historical events and figures, its role in allowing readers to form a connection with people and events of the distant past – inaugurated nineteenth-century debates about the role of history in fiction. Orel argues that it was Scott's linking of his characters with specific situations, a time period and way of life which found most favour among practitioners of the historical novel in the nineteenth century rather than the accurate detailing of historical minutiae.

Tom Mole attributes the birth of the first modern literary celebrities – Romantic writers like Byron, Ann Yearsley and

Letitia Landon – to the English print industry. He argues that writers like Byron were precursors to our present-day celebrities whose public images would take on a life of their own. With access to mass printing technologies and expanding readership at the time, the Romantic writer could create and manage their public persona as an independent commodity for sale alongside their works. Landon and Byron's images, in the form of engravings and portraits, would often themselves become commodities and an industry of printing and distribution ensured that their celebrity spread far wider than even their popular literary predecessors did. These writers were also the first to recognise that the presence of a print industry and a growing audience (many of whom were unknown to them) could result in a conflating of their real selves and the characters and voices in which they wrote.

Moreover, at a time when the number of new books and writers flooding the market was unprecedented, readers required a mode of staying unique or true to their individuality in choosing the mode and content of print media consumed. The Romantic celebrity solved this problem through a careful management of their image, both in their writing and everyday life, such that their works, images of them and stories about their private lives, sought to establish a sense of intimacy with readers who were otherwise alienated in a literary landscape where several names and works jostled for attention. The protagonists of Byron's "Childe Harold's Pilgrimage" and "Don Juan" for example were received by critics as well as readers as a version of Byron himself. Reading Byron's works during the Romantic period was also supplemented by consumption practices peculiar to the print-culture industry – looking at his portrait, illustrations accompanying his works where the hero resembled him, writing to him or even dressing like him. Landon was better known by the initials "L.E.L", which heightened the enigma surrounding her personal life. The female characters of her poetry too, as in Byron's case, were often read as mirrors of Landon's real self.

Byron and Landon would create personas in their writing that both shaped and relied on these practices of print consumption. The closure of any distinction between the celebrity's industrially produced public image and their own sense of subjectivity set new norms for making sense of the self, a point I will return to while discussing the development of ideas related to the Romantic-era individual in Chapter Five.

This Romantic-era notion of authorial genius and a persona for the writer, which sets them apart as divine or immortal would impact how subsequent generations of writers, critics and readers interpreted their works. Moreover, the linking of authorship with genius would also take on gendered connotations in the nineteenth century. As Deidre Lynch shows in her overview of nineteenth- and twentieth-century scholarship about Jane Austen, the idea of genius as applied to an author was often masculinised. At various points in this period Austen's "quiet, domestic" life is contrasted with the infamy of Byron's, and her works are even considered safe reading material for girls. The figure of Austen-as-author develops in a mode different to that of Byron owing to subsequent biographers' (including some of Austen's family members) negotiation of her gender as well as her own ambivalence towards the practice of author-worship prevalent in her time. Lynch's essay forms part of a growing body of scholarship that seeks to interrogate several modern notions about literature this chapter began with – the professional writer, the solitary artist struggling against the tide of commercial book production, and the formation of tastes and reading publics – through the lens of gender. As Feldman, Schellenberg and Levy have shown, histories of the eighteenth-century print industry and the resultant analytic frames applied to notions of authorship have suffered on account of an exclusive focus on the literary careers of very few men and women. They raise questions that are important for any historical understanding of literary production in the Romantic era – how representative are the cases of widely-studied or canonical authors in understanding the print industry; what other aspects of the print industry, outside of the content of books and periodicals, contribute meaningfully to our understanding of ideas of authorship, reading publics and literary taste; to what extent does an understanding of the material conditions of book production (demand, supply, cost of production, copies sold) influence the perceived literary merit of an author and his/her works?

In looking closely at the careers of both widely studied and lesser-known women authors, these scholars challenge our belief in the wide-applicability of the Romantic idea of individualised authorship as illustrated by the works of several canonised male poets.[8] The start of the Romantic period, as argued earlier, coincides with a rise in new kinds of readers – those from middle and lower classes. Women comprise another category of new readers in this period while also, interestingly enough, entering the publishing industry in unprecedented numbers. Several women turned to publishing because it was one of few genteel ways available to them to earn money. There were, however, several obstacles to being published – being a married woman (since women could then not own any property legally or enter into contracts), a male-dominated publishing industry where women-writers were perceived as competitors and prevailing publishing models available to new writers requiring significant capital investment. It is in the context of these conditions that women become professional writers where earning an income through writing required not only literary genius but a shrewd understanding of the print industry's operations. Austen herself was not as successful (in terms of being reviewed in the periodical press and number of copies of books sold in her lifetime) as contemporaries like Ann Radcliffe, Frances Burney and Maria Edgeworth and these novelists too are not representative of the professional literary life of women. Several women would, in fact, write across multiple genres and send works to a variety of publishers with promises to make necessary alterations that would suit market needs.

Finally, the figure of the woman writer in the Romantic period is particularly fraught given our access to her via the interpretative lenses of subsequent generations of biographers, critics and historians. Re-examining the history of print in the Romantic period allows us to call into question some of the generalisations often made about the professional woman writer. These include the idea that she had no desire to earn profit and shied away from fame, that her relationships with contemporary male authors was either competitive or submissive, or that genius rather than financial distress motivated writing and publishing.[9] Additionally, contestations over the interpretation of works by Austen and Byron that have sprung up in the centuries following their lives among communities of fans and scholars contribute a further dimension to studying the reception of English Romanticism.

This chapter has allowed us to view literary works as being embedded in a printing and publishing economy that contributed to how they were valued. In addition, as we have seen, literary works and their authors are far from being isolated sites of meaning. Ideas in the present that inform our cultural attitudes towards determining literary merit or building our identities as readers can be traced back to the Romantic period where too they were contested just as fiercely. The media continues to be responsible, as it was with English Romantic writing, for creating and regulating communities of readers with shared norms for reading and interpretation.

Works Cited

"Advertisement." *The Edinburgh Review*, vol. 1, A and C Black, October 1802, *Hathi Trust Digital Library*, https://hdl.handle.net/2027/uc1.b2973109. Accessed 31 December 2019.

Altick, Richard Daniel. *The English Common Reader: A Social History of the Mass Reading Public, 1800–1900*. U of Chicago P, 1957.

Behrendt, Stephen C. "The Romantic Reader." *A Companion to Romanticism*, edited by Duncan Wu, Blackwell, 2017, pp. 99–108.

Butler, Marilyn. "Culture's Medium: The Role of the Review." *The Cambridge Companion to British Romanticism*, edited by Stuart Curran, Cambridge UP, 1993, pp. 120–47.

Byron, George Gordon. *English Bards and Scotch Reviewers: A Satire*. http://www.victorianweb.org/previctorian/byron/reviewers.html. Accessed 1 January 2020.

Chandler, James. "History." *An Oxford Companion to the Romantic Age: British Culture 1776–1832*, edited by Iain McCalman, 1999, 354–61.

"Christabel & c." *The Antijacobin Review*, vol. L, C Cradock, July 1816, *Hathi Trust Digital Library*, pp. 632–36, https://hdl.handle.net/2027/inu.30000080767027. Accessed 31 December 2019.

Coleridge, Samuel Taylor. *Biographia Literaria*, 2004, *Project Gutenberg*, https://www.gutenberg.org/ebooks/6081. Accessed 31 December 2019.

Feldman, Paula R. "Women Poets and Anonymity in the Romantic Era." *New Literary History*, vol. 33, no. 2, 2002 pp. 279–89.

Fergus, Jan. "The Professional Woman Writer." *The Cambridge Companion to Jane Austen*, edited by Edward Copeland and Juliet McMaster, Cambridge UP, 1997, pp. 12–31.

Flynn, Phillip. "Early 'Blackwood's' and Scottish Identities." *Studies in Romanticism*, vol. 46, no.1, 2007, pp. 43–56.

Jeffrey, Francis. "Thalaba the Destroyer: A Metrical Romance." *The Edinburgh Review*, vol. 1, A and C Black, October 1802, *Hathi Trust Digital Library*, pp. 63–83, https://hdl.handle.net/2027/uc1.b2973109. Accessed 31 December 2019.

———. "The Excursion, being a portion of The Recluse, a Poem by William Wordsworth." *The Edinburgh Review*, vol. 24, A and C Black, November 1814, *Hathi Trust Digital Library*, pp. 1–4, https://hdl.handle.net/2027/uc1.$b623336. Accessed 19 February 2021.

Kandl, John. "Private Lyrics in the Public Sphere: Leigh Hunt's 'Examiner' and the Construction of a Public 'John Keats'." *Keats-Shelley Journal*, vol. 44, 1995, pp. 84–101.

Klancher, Jon P. *The Making of English Reading Audiences, 1790–1832*, U of Wisconsin, 1987, *Internet Archive*, http://archive.org/details/makingofenglishr00klan. Accessed 1 January 2020.

Levy, Michelle. "Do Women Have a Book History?" *Studies in Romanticism*, vol. 53, no. 3, 2014, pp. 296–317.

Lockhart, John Gibson. "Cockney School of Poetry. No. IV." *Blackwood's Edinburgh Magazine*, vol. 3, William Blackwood, August 1818, *Hathi Trust Digital Library*, pp. 519–24, https://hdl.handle.net/2027/hvd.hxq6vz. Accessed 14 January 2020.

Lorraine de Montluzin, Emily. *The Poetry of the Gentleman's Magazine, 1731–1800: An Electronic Database of Titles, Authors, and First Lines*, 2012, http://www.gmpoetrydatabase.org/db/intro.php. Accessed 4 March 2021.

Lynch, Deidre. "Jane Austen and Genius." *A Companion to Jane Austen*, edited by Claudia L. Johnson and Clara Tuite, Blackwell, 2009.

"Lyrical Ballads, With a Few Other Poems." *The Analytical Review, or History of Literature, Domestic and Foreign, on an Enlarged Plan*, vol. 28, J. Johnson, December 1798, *Hathi Trust Digital Library*, pp. 583–87, https://hdl.handle.net/2027/nyp.33433087364810. Accessed 31 December 2019.

"Lyrical Ballads, With a Few Other Poems." *The British Critic and Quarterly Theological Review*, vol. 14, F and C Rivington, October 1799, *Hathi Trust Digital Library*, pp. 364–69, https://hdl.handle.net/2027/chi.79237046. Accessed 31 December 2019.

Mole, Tom. *Byron's Romantic Celebrity: Industrial Culture and the Hermeneutic of Intimacy*. Palgrave Macmillan, 2007.

Orel, Harold. *The Historical Novel from Scott to Sabatini: Changing Attitudes Toward a Literary Genre, 1814–1920*, Palgrave Macmillan, 1995.

Parker, Mark. *Literary Magazines and British Romanticism*. Cambridge UP, 2001.

Perkins, Maureen. "Street Literature." *An Oxford Companion to the Romantic Age: British Culture 1776–1832*, edited by Iain McCalman, 1999, pp. 720–21.

Reiman, Donald H, editor. *The Romantics Reviewed: Contemporary Reviews of British Romantic Writers, Part B: Byron and Regency Society Poets–Vol. 2*, Routledge, 2016.

Roberts, Daniel S and Robert Morrison, editors. *Romanticism and Blackwood's Magazine*, Palgrave Macmillan, 2013.

Schellenberg, Betty A. *The Professionalization of Women Writers in Eighteenth-Century Britain*, Cambridge UP, 2005.

Shelley, Percy Bysshe. "Adonais: An Elegy on the Death of John Keats, author of Endymion, Hyperion, etc." *Romanticism: An Anthology*, edited by Duncan Wu, 4th ed., Wiley-Blackwell, 2012, pp. 1248–65.

Southey, Robert. "Lyrical Ballads, With a Few Other Poems." *The Critical Review, or, Annals of Literature*, vol. 24, W. Simpkin and R. Marshall, October 1798, *Hathi Trust Digital Library*, pp. 197–204, https://hdl.handle.net/2027/nyp.33433066596317. Accessed 31 December 2019.

St Clair, William. *The Reading Nation in the Romantic Period*. Cambridge UP, 2004.

Wheale, Nigel. *Writing and Society: Literacy, Print and Politics in Britain 1590–1660*, Routledge, 1999.

Williams, Raymond. *Culture & Society 1780-1950*. Doubleday & Company, Inc., 1960.

Williamson, Gillian. *British Masculinity in the Gentleman's Magazine, 1731–1815*, Palgrave Macmillan, 2016.

Notes

1. This is not including prints, street literature like chapbooks, broadsheets and broadsides (Perkins, "Street Literature", 720).
2. See Gillian Williamson's *British Masculinity in the Gentleman's Magazine, 1731–1815* for a study of how codes of masculine conduct were indexed and negotiated in this long-running magazine. Williamson uses the records of births, deaths, marriages and obituaries to study the modes through which masculinity was made sense of at varying points in the eighteenth century. The late eighteenth century, she notes, is marked by a shift in the "gentlemanly" masculine ideal owing to pressures exerted by events like the publication of Paine's *Rights of Man* and the French Revolution. Readership and social perceptions of *The Gentleman's Magazine* suffered in the early nineteenth century precisely because it was now split between masculine ideals put forward by opposed class-based groups – middle-class businessmen and the old landed elite. Neither group was egalitarian enough, in Williamson's view,

to accept the implications of *Rights of Man* for the lower social orders and its impact on the eighteenth century gentlemanly ideal of distinction earned through rank or trade.

3. See for instance, The Poetry of the *Gentleman's Magazine* database compiled by Emily Lorraine de Montluzin (available at http://www.gmpoetrydatabase.org/db/index.php). The database illustrates a great diversity of content and contributors – of 12561 poems published in the magazine, only 4929 are by known authors. Montluzin's introductory note in the database offers valuable information on the social backgrounds and professions of contributors, many of whom were not primarily writers or poets. Other than letters to the editor, the database offers plentiful evidence for the magazine's readers (often anonymously) contributing translations of famous works in response to its verse composing competitions and poems on silly and serious subjects celebrating events of national and personal significance.
4. See also Nigel Wheale's *Writing and Society: Literacy, Print and Politics in Britain 1590–1660* for a longer history of book publishing and reading publics in Britain. Wheale identifies in sixteenth and seventeenth century pre-industrial Britain, early trends for several aspects of the modern, industrialised print economy detailed in this chapter. Among these are the increased value attached to literacy and learning across social classes, the practice of reading aloud, the existence of a book trade (though monopolistic), attempts at state regulation of publishing and reading practices amid fears of its impact on religious and political beliefs. Wheale even details the case of the "sculler-scholar" John Taylor, the earliest instance of a writer from a working-class background (Taylor was a waterman, someone who ferried passengers across the Thames for a fee) to have become well-known and made a living by writing. Taylor is distinguished from working-class Romantic poets like Burns owing to the very urban nature of the form, content and readership of his works. Burns' poetic identity on the other hand would be seen as rural and by extension, "unspoiled" by the intervention of education. Wheale's study looks *prospectively* at the sixteenth and seventeenth centuries to see in them early modern tendencies rather than view them retrospectively as the Renaissance.

5. See for instance, St Clair's chapter on the effect of pricing and copyright on sales and the access to books and the chapter on *Frankenstein's* publication history in *The Reading Nation in the Romantic Period* (2005). He refutes common misconceptions about *Frankenstein's* publishing success by demonstrating how poorly its sales figures compare with those of contemporary novelists like Scott. Interestingly, sales figures and print are not the only measure of the public's knowledge of *Frankenstein*. St Clair also documents the role played by stage versions of the novel in sustaining a demand for its print version, finally only fulfilled in the late nineteenth century, almost 80 years after it was first published and in a range of textual formats.
6. Poets like Samuel Johnson and Thomas Gray were commissioned to make contributions for Dodsley's collection thus also signaling the rise of the publisher as patron.
7. See "John Gibson Lockhart and *Blackwood's*: Shaping the Romantic Periodical Press" in Morrison and Roberts' (ed.) *Romanticism and Blackwood's Magazine*.
8. My chapter titled Gendering Romanticism also details how theories of authorship, put forward by Romantic writers themselves, articulate gendered modes of being in the world.
9. See Jan Fergus' "The Professional Woman Writer" in *The Cambridge Companion to Jane Austen*, eds. Edward Copeland and Juliet MacMaster for a detailed account of Jane Austen's adept management of her publishing career and resulting remuneration. See also Feldman, Schellenberg and Levy for a detailed survey of various "myths" about the professional woman writer in scholarship about the eighteenth and nineteenth centuries in Britain.

FOUR

English Romanticism and Empire

Even so, my countrymen! have we gone forth
And borne to distant tribes slavery and pangs,
And, deadlier far, our vices, whose deep taint
With slow perdition murders the whole man,
His body and his soul!

(Coleridge, *Fears in Solitude*, lines 50–54)

And lucent syrops, tinct with cinnamon;
Manna and dates, in argosy transferr'd
From Fez; and spiced dainties, every one,
From silken Samarcand to cedar'd Lebanon.

(Keats, *The Eve of St. Agnes*, lines 267–70)

Our focus on understanding the term Romanticism has so far led us to sociopolitical events (both global as well as local) and their enunciation in writing between the late eighteenth and early nineteenth century. Events like the French Revolution had a significant impact on this period by overturning notions of how we understand individuals and the way they come together in social and political formations. Writing designated as Romantic, at least in regards to the historical context in which it arose, shares some literary traits like themes, tropes and aesthetic conventions of writing, and even interpretation. In addition, our understanding of Romanticism must necessarily include the many material contexts discussed so far: the social context of writers, debates about authors and readers in the public sphere and events that crystallise modern notions of the individual and citizenship like war, revolution and nation-formation. This chapter will attempt to bring together Romanticism in England within the context of the Empire such that both can meaningfully inform our understanding of writing produced at this time.

Any story tracing the emergence of the English Empire tends to begin well before the period generally studied as the Romantic age. For instance, if we understand Empire as one country establishing a dominating militaristic-economic relationship with a host of other entities spread across the world, then the history of the British Empire begins with the setting up of their colonies in America in the sixteenth and seventeenth centuries. The Romantic period however, does coincide with the history of Empire in interesting ways, allowing us to see this history as formative rather than constitutive. In other words, the changing course of the British Empire at this time gives rise to several typically Romantic themes, genres and modes of writing. For instance, the American Revolution would end in 1783 and mark a new phase for British imperial expansion. The loss of the American colonies would drive Britain towards strengthening their presence in India and China, with whom their engagement thus far had been primarily for the purposes of trade. Oriental[1] themes and settings would become a feature of writing in the eighteenth century in England, reflecting their changing relationships with regions overseas. As Saree Makdisi notes however, there are distinct phases in England's relationship with the East or the Orient (as it was titled at the time) as seen in writing from this period. Prior to the eighteenth century, tales about lands to the East – where explorers and traders travelled – signified adventure and exoticism and were rarely backed by verifiable information. Many of these accounts served as entertainment rather than sites of knowledge about these far-flung places. The early part of the eighteenth century continued to see publications that featured Oriental characters, themes and settings but these again were exploiting the popularity of a newly emerging genre rather than building the reader's expertise or interest in cultures other than their own. Serious study of Eastern cultures and ways of life would only begin after 1757, when Britain's relationship with India via the East India Company changed to necessitating administration and governance rather than solely trade.

If the French Revolution provides a framework with which to contextualise England's anxieties over comparisons with France, then a study of the British Empire in the Romantic period offers a way of framing the diverse and plentiful writing produced about the East at this time. English writing about and as an Empire thus was coming to terms with the diverse people and cultures that now formed a part of it. A comprehensive overview of Romantic writers' engagement with the many places and cultures they encountered during eighteenth- and nineteenth-century imperial expansion is outside the scope of this chapter.[2] In lieu of a global context for the British Empire, the focus in this chapter will be on Britain's military and economic takeover of India to illustrate how this relates to literary production. Imperial contexts outside India also find mention here when a major work or writer in the period has engaged with it. The following section offers a framework for analysing the relevance of Romantic writing about a single British colony, but with the caveat to readers that every erstwhile colony possesses its own local and historical peculiarities. Moreover, the term Empire does not mean a monolithic entity that was organised, cohesive and static. Instead, as this chapter will suggest, it can be understood as a range of material and cultural aspects of Britain's (among other colonial powers) expansion of their territories abroad. Literature was one such key site whether in terms of representing faraway lands to those at home or as a means for evaluating Britain's changing power relationships with the rest of the world. An examination of Romantic literature alongside the contexts of Empire, this chapter will demonstrate, reveals a transformation in attitudes towards other cultures over the course of the late eighteenth and early nineteenth centuries in England.

Romantic Aesthetics and the Colony: India and the East

The Battle of Plassey in 1757 helped the British East India Company secure Bengal and marked the beginning of the English reign in India. Over the next hundred years, English rule would spread to the rest of the Indian subcontinent from Bengal, primarily through a strengthening of military and economic resources. The defeat of the Nawab of Bengal allowed the East India Company to situate themselves in a position of administrative power in the region, collecting tax revenue and supplementing their military ranks with Indian soldiers. At the time, India was a trading hub that not only the British but other European powers like the French and Dutch also sought to monopolise. However, with English military and economic strength bolstered by the East India Company's administration of Bengal (whose tax revenues were now used to purchase Indian goods for export to Britain), the Dutch and French would be ousted from India.

What is of interest to us here, in our study of literature that responds to and arises from this context, is the establishment of cultural power, in addition to military and economic power, in newly acquired parts of the Empire in this period. English imperial power manifested in the late eighteenth and early nineteenth centuries via cultural institutions like religion, literature, law and the arts as much as military and economic administration. A key illustration of this was the establishment of the Asiatic Society in Calcutta in 1784 with a view to promote serious study of Oriental systems of knowledge. The founder of the Asiatic Society, William Jones, was a judge appointed to the Supreme Court at Bengal and a key figure in the early phase of Empire and Romantic writing in England. This early phase, as we will see in Jones' writing, is characterised by a very different attitude towards the language, literature and arts of cultures outside England compared to the one that would crystallise towards the end of the Romantic period in the early nineteenth century.[3] Jones' *Poems, Consisting Chiefly of Translations from the Asiatic Tongues* (1772) is illustrative of his view of the cultural accomplishments of Asia and the Middle East. In an essay titled "On the Poetry of the Eastern Nations" accompanying this volume, Jones addresses the criticisms levelled against the languages and literatures of the East by his contemporaries. In response to them, he argues that not only do the literatures produced in Persian, Arabic and Turkish share similarities with their European counterparts, they also possess several distinctions – a result of their linguistic, cultural and geographic particularities – that make them superior.

Jones' essay is interesting for the insights it offers in studying the dual theme of Empire and Romanticism. In the descriptions of the natural bounty of Arabia – the "valuable" spice trees of Yemen and its naturally "secure" and defensible geographic location "enclosed on one side by vast rocks and deserts, and defended on the other by a tempestuous sea" – an seems evident (75). In other words, there is a careful detailing in the description of the natural and human resources of the region, creating an informational map at precisely the time when English imperial aspirations were beginning to turn East following opposition in the American colonies. An imperial gaze is also discernible in the translating (and in the process, subsuming) of Eastern aesthetic categories in very English terms. For instance, Jones supplies several illustrations from Arabian poetry to demonstrate their frequent use of objects found in nature. He contends that the kind of objects that poetry describes has an impact on the form. Here, interestingly, he invokes the very English and Romantic aesthetic categories of the beautiful and the sublime to evaluate Eastern poetry. He says,

> we must not believe that the *Arabian* poetry can please only by its descriptions of *beauty*; since the gloomy and terrible objects, which produce the *sublime*, when they are aptly described, are no where more common than in the *Desert* and *Stony Arabia's*; and,

> indeed, we see nothing so frequently painted by the poets of those countries, as wolves and lions, precipices and forests, rocks and wildernesses. (76)

The dual operation of Empire and Romanticism is visible here in Jones' arguments about the universal nature and conditions of aesthetic productions that he nevertheless evaluates in English terms. He argues that Arabian poetry cannot be inferior to its Western counterpart owing to the presence of natural beauty in the region that then becomes the primary imagery and metaphor for speaking of all beauty (that of the beloved, for instance). Poetry that represents the beauty of nature, for Jones, is common to the literature of the East and the West, just by virtue of the inhabitants of these regions living in proximity to nature. Similarly, following his translation of an "Ode" written by the Persian poet Mohammad Shams Od-Din Hafez, Jones notes the parallels between this text and a Shakespearean sonnet. Eastern imagery, Jones states, is thus not quite so different from the imagery employed by poets in England. However, in translating and categorising the works of Arabian poets as being *beautiful* and *sublime* and similar in imagery to a celebrated English poet, Jones subsumes Eastern poetry under an English Romantic lens. Jones' depiction of Eastern literature thus stays close to several other themes and ideas that are characteristic of the Romantic period. His close attention to the manner and mode of representing nature in poetry is perhaps the first hint of a Romantic theme.

Further, in an appraisal of the history of Arabic literature from the seventh century onwards, Jones persuades his reader to see the Arabian tendency to celebrate poetry and the poet with the highest regard. As we have seen in the chapter on gender and the one on the public sphere, the Romantic period in England saw the rise of the poet and poetry as occupying a far superior position to several other forms and their practitioners. Jones also highlights the closeness to nature and agricultural mode of living that he observes in the people of this region, echoing yet another Romantic sensibility. English scientists and explorers too, like Jones, translated local flora and fauna, customs and traditions such that they could become mobile and travel outside their native environments to England. I will return to the context of translating natural knowledge from the colony into English in the chapter on science. The next section examines how London takes on the characteristics of an imperial city once it is suffused with the many people, commodities and ideas that now begin to flow into it from all over the world.

The Character of an Imperial Metropolis: Foreigners and Exotic Commodities in London

Early Romantic poets like Wordsworth and Coleridge would respond to the contexts of Empire in ways different from those like William Jones who travelled to England's colonies. These poets, like several other Englishmen of the upper classes, would encounter the Empire in the form of its material consequences at home. How London appeared to a visitor in the late eighteenth and early nineteenth century had changed dramatically because of imperial expansion. In his *Prelude* for instance, Wordsworth notes about his visit to London in 1791 that

> Among the crowd all specimens of man,
> Through all the colours which the sun bestows,
> And every character of form and face:
> The Swede, the Russian; from the genial south,
> The Frenchman and the Spaniard; from remote
> America, the Hunter-Indian; Moors,
> Malays, Lascars, the Tartar, the Chinese,
> And Negro Ladies in white muslin gowns (Wordsworth, *The Prelude*, Book VII, lines 221–25)

Wordsworth describes London as clearly interspersed with the presence of many "colours" and "specimens" – this is also indicative of how the city was considered at the time to be a haven for slaves from the British West Indies.[4] The Black population in Britain was a direct consequence of the slave trade and at the time of Wordsworth's visit, the debate over the abolition of slavery was at its peak. It is thus interesting that in the lines that follow, Wordsworth juxtaposes the many "specimens" of man he sees on his London visit with other objects that Empire makes possible –

> The spectacles within doors,
> —birds and beasts
> Of every nature, and strange plants convened
> From every clime (*The Prelude*, Book VII, lines 230–32)

As noted in Chapter One, the Romantic poets came of age at a time when there was widespread public participation in the campaign against ending the slave trade. Several of the major poets of the period would record in their works, disillusionment over the continued support of slavery and slave-produced commodities in England. Wordsworth's portrait of "Negro Ladies", in anticipating the lines about "spectacles" that are "within", marks them as objects brought from outside domestic borders such that they can never be anything other than extraordinary.

There is a sense of "foreignness" in Wordsworth's naming of the many races and nationalities he sees in England. His poetic representations of London seek to tame the monstrous imperial cityscape where many-coloured individuals are on display for visitors.[5] Wordsworth's picture of London in his *Prelude* contrasts city-life with the simple and uncorrupted ways of the peasant in the countryside. For Heffernan, Wordsworth's London symbolises the epitome of imperial conquests abroad because of its potential for exhibiting and viewing material possessions. In fact, Wordsworth's gaze (or his way of looking at scenes in London) in *Prelude* is very similar to London's gaze on the world, made clear in the poem's descriptions of panoramic paintings and scale models of other cities (Rome and Tivoli are specifically named). Among the many attractions in London that Wordsworth chooses to describe, the panoramic paintings and city models are significant for the way they offer a vantage point for a viewer in a foreign landscape. What Wordsworth offers in his view of London's multiracial crowds is a similar vantage point for the reader to evaluate his/her own position with respect to a place/culture/lifestyle that may be different to his/her own.

Consider the following extract from Book VII of *The Prelude* that describes in detail what the traveller to London can hope to experience in the late eighteenth and early nineteenth centuries:

> But imitations, fondly made in plain
> Confession of man's weakness and his loves.
> Whether the Painter, whose ambitious skill
> Submits to nothing less than taking in
> A whole horizon's circuit, do with power,
> Like that of angels or commissioned spirits,
> Fix us upon some lofty pinnacle,
> Or in a ship on waters, with a world
> Of life, and life-like mockery beneath,
> Above, behind, far stretching and before;
> Or more mechanic artist represent
> By scale exact, in model, wood or clay,
> From blended colours also borrowing help,
> Some miniature of famous spots or things,—
> St. Peter's Church; or, more aspiring aim,
> In microscopic vision, Rome herself; (lines 238–53)

The traveller to London at this time, especially one who hails from the Lake District, is immediately struck by a *mode* of seeing rather than the many sights alone. Outside of the many-coloured people, who are spectacles to the rural traveller, the capacity to see directly into the locations outside England where travel was now possible was a novel experience. Wordsworth, however, is very conscious that the capacity for "power" and a "lofty pinnacle" is what makes these paintings and model cities imperial and alluring to the viewer. Moreover, as he states at the start of this extract, man's "weakness" results in a dependence on these modes of entertainment, which, even with their life-like quality, are ultimately "imitations" and "mockery".

Some of Wordsworth's other poems on London register a more explicitly pessimistic view of what the city represents to England. In "Written in London, September, 1802" (1807) he says that at present in England,

> The wealthiest man among us is the best,
> No grandeur now in nature or in book
> Delights us. Rapine, avarice, expence,
> This is idolatory; and these we adore (lines 8–10)

Similarly, in his "London, 1802" (1807), he describes the city as a "fen of stagnant waters" where

> the heroic wealth of hall and bower
> have forfeited their ancient English dower
> Of inward happiness (lines 4–6)

In these descriptions of London, Wordsworth is mourning the loss of "inward" happiness (understood here as an "English inheritance" that pre-existed the present time which could include the appreciation of nature or even learning) at the cost of the "external" benefits (like the accumulation of material wealth).

Coleridge would make similar links between the city, accumulation of wealth and imperialism in his poetry as well as his lectures. As part of his Bristol Lectures on the topics of religion and politics, meant to raise money for his scheme of starting an egalitarian commune in America,[6] Coleridge would say about cities that in them "God is everywhere removed from our Sight and Man obtruded upon us – not Man, the work of God, but the debased offspring of Luxury and Want" (Lecture Six, 689). Like in Wordsworth's case, Coleridge associates the show of wealth in cities with a decline in one's faith ("inward happiness"). He later makes explicit links between Empire and the city when he speaks about the most conspicuous aspects of consumption in London at the time:

> It has been openly asserted that our commercial intercourse with the East Indies has been the occasion of the loss of eight million Lives—in return for which most foul and heart-inslaving Guilt we receive gold, diamonds, silks, muslins & callicoes for fine Ladies and Prostitutes, Tea to make a pernicious Beverage, Porcelain to drink it from, and salt-petre for the making of gunpowder with which we may murder the poor inhabitants who supply these things. Not one thing necessary or even useful do we receive in return for the horrible guilt in which we have involved ourselves. Africa and the West India Islands, on these fearful subjects I shall observe nothing at present. I hang my head when I think of them, they leave an indelible stain on our national character— (Lecture Six, 689)

Coleridge also names Lord Clive and Warren Hastings in his speech to criticise their treatment of Indians and makes specific reference to the Bengal famine of 1770.[7] His reference to the activities of the East India Company as well the listing of consumables that now flooded the English market because of the Company's takeover of India and China makes the links between Empire and Britain very clear. In addition, what is interesting to note about this extract from his speech is the separation that Coleridge also seeks to create between a nation's character before and after its enslavement of other nations. A reference to "Christian Scriptures" precedes this extract and along with the reference to the "work of God" asserts another important theme within Romantic writing about Empire – religion or religious character.

Coleridge's speech is one of several Romantic-era writings which introduce the idea that Empire and its by-products, whether in the form of slavery, the decimation of populations in England's colonies or the products of colonial trade, are unchristian. The Church was an important institution through which control over England's various colonies was possible with due alterations in institutional activities to suit local conditions. Various denominations of Christians in England would raise funds for and create missionary societies whose task it was to spread the religion via its scriptures in the colonies. The local networks and institutions set up by these missionary societies were also crucial in the abolition campaign. Christianity was thus not only a tool of colonial conquest but often enlisted as a critique of England's imperial aspirations as well. So widespread was the religious rhetoric in the campaign to abolish slavery that Ottobah Cugoano, a former slave, would also invoke the "unchristian" character of continuing the slave trade while recounting the story of his own capture into and eventual escape from slavery in his *Thoughts and sentiments on the evil and wicked traffic of the slavery: and commerce of the human species, humbly submitted to the inhabitants of Great-Britain* (1787). Peter J. Kitson has observed that prominent dissenters (like the Quaker William Wilberforce or even Coleridge in his early embracing of Unitarianism)[8] would find the abolitionist cause to be a way of mounting not only a critique of Empire but of the suppression of Christian religious minorities at home. Those whose faith and beliefs differed from those preached by the Church of England were at this time forbidden from holding public office and could be denied education by institutions that upheld Anglicanism. Dissenters who faced an oppressive government at home would thus find common cause with the plight of slaves and the inhabitants of Britain's colonies who were similarly subject to centralised and alienating principles of governance.[9]

The Moral Burden of Empire

As a final note about Coleridge's speech, I want to draw attention to the line where he speaks about "horrible guilt" and the "indelible stain" of the consequences of imperial expansion in Africa and Asia. Guilt is another significant theme in the Romantic response to Britain's imperial activities and manifests in various forms in the writing of the time. Prominent examples of writing that seek to evoke the reader's guilt while also expressing that of the author have been mentioned already: abolitionist writing as well as a critique of Britain's imperial activities whether in the form of maritime exploration, setting up of colonies overseas or the rising domestic consumption of goods procured through slavery.

I will offer a few more examples of these kinds of writings here grouped under the theme of guilt in the context of Empire. Coleridge's famous "The Rime of the Ancient Mariner" has been studied for instance as demonstrating European guilt over their treatment of other cultures (Empson; Ebbatson). At the time of its publication, Coleridge's poem received negative attention for being very different from the other poems in *The Lyrical Ballads*, of which it formed a part. In the nineteenth and twentieth centuries, when scholarship about the Romantic period was growing, the poem was studied for precisely those "odd" characteristics that have now come to be closely associated with this movement. Most significant of these was the exploration of themes – otherwise absent in English poetry until the Romantic period – like the supernatural. The mariner, for instance, encounters a ghost ship on his journey in addition to seeing the death and subsequent resurrection of all his crew. Reading Coleridge's poem as an illustration of guilt over colonial conquest and expansion is an important mode of revisiting Romanticism and bringing its major works closer to political contexts of the time. Critics have read the motiveless "crime" (the killing of an albatross) featured in the poem as paralleling late eighteenth-century contexts of news about European contact with far-off lands and people, its impact on their cultures, accounts of maritime voyages that were often dangerous and the public outcry against slavery. Ebbatson, for instance, notes the parallels between the central events of the mariner's account of his journey in Coleridge's poem and those undertaken by Captain Cook, Columbus, Magellan and Vasco da Gama prior to the eighteenth century. These parallels are especially discernible in how the poem sets up the hostility of the territories into which the mariner and his crew venture.

In account in the poem, right after Coleridge's mariner shoots down the albatross, he remembers that there was an ambivalence among the crew about what this act meant. At first, the ship's crew blames the mariner for stopping the breeze by shooting the albatross. Soon after, however, when faced with bright sunshine, the crew concedes that killing the albatross was a good act since it is such birds that cause mist and fog. This ambivalence over the nature of the act soon passes when the mariner and his crew would both "become the first that ever burst / into that silent Sea" but also find this very region to be the cause for their doom as described in the famous lines:

> Water, water, every where
> And all the boards did shrink,
> Water, water, every where
> Ne any drop to drink.
> The very deeps did rot: O Christ!
> That ever this should be!
> Yea, slimy things did crawl with legs
> Upon the slimy Sea. (lines 115–20)

At the very moment that they become the "first" to venture into a foreign land, the mariner and his crew find that they are unwelcome here and in immense danger. The voyage is thus not without its costs and the poem demonstrates a kind of "repentance" the mariner must undertake to be deemed ready to return to his own home. The poem codes this repentance as the mariner discovering love for the very creatures he finds abhorrent in the above extract, thus resolving conflict with a foreign land by learning to accept and love these "others" who are not like us. However, this voyage also changes the mariner, the only survivor from his journey, now infected by sudden and uncontrollable fits of a need to share his story with others. He now passes "like night, from land to land" only to pass on the tale of his experiences at sea after he has returned home. An act that is committed in a far-off land thus returns to taint the mariner in his own country and his remembrance of this is almost pathological, requiring alleviation in the form of talking about and reflecting on what he did.

Coleridge speaks more explicitly of the crime of colonial expansion in his "Fears in Solitude" where he says that despite knowing the consequences of their actions, Englishmen have

> gone forth
> And borne to distant tribes slavery and pangs,
> And, deadlier far, our vices, whose deep taint
> With slow perdition murders the whole man,
> His body and his soul! (lines 50–54)

He may well be speaking here of Captain Cook's voyages to Tahiti, Hawaii and even the Antarctic whose native human and animal populations would suffer the ravages of disease and commerce that would continue with subsequent travellers.

"Englishness" in the Context of Empire

As observed in the chapters on gender and the public sphere, it was a common theme in Romantic writing to describe and make sense of the writer's creative process. In various treatises about poetry and the nature of writing and inspiration, most notably in the case of the preface to the *Lyrical Ballads*, *Biographia Literaria* and a *Defence of Poetry*, the poet is someone whose capacity for imagination (understood as the power to fuse into something new those images and ideas they had seen and experienced) set him apart from others. This interest in how the poet creates something new in both the form and content of poetry is a characteristically Romantic trait. Descriptions of the poet's capacity for creation thus also demonstrates interesting intersections with contexts of Empire during this time. While the images of London as an imperial city are illustrative of national ambitions, poetic treatises or descriptions of what writers could create perhaps tell us something about ambition at a more individual level. A significant connection between the contexts of colonial expansion and aesthetic theories is the linking of opium with creative powers. Several commodities produced in Britain's overseas colonies came to define English cultural practices at the time: tea, sugar, tobacco, chocolate and by the early nineteenth century, opium. Opium was responsible in the eighteenth century for correcting England's diminishing balance of payments with China. In other words, while there was a huge demand for Chinese goods in England's domestic market, there was little that Britain produced that the Chinese needed. Eventually, cheaply produced opium in India traded secretly to China via the East India Company was what enabled England to earn the gold required to trade profitably in Chinese goods. Opium was thus available plentifully in England and was used both recreationally and prescribed medicinally for a host of ailments. Several writers would record their experiences of using opium and its related by-products like laudanum when prescribed to take these for ailments ranging from dysentery to cough and insomnia. Some famous responses to the use of opium tell us a great deal about how Romantic writers felt about dependence on a substance of foreign origin while also making sense of how it altered one's state of mind. This economic dependence on a foreign commodity would result in literary representations that sought to keep apart identities – the East and Britain – that were threatening to merge. Romantic writers would create an English context for commodities like opium by describing differences in modes of use and its physical effects.

In his *Confessions of an English Opium Eater* (1821) for instance, De Quincey claims to have an "authoritative" stance on the effects of opium. He says that opium's effects have thus far been shrouded in mystery and only medical practitioners claim knowledge about this. His autobiographical account gathers this authority through a commitment to detail about his experiences which offer several insights into ideas surrounding this colonial commodity. He remembers, for instance, his very first experience of consuming opium and describes this as not belonging to the material realm. Referring to his first act of purchasing opium from a druggist, De Quincey says it is a moment of "mystic importance". At the same time he finds the act so other-worldly in its effects on him that he chooses to think of the druggist as "a sublunary druggist; it may be so, but my faith is better – I believe him to have evanesced, or evaporated. So unwillingly would I connect any mortal remembrances with that hour, and place, and creature, that first brought me acquainted with the celestial drug" (854). This import to London has thus clearly been distanced for the reader, to such an extent that the commodity as well as its trade do not even belong in the "mortal" realm. Further, De Quincey also works to separate the "English" uses of opium from its "Oriental" contexts and refers specifically to the "pictures of Turkish opium-eaters" with which his readers may be familiar as a point of reference. Speaking of the Turkish he says that they are "absurd enough to sit, like so many equestrian statues, on logs of wood as stupid as themselves" but requests that his readers look to his own experiences to think about consuming opium in an English style. This style is not imbued with the connotations built into the Turkish who (at least according to various visual representations that the English were accustomed to) seemed affected by "torpor". Instead, in comparison, as De Quincey strives to show his readers, he excelled at his studies and partook in refined activities like attending the opera while having consumed opium.

De Quincey thus creates an entirely new context for the consumption of opium while simultaneously distancing this from other contexts or associations it may have had in England at the time. In addition to a description of differences in the lifestyle of the English and the Turkish, even while they consumed the same commodities, De Quincey also explores the differences at the level of the individual. He meets a Malay in London and describes him as not really "belonging" there, unlike Wordsworth's depiction of many races suffusing the city. The Malay visits De Quincey at his lodgings and is permitted to stay a night. In De Quincey's narrative the Malay is alone (unlike those who are part of a faceless crowd in Wordsworth's London portrayal) and is seen to represent a veiled danger that he only decodes later on (the Malay would become a recurring feature of his nightmares, a part of the negative features De Quincey attributes to opium):

> In a cottage kitchen, but panelled on the wall with dark wood that from age and rubbing resembled oak, and looking more like a rustic hall of entrance than a kitchen, stood the Malay—his turban and loose trousers of dingy white relieved upon the dark panelling. He had placed himself nearer to the girl than she seemed to relish, though her native spirit of mountain intrepidity contended with the feeling of simple awe which her countenance expressed as she gazed upon the tiger-cat before her. And a more striking picture there could not be imagined than the beautiful English face of the girl, and its exquisite fairness, together with her erect and independent attitude, contrasted with the sallow and bilious skin of the Malay, enamelled or veneered with mahogany by marine air, his small, fierce, restless eyes, thin lips, slavish gestures and adorations. (859–60)

The Malay presents a danger that De Quincey's servant girl is unaware of while also exhibiting signs of poor health and "slavishness". Referring to him as a "tiger-cat", De Quincey further dehumanises him by making him an object that the English girl "gazes" at. Moreover, while the English girl possesses features of a "native" mountain dweller, the Malay is characterised as being itinerant through a reference to "marine air" and has clearly developed a "veneer" of "slavish gestures and adorations" necessary to survive his uncontrollable mobility.

De Quincey continues to report that he shared some opium with the Malay who would then "suddenly raise his hand to his mouth, and (in the school-boy phrase) bolt the whole, divided into three pieces, at one mouthful. The quantity was enough to kill three dragoons and their horses... (860). The separation between modes of consumption continues but here, the Malay's use of opium far exceeds what De Quincey feels an average human can tolerate and he even expresses some concern about whether the Malay will survive this dosage. Subsequently however, he confirms for the reader that this is something the Malay is no doubt "used to" but the incident (one of excessive consumption) leaves De Quincey altered. He seems infected by contact with the Malay who "fastened afterwards upon my dreams, and brought other Malays with him worse than himself, that ran 'a-muck' at me, and led me into a world of troubles" (860). De Quincey is thus irreversibly changed by his encounter with the Malay, not unlike Coleridge's mariner who returns changed from his voyage into strange lands. In the section that explores the "pains of opium", De Quincey is mainly evoking for the reader, the "horrors" of "Asiatic" scenes that he begins to view in his nightmares. The "waking" and "sleeping" state fuse for De Quincey, allowing him no agency in "gazing" upon scenes in his dreams where he finds himself in China but also in several ancient empires at once –

> Under the connecting feeling of tropical heat and vertical sun-lights, I brought together all creatures, birds, beasts, reptiles, all trees and plants, usages and appearances, that are found in all tropical regions, and assembled them together in China or Indostan. From kindred feelings, I soon brought Egypt and all her gods under the same law. I was stared at, hooted at, grinned at, chattered at, by monkeys, by paroquets, by cocakatoos. (863)

This description of his nightmares, which he prefaces as being "Oriental imagery" that impose "unimaginable horror" and "mythological torture" on him, is interesting for how it reverses his own encounter with the Malay. He is now the one who is "stared at", he faces an uncontrollable mobility when he repeatedly arrives in dreams inside Chinese houses against his will and cannot distinguish his identity in the face of these ancient civilisations and regions where "man is a weed" (863).

The dependence on a commodity that arises in an Oriental context thus returns to haunt De Quincey in the form of "Oriental dreams". The form of the dream, moreover, allows him to explore the very complex relationship shared by England, India and China at the time.[10] While England dominated these regions through trade and military power, images from these regions found their way into the consciousness of Englishmen and women, even those who had never travelled to the colonies. De Quincey is thus interesting for his focus on images of Eastern regions and people as the primary source of knowledge he relies on and experiences in his opium-fuelled dreams.[11] His writing is also fascinating for the links it makes between the writer's capacity to imagine a world where he is not physically present and the effects of opium – the commodity itself appears to impose geographical limitations on the writer's imagination. The horrors and the oppression of De Quincey's Oriental dreams seem to also arise from his inability to control the reach or direction of his visions.

As evidenced by the passages from De Quincey, Romantic writers engaged with the question of Empire by exploring the relationship between their own culture and the others they now routinely met and interacted with. By the early nineteenth century, as is also evident in Wordsworth's portrayal of multicultural London, the city was also home to cultures other than English and was also driven economically by colonial expansion. Anxieties such as those faced by De Quincey pertained mainly to the difficulty in distinguishing what was "English" from the other cultures that colonialism sought to conquer through cultural means (like propagating Christianity and the teaching of the English language) as much as through trade and military might. Likewise, in Coleridge's "Kubla Khan", the poet's creativity and imaginative potential is driven by a commodity that is not English and thus a "new" kind of landscape is made possible. In his headnote to the poem, Coleridge describes how he composed the poem in a dream induced by opium while also reading a seventeenth-century travelogue. The headnote thus clearly invokes the dual context of travel and opium and goes on to suggest that Coleridge remembers the scale of his dream being much grander than what he can recreate in the poem inspired by this dream. The "fragment" as Coleridge calls it, offers him Oriental visions of a very different kind from De Quincey. Rather than fear and anxiety, Coleridge's vision of a Mongol King, his palace, the lands he inhabits, and the Abyssinian maid are a "deep delight" that inspire him to recreate the same experience for others. Although induced by opium, the Oriental landscape that Coleridge finds himself in is not one that is hostile to him – rather, it fills him with awe and wonder. However, Coleridge too fears that this capacity to "see" an Oriental vision and attest even to "half-remembered" details are a danger to those who can also now see and imagine the same. His exclamation of "Beware! Beware! His flashing eyes, his floating hair!" are a reference to the poet, who, after seeing other worlds seeks to recreate them for his readers. Coleridge too fears the "infecting" power of his Oriental vision and worries how he will now contain what he has seen and learned without impacting the world he inhabits.

The visions of Eastern countries are thus not always directed by a "gaze" that conquers – often, the Romantics also explored what it meant to be "gazed at" in return and the sheer distance (both geographic as well as cultural) that existed between themselves and the people and lands their countrymen came into contact with. "Kubla Khan" is also interesting for the kind of distancing that it imagines for a far-away empire. While the poem attempts to evoke the feeling of being physically present in a space that is far-removed in time (Kublai Khan ruled China in the thirteenth century), it uses several other ideas to indicate how inaccessible it is. The poem for instance features aspects that are hard to grasp mentally – "measureless" caverns, a historical figure (Kubla Khan) hearing his ancestors speak at an unspecified moment and place and a half-remembered vision (of music played by an Abyssinian woman) inside a half-remembered dream. The Orient appears to represent a great degree of unknowability for the poet which is precisely what makes it alluring for him.

Shelley's "Alastor" similarly features a vision experienced by the eponymous wandering poet in the "vale of Cashmire" where a "veiled maid" would recite poetry and music to him. In contrast to Hazlitt's view of the Malay however, and Coleridge's unspeaking Abyssinian maid, Shelley's wandering poet finds his "veiled maid" to have a voice like the "voice of his own soul". Moreover, the content of what she says is dear to the poet's heart:

> Knowledge and truth and virtue were her theme,
> And lofty hopes of divine liberty,
> Thoughts the most dear to him, and poesy,
> Herself a poet. (lines 158–61)

Shelley's encounter with foreign lands contains several features of Romantic writing about the Empire identified so far. It shares with the passages in De Quincey and Coleridge its exotic modes of distancing through a narrative that comprises many mysteries and sudden turns and is also similar to Jones' view of an affinity between England and the cultures of Persia and India.

The associations between poetic inspiration, visions of the East and their reconstitution in poetry and prose establish a further idea about Romantic imperialism – the lands and cultures Englishmen encountered at this time, especially in the context of colonialism, were very much a part of their cultural imaginary. By cultural imaginary I mean a set of images (De Quincey's reference to pictures and statues) and other modes of representation – travellers' accounts and stories from other lands translated into English (*The Arabian Nights Entertainment*, for example, was first translated into English in the eighteenth century and fuelled public interest in the genre of Oriental tales) – that become another register in which lands outside England exist. In addition to exploring the consequences of a close association with the East for poetry and aesthetics, English writers also described for their readers, encounters with different modes of power and governance. These writings did not have an explicit focus on the East geographically but sought to respond to the prevalent criticism of monarchical rule at this time. As noted in Chapter One, this was perhaps also driven by English dissatisfaction over events in France following the initial years of the revolution. Many writers viewed Napoleon's rise to power, for instance, as a return to a tyrannical form of rule and his coronation as emperor in 1804 confirmed France as an empire rather than as the republic it was imagined to be following revolution. Many of England's elite (of whom the major Romantic writers were a big part) were critical of forms of government they perceived as repressive both within and outside England and Europe.

British imperial expansion in this period, especially in the Indian subcontinent, complicated questions about forms of government even more. Maintaining authority in a geographical region that was no longer confined to the borders of Britain and "Englishness" meant diverse interpretations of good government. Englishmen who travelled to far-off colonies had to contend with culturally different modes of executing and maintaining authority before asserting their own. Even English missionaries, who travelled to spread religious teachings in the colonies, had to adapt Anglicanism to adequately survive regional languages and religious practices. Empire thus also coincided with the thinking and reflecting on the best mode of governing a culture other than one's own. This would manifest sometimes in a condescending attitude towards forms of government in Asia influenced by eighteenth-century theories about "despotic" rulers[12] and at other times, as an anxiety over how European powers compared to the rulers they would come to replace in the colonies. One of the most prominent instances in this period of the interplay between Oriental themes and an exploration of new and foreign modes of rule is the Gothic novel. In the most characteristic works of this genre, tyranny and oppression are present in the form of an aristocrat or ruler in a distant land (often also distant in time since many of these novels were set in the medieval period) and the horrors of daily life under these circumstances are visualised for the reader.

William Beckford's *Vathek* (1786) for instance, describes its titular caliph's relationship with his subjects and kingdom thus:

> Notwithstanding the sensuality in which Vathek indulged, he experienced no abatement in the love of his people, who thought that a sovereign immersed in pleasure was not less tolerable to his subjects than one that employed himself in creating them foes. But the unquiet and impetuous disposition of the Caliph would not allow him to rest there: he had studied so much for his amusement in the life-time of his father as to acquire a great deal of knowledge, though not a sufficiency to satisfy himself; for he wished to know everything; even sciences that did not exist. He was fond of engaging in disputes with the learned, but liked them not to push their opposition with warmth. He stopped the mouths of those with presents, whose mouths could be stopped; whilst others, whom his liberality was unable to subdue, he sent to prison to cool their blood; a remedy that often succeeded. Vathek discovered also a predilection for theological controversy; but it was not with the orthodox that he usually held. By this means he induced the zealots to oppose him, and then persecuted them in return; for he resolved, at any rate, to have reason on his side. (10)

This passage makes clear what little say the subjects in Vathek's kingdom have in its daily affairs while also emphasising the boundless nature of Vathek's power. Vathek strove to control even the fields of knowledge "that did not exist" and did not respect any institutional boundaries to his learning – later in the novel he would destroy a religious relic for his amusement. Most of what Vathek desires in the novel he can obtain through the exercise of tyranny, but his ambition does not abate even when it comes at the cost of sacrificing several of his subjects.

The Eastern ruler would again make an appearance in Shelley's "Ozymandias" published in 1818 at a time when the British Museum would announce their impending acquisition of a statue fragment of Rameses II. Shelley's source for how the statue looked, however, was from an account by an ancient Greek historian translated into English in 1814 (*The Historical Library of Diodorus the Sicilian*). In Shelley's poem, the ruler, even as seen in the statue fragment, is clearly despotic: his "frown, / And wrinkled lip, and sneer of cold command, / which yet survive (lines 4–5). His only remark inscribed on the statue reads, "My name is Ozymandias, King of Kings; / Look on my works ye Mighty, and despair!" (lines 10–11). Shelley, however, visualises his ruler's tyranny as transient with the closing lines of

> Nothing beside remains. Round the decay
> Of that colossal Wreck, boundless and bare
> The lone and level sands stretch far away (lines 12–14)

The statue fragment, its imposing inscription and the expression of the tyrant it preserves is situated in the present amidst an empire that did not survive. For Shelley, the work of art (the sculptor's portrayal of a ruler) is what survives but the empire it signifies is no more.

This idea of the transience and futility of the Empire is echoed yet again in the third canto of Byron's "Childe Harold's Pilgrimage" (1816). Interestingly, Childe Harold is a tourist who visits the sites of bygone empires and the battles fought to consolidate them in various parts of southern and western Europe. In the third canto, Harold visits Belgium and the site of the Waterloo battle made iconic at the time for being the place where Britain – allied with Belgium, Prussia, the Netherlands and Germany – defeated Napoleon. This victory was hailed as the end of not just a tyrannical form of monarchy but also Napoleon's unchecked ambition that had threatened to destroy the early promises of the French Revolution. Byron's Harold, however, looks upon the site of Waterloo with the characteristic Romantic melancholy over the cost of war:

> And Harold stands upon this place of skulls,
> The grave of France, the deadly Waterloo!
> How in an hour the power which gave annuls
> Its gifts, transferring fame as fleeting too! (lines 154–57)

Like with Shelley's image of Rameses II, Napoleon is absent here except for the account of his defeat and the mention of lives that were lost in overthrowing him. Harold remarks that there is not even a "colossal bust" or "column trophied for triumphal show" to mark the end of Napoleon's reign. This victory too is perceived as hollow since

> Gaul may champ the bit
> And foam in fetters;—but is Earth more free?
> Did nations combat to make One submit;
> Or league to teach all kings true sovereignty?
> What! shall reviving Thraldom again be
> The patched-up idol of enlightened days?
> Shall we, who struck the Lion down, shall we
> Pay the Wolf homage? proffering lowly gaze
> And servile knees to thrones? No; prove before ye praise!
> (lines 163–71)

For Byron, a united league of nations bringing down a single despot is not sufficient proof of a return to the principles promised by the French Revolution. In his view, this defeat symbolises a further consolidation of power in a few hands – the "true sovereignty" that kings now enjoyed – and one mode of empire-building is merely being exchanged for another. The human costs of raising and subsequently competing to secure the limits of imperial expansion seem to Byron a cycle that never ends as evidenced by the many ancient and contemporary battle sites visited by his touring protagonist.

In Byron and Shelley's view, the ruins of empire, when viewed from the vantage of the present, appear to symbolise ill-gotten power that is doomed not to last. In his poem "On Seeing the Elgin Marbles" (1817), following the acquisition of several artefacts from Parthenon by the British Museum, Keats would echo similar sentiments. Rather than celebrate the preserved beauty of these artefacts, Keats uses the occasion to reflect on his own mortality. The poem uses several images of impending and uncontrollable circumstances that may bring a living thing to its end, especially disease and the passing of time, to convey a sense of transience in the majesty of ancient Greek ruins. He uses the image of being struck down in flight to describe his feelings when he sees the marbles:

> each imagined pinnacle and steep
> Of godlike hardship tells me I must die
> Like a sick eagle looking at the sky (lines 3–5)

The perspective that Keats offers the viewer is one that almost serves as a warning – looking on the achievements of past empires in the present can only feel like an insurmountable feat. The distance travelled by these artefacts as well as their distance from Keats' time seem to him an "imagined pinnacle and steep" that he does not have the energy to scale. The sick eagle dying while looking at the sky serves as an interesting image here. It conveys the sense of mortality holding us back from achieving what would otherwise seem a natural task.

Empire and Travel: From Expansion to Governance

Objects, people and images of places outside Britain clearly played a role in how Romantic-era writers and readers imagined the Empire. The literary works examined here and their framing of the content of Empire, not just its political-economic landscape but what it meant, how it made one feel and what it meant for one's sense of self and place in the world, played a role in anticipating many events that followed. For instance, Britain's governing of India in the nineteenth century as a region that needed education in the English language and the values espoused by English literature and culture was anticipated by events at the end of the Romantic period. The East India Company in 1813 would no longer have a trading monopoly in India but with a renewed charter from the Crown would now become responsible for the education and general improvement of Indian society. Several Romantic-era writers would contribute to building a sense of responsibility Britain owed to its most profitable colony. Additionally, the late eighteenth and early nineteenth centuries saw a proliferation in the genre of travel writing which allowed Englishmen and women to make sense of their own country as well as the world outside in specific ways.

As demonstrated in the passages from "Childe Harold's Pilgrimage", travel in this period was unique when compared with earlier times – the Romantic traveller sought solitude as well as a *way* of looking at landscapes. Inspired by the visual aesthetics of European painters like Claude Lorraine (known for his scenes of pastoral beauty) and Salvator Rosa (his landscapes were often visualised as places of danger and mystery), Romantic writers would apply similar frames to their travels within and outside England. Travel writing was a well-known and much-loved genre in the Romantic period that would also play an important role in assisting the expansion of Empire. Much like present-day travel writing, Romantic travel writing found a way to evoke in readers' minds, ways of imagining a place, modes of conduct to follow there, how one ought to make sense of the place and how one was likely to feel when they were there, even in advance of having travelled there. It is in these contexts that we can look at some of the writings about other cultures, places and people that were produced in England in the early nineteenth century.

To illustrate the related contexts of travel writing and empire building in this period, I will examine a few poems focusing on British-ruled India. Amelia Alderson Opie in her "Song of a Hindustani Girl" (1801) adopts the perspective of an Indian girl in love with an "English Gentleman" and explores the tragedy of this relationship. In her footnote to the title, she says of the girl, "She had lived several years in India with an English gentleman to whom she was tenderly attached: but when he was about to marry, sent his Indian favorite up the country; and, as she was borne along in her palanquin, she was heard to sing the above-mentioned melody" (Opie). The Indian girl was clearly only a "favorite", never meant to be married to the gentleman as indicated by the separation in the statement between one who is "tenderly attached" and the future condition of being "about to marry". The girl is thus distanced at the very outset, like De Quincey's Malay in his English cottage, as someone who cannot cross the cultural threshold into an English gentleman's life when he is about to marry. The poem is a melancholy refrain by the Indian woman about how her life will now be meaningless while the Englishman will find himself an English wife. Several contrasts are evoked in the poem between the English bride and the Indian girl that set up irreconcilable differences between the two cultures. The English bride loves by "anxious duty" while the Indian girl is characterised by a "passion warm", the Indian girl believes the English bride likely to have an ambition to "rule" and "her own desires pursue" while she herself had shown "fond submission" (Opie). The song ends with the Indian girl contrasting her own purpose and capacity for love with the Englishman's saying that while "death will endear her", he will "every heart subdue" and "each maid" that sees him will love him, not only his English bride.

Several interesting themes and contexts characteristic of the genre emerge in this poem. While not strictly speaking in the genre of travel writing, Opie's poem belongs in a mode of writing by women Romantic writers who engage with the theme of Empire in very different ways from the male writers surveyed so far. Scholars[13] have noted that male Romantic writers often characterise the regions they encounter on their travels in feminine terms, thus asserting a degree of authority and control over them. In addition, this feminising also applies to the people in these regions who are then assumed to require the intervention and improvement provided by colonial rule. The women who appear in the writing of male poets at the time, especially Eastern women, are often visualised as commodities to be possessed. They are described as beautiful, mysterious and evoke a certain temptation in the male poet that he must eventually overcome. Women writers attempt to work against this masculine aesthetic even as several of them continue to assist and perpetuate the established ways of looking at Empire in this period. In the case of Opie, her Indian girl is given a voice with which to concretise a liaison with an Englishman, which is otherwise being erased by sending her up the country against her will. Although creating a negative contrast with an English bride, Opie's Indian girl ends the poem with an uncharacteristically assertive "And thou'lt mourn thy Poor Indian" thus transforming into a guilt-ridden memory even after she is sent away. The poem also throws light on an under-represented aspect of Indo-British relationships at the time by making clear the additional vulnerability of women in the colonies at the time of colonial occupation.

Felicia Hemans' "The Indian City" (1828) and Letitia Elizabeth Landon's numerous poems about India in the literary annual *Fisher's Drawing Room Scrapbook* also illustrate very different views on Empire from those we have examined so far. On the one hand, they are representative of changing attitudes in England over its relationship with India. They anticipate for instance, Macaulay's often-cited views in his *Minute on Indian Education* (1835) that the focus of British public expenditure in India ought to be on English education rather than the study of vernacular languages. This is in contrast with the attitudes of earlier British governors in India like Warren Hastings who along with William Jones encouraged the serious study of native antiquity, customs, languages, literatures and scientific treatises. The English Education Act of 1835 would declare English as the medium of instruction in all but two institutions of learning as well as the language of administration and law in India. Macaulay would assert that the continued funding of studying vernacular languages, literatures and sciences in India would be futile since

> the dialects commonly spoken among the natives of this part of India contain neither literary nor scientific information, and are moreover so poor and rude that, until they are enriched from some other quarter, it will not be easy to translate any valuable work into them. It seems to be admitted on all sides, that the intellectual improvement of those classes of the people who have the means of pursuing higher studies can at present be affected only by means of some language not vernacular amongst them.

He would then proceed to offer English as the best possible "foreign" tongue that can, through an education in its literatures and culture offer "access to all the vast intellectual wealth which all the wisest nations of the earth have created and hoarded in the course of ninety generations". Here again, it is important to note the differences in the ways in which Macaulay discusses Indian languages and literatures as being inferior to English and the view about an equivalence between the two cultures taken by writers like William Jones in the previous century.

The goal of British governance appears much clearer in the work of a writer like Macaulay who explicitly links the idea of Empire (comprising geographically and culturally disparate communities) through the speaking of English. For him, it is "the language of two great European communities which are rising, the one in the south of Africa, the other in Australia,— communities which are every year becoming more important and more closely connected with our Indian empire". Through education in English, a geographically dispersed Empire and its culturally diverse subjects could become consolidated as a class "of persons Indian in blood and colour, but English in tastes, in opinions, in morals and in intellect" (Macaulay). It is in the context of debates over the mode of rule to be exercised in India that poems like Hemans' and Landon's ought to be read. Having never visited India, these writers nevertheless draw upon the extensive writing about India that was available at this time. "The Indian City" for instance, borrows from Forbes' *Oriental Memoirs* which contained the artist's extensive sketches of India from his travels there as an employee of the East India Company. All of Landon's India poetry was similarly written to accompany sketches made by naval officers from their time in India and China. She would also frequently supplement her poems with extensive scholarly footnotes informed by the publications of well-known English oriental scholars. *Fisher's Drawing Room Scrapbook* thus featured Landon's poems as accompaniments rather than the main feature, which were picturesque sketches of places of note in exotic travel locations. Several of these pictures were of ruins of past empires in India and provided a new perspective about this colony. Increasingly towards the end of the Romantic period, there was a debate over whether Britain is a "benefactor" or "ruler" of colonies like India. Pictures of ruined landscapes in India allowed the region to be viewed as one that necessitated improvement through an English administrative intervention. I will offer here a brief analysis of a few of Landon's and Hemans' poetry to make explicit the connections between women writers in the early nineteenth century and the anticipation and rejection of some of the themes relating to Empire discussed so far.

Hemans' "The Indian City" deals with interreligious conflict and its consequence on individuals by detailing the death of a "Moslem" boy at the hands of "the children of Brahma born" and how this led to an exacting of vengeance by the boy's community. The poem sets up a contrast between the idyllic locations of the city in the opening stanzas – the "graceful Hindoo maid" fills water with a "cool sweet plashing" and the Brahmin murmurs his prayers – and the images of the revenge-fuelled war towards the end – "the sword of the Moslem, let loose to slay, / Like the panther leapt on its flying prey" (lines 219–20). In addition, the central event of the poem, the Muslims boy's punishment by death for straying into Hindu temple grounds, is set up as an act committed upon an "outsider" to the city. At the very outset for example, even as the poem spends considerable narrative time on the mother mourning her son's death, his act is clearly indicated as trespassing. We are told that the boy and his mother are passing through the city on their way to Mecca and only stop here for rest before resuming their journey. In addition, consider the following lines that describe the Muslim boy's entry into the temple-grounds or "the very heart of the holy ground":

> And there lay the water, as if enshrin'd
> In a rocky urn, from the sun and wind,
> Bearing the hues of the grove on high,
> Far down thro' its dark still purity.
> The flood beyond, to the fiery west
> Spread out like a metal-mirror's breast,
> But that lone bay, in its dimness deep,
> Seem'd made for the swimmer's joyous leap,
> For the stag athirst from the noontide chase,
> For all free things of the wild-wood's race. (lines 37–46)

The boy clearly sees no religious significance to the secluded spot and views it very differently from how the Brahmins or Hindus see the same space at the start of the poem. They make no sounds or movements to disturb this landscape and seem almost to belong to it naturally. The Muslim boy, however, "leaps" into the water and is seen "dashing the spray-drops". Several comparisons are made between his movements and those of wild animals, thereby somehow evoking a sense of his animal-like or uncivilised nature.

Hemans can be seen buttressing the British viewpoint on India at this time as a place that was mired in interreligious conflict owing to long-term oppression of the "effeminate" Hindu race by "barbaric" Muslim invaders. Jean Fernadez makes a similar argument about Landon's "Hindu and Mahomeddan Buildings" in which Hindus are perceived as "colonised insiders" whose glorious past has been converted into "ruins" by Islamic invaders. Hemans' "The Indian City" also ends with the city being laid waste by the "Tartar steed" that brings "flame thro' the idol fanes" and the ruins that remain of this once-glorious city are attributed to "one deep heart wrung" (line 228). While Hemans can be seen exploring and finding common cause with the perspective of the grieving and avenging mother (the boy's mother is the one who rallies her clansmen to wage war on the Hindu city) in this poem, there is also a certain disproportionality ascribed to the violence of the Muslims in the poem.

Some of Landon's India poems can also be seen to negotiate this kind of space within writing about Empire. In her "Hindoo Temples and Palace at Madura" she finds common cause with a female poet from south India[14] to demonstrate that there are "lessons" for her British readers in reading about a woman who achieved immortality through her verse against all odds. She parallels this immortality with the work of Empire and asks if this is as "noble" a conquest as the "mind's ethereal war". Even as Landon, like Hemans and Opie, immortalises the voice and perspective of women who are otherwise not seen and heard the same way as the male poets we have examined, she nevertheless assists in the imperial project by transforming India and Indian subjects into objects for consumption. In her "A Suttee" (1836), Landon writes in the tradition of a blazon and describes individual parts of the Indian woman's body as she prepares to immolate herself on her husband's funeral pyre. The poet's gaze slowly unveils the female subject in the poem and thus transforms the reader into a spectator. In a prefatory note to a poem titled "The Nizam's Daughter", written to accompany an engraving of the British Residency at Hyderabad, Landon says,

> The edifice here represented is the residence of the English Minister at the Court of the Nizam, or native prince. The party entering the gate shews the species of state, and the retinue, with which persons of rank appear in public. The curtains of the palanquins, in which females go forth, are always closely drawn: seclusion in the East is, as it were, the element of beauty. It is quite in human nature to admit that—"such must be / Dear—and yet dearer for its mystery".

It is thus precisely the seclusion of the Indian woman that adds to her charm and sense of mystery. The poem itself performs yet another "unveiling", as in "A Suttee", and offers a very elaborate description of the young Nizam princess. In this particular poem, parts of the girl's body are visualised together with the ornaments and precious metals that adorn them, making explicit the girl's value in two registers – as being thus far hidden and thus more desirable as well as being adorned with precious cargo. Her hair for instance is braided with "silver and with gold" and "one large pearl", her ankle and wrists sport a "band of gold" and around her waist is a girdle of "red rubies". At these moments it appears that Landon follows in the tradition of other Romantic poets who evoke a sense of richness and luxury in the East and perpetuate the notion of this region as being visible only as a commodity or status symbol. As illustrated by the lines preceding this chapter from Keats' "The Eve of St. Agnes" (1820), by the early nineteenth century in England, Empire is synonymous with trade and opulence.

Even as they make visible the plight of women in Eastern nations and communities, women writers in the Romantic period would simultaneously assist in consolidating the view that India required a more invasive form of administration and governance in the period following the Education Act of 1835. By representing a nation in ruins, where widows were burned and where communities clashed over irreconcilable differences in religion and caste, as with the poems in this section, the work of restoration and improvement was increasingly felt to be an English responsibility. Travel writing in this period would also commodify England's colonies, inviting Englishmen and women to view these faraway places as objects and lifestyles to be possessed.

This chapter has demonstrated how English Romantic writers occupied a range of positions with respect to British imperial expansion during the late eighteenth and early nineteenth centuries. English Romantic writing can offer us an insight into how the material conditions of Empire, in terms of changing political and economic relations between Britain and her colonies, interact with cultural and social factors as well. English identity would come under threat during this period when people and commodities flowed outside and into colonial Britain, forcing writers to contend with a transforming national character. Many rebellions against British rule, some successful and others unsuccessful, would also necessitate an evaluation of the nation's morals, culture and values against those over whom they sought control. These distant lands that Britain sought to integrate into an Empire would feature routinely in the writing of the period; initially as exotic locales that elicited wonder and curiosity but later as a range of complex representations: as sites of strategic economic and military importance, a source of guilt, sites of incomprehensible difference, a threat to the unity of Empire and an opportunity for establishing cultural supremacy.

Works Cited

Barrell, John. *The Infection of Thomas de Quincey: The Psychopathology of Imperialism.* Yale UP, 1991.

Beckford, William. *Vathek,* 1849, *Project Gutenberg,* https://www.gutenberg.org/files/42401/42401-h/42401-h.htm#citation9. Accessed 30 August 2020.

Butler, James A. "Travel Writing." *A Companion to Romanticism*, edited by Duncan Wu, Blackwell, 1999, pp. 393–400.

Coleridge, Samuel Taylor. "Fears in Solitude." *British Literature 1780–1830*, edited by Anne K Mellor and Richard E Matlak, Harcourt Brace, 1996, pp. 695.

———. "Kubla Khan: or, A Vision in a Dream." *British Literature 1780–1830*, edited by Anne K Mellor and Richard E Matlak, Harcourt Brace, 1996, pp. 729–30.

———. Excerpt from Lecture Six of the *Bristol Lectures*. *British Literature 1780–1830*, edited by Anne K Mellor and Richard E Matlak, Harcourt Brace, 1996, pp. 689.

———. "The Rime of the Ancyent Marinere". *British Literature 1780–1830*, edited by Anne K Mellor and Richard E Matlak, Harcourt Brace, 1996, pp. 700.

Cugoano, Ottobah. *Thoughts and sentiments on the evil and wicked traffic of the slavery: and commerce of the human species, humbly submitted to the inhabitants of Great-Britain, by Ottobah Cugoano*. London, 1787. *Eighteenth Century Collections Online Text Creation Partnership*, 2011, http://name.umdl.umich.edu/K046227.0001.001. Accessed 17 December 2019.

Davis, D.B. *The Problem of Slavery in the Age of Revolution, 1770–1823*. Oxford UP, 1999.

De Quincey, Thomas. Extract from *Confessions of an English Opium Eater*. *British Literature 1780–1830*, edited by Anne K Mellor and Richard E Matlak, Harcourt Brace, 1996, pp. 848–65.

Drew, John. *India and the Romantic Imagination*. Oxford UP, 1998.

Ebbatson, J. R. "Coleridge's Mariner and the Rights of Man." *Studies in Romanticism*, vol. 11, no. 3, 1972, pp. 171–206.

Empson, William. "The Ancient Mariner." *Critical Quarterly*, vol. 6, no. 4, 1964, pp. 298–319.

Fernandez, Jean. "Graven Images: The Woman Writer, the Indian Poetess, and Imperial Aesthetics in L.E.L.'s 'Hindoo Temples and Palaces at Madura.'" *Victorian Poetry*, vol. 43, no.1, 2005, pp. 35–52.

Fulford, Tim. *Romantic Indians: Native Americans, British Literature, and Transatlantic Culture 1756–1830*.Oxford UP, 2006.

Fulford, Timothy, and Peter J. Kitson, editors. *Romanticism and Colonialism: Writing and Empire, 1780–1830*. Cambridge UP, 1998.

Gascoigne, John. "Empire." *An Oxford Companion to the Romantic Age: British Culture* 1776–1832, edited by Iain McCalman, Oxford UP, 1999, pp. 51–58.

Heffernan, James A W. "Wordsworth's London: The Imperial Monster." *Studies in Romanticism*, vol. 37, no. 3, 1998, pp. 421–43.

Hemans, Felicia. "The Indian City." *British Literature 1780–1830*, edited by Anne K. Mellor and Richard E. Matlak, Harcourt Brace, 1996, pp. 1234–36.

Jones, Sir William. *Poems, Consisting Chiefly of Translations from the Asiatick Tongues* (1772), edited by Rudolf Beck, Universitat Augsburg, 2009.

Keats, John. "The Eve of St. Agnes." *British Literature 1780–1830*, edited by Anne K. Mellor and Richard E. Matlak, Harcourt Brace, 1996, pp. 1283.

———. "On Seeing the Elgin Marbles." *British Literature 1780–1830*, edited by Anne K. Mellor and Richard E. Matlak, Harcourt Brace, 1996, pp. 1261.

Kitson, Peter J. "Romanticism and Colonialism: Races, Places, Peoples, 1785–1800." *Romanticism and Colonialism: Writing and Empire, 1780–1830*, edited by Timothy Fulford and Peter J. Kitson, Cambridge UP, 1998, pp. 13–34.

Landon, Letitia Elizabeth. "Hindoo Temples and Palace at Madura." *Letitia Elizabeth Landon (L. E. L.) in Fisher's Drawing Room Scrap Book, 1836/Madura compiled by Wikisource contributors,* https://en.wikisource.org/w/index.php?title=Letitia_Elizabeth_Landon_(L._E._L.)_in_Fisher%27s_Drawing_Room_Scrap_Book,_1836/Madura&oldid=7095512. Accessed 31 August 2020.

———. "The Nizam's Daughter". *Letitia Elizabeth Landon (L. E. L.) in Fisher's Drawing Room Scrap Book, 1835/Nizam's Daughter compiled by Wikisource contributors, https://en.wikisource.org/wiki/Letitia_Elizabeth_Landon_(L._E._L.)_in_Fisher%27s_Drawing_Room_Scrap_Book,_1835/Nizam%E2%80%99s_Daughter*. Accessed 31 August 2020.

———. "A Suttee". *Letitia Elizabeth Landon (L. E. L.) in Fisher's Drawing Room Scrap Book, 1836/Immolation compiled by Wikisource contributors,* https://en.wikisource.org/wiki/Letitia_Elizabeth_Landon_(L._E._L.)_in_Fisher%27s_Drawing_Room_Scrap_Book,_1836/Immolation. Accessed 31 August 2020.

Lawson, Philip. *The East India Company: A History*. Routledge, 2014.

Leask, Nigel. *British Romantic Writers and the East: Anxieties of Empire*. Cambridge UP, 2004.

Macaulay, Thomas Babington. *Minute on Education (1835). South Asia Study Resources compiled by Frances Pritchett*, http://www.columbia.edu/itc/mealac/pritchett/00generallinks/macaulay/txt_minute_education_1835.html. Accessed 31 August 2020.

Makdisi, Saree. "Romanticism and Empire." *A Concise Companion to the Romantic Age*, edited by John Klancher, Wiley-Blackwell, 2009, pp. 36–56.

Mellor, Anne K. "Romanticism, Gender and the Anxieties of Empire: An Introduction." *European Romantic Review*, vol. 8, no. 2, 1997, pp. 148–54.

Opie, Amelia Alderson. "A Hindustani Girl's Song." *The Amelia Alderson Opie Archive*, https://ameliaopiearchive.com/a-hindustani-girls-song/. Accessed 31 August 2020.

Shelley, Percy Bysshe. "Alastor; or, The Spirit of Solitude." *British Literature 1780–1830*, edited by Anne K. Mellor and Richard E. Matlak, Harcourt Brace, 1996, pp. 1056.

———. "Ozymandias." *British Literature 1780–1830*, edited by Anne K. Mellor and Richard E. Matlak, Harcourt Brace, 1996, pp. 1066.

Warne, Vanessa. "'What Foreign Scenes Can Be': The Ruin of India in Letitia Landon's Scrapbook Poems." *Victorian Review*, vol. 32, no. 2, 2006, pp. 40–63.

Warren, Andrew. *The Orient and the Young Romantics*. Cambridge UP, 2014.

Wordsworth, William. "London, 1802." *British Literature 1780–1830*, edited by Anne K. Mellor and Richard E. Matlak, Harcourt Brace, 1996, pp. 599.

———. *The Prelude 1799, 1805, 1850*, edited by Jonathan Wordsworth, M.H Abrams and Stephen Gill, Norton, 1979.

———. "Written in London, September, 1802." *British Literature 1780–1830*, edited by Anne K. Mellor and Richard E. Matlak, Harcourt Brace, 1996, pp. 598.

Notes

1. The term "oriental" at this time referred to any person or thing belonging to the eastern and southern part of Europe. Edward Said would note in his *Orientalism* (2003) that the term carries connotations beyond just descriptions of people belonging to regions to the East of Europe. For him, terms like the Orient (referring to regions like Asia, Egypt and the Middle East) and Oriental are products of a body of knowledge called "Orientalism" that *created* specific (often stereotypical) notions about non-European cultures by treating the European as the norm.
2. For a more detailed overview of Romantic responses to Empire, classified according to regions abroad where Britain had a colonial presence, see *Romanticism and Colonialism* edited by Timothy Fulford and Peter Kitson. For a discussion of English writers' interest in and representation of Native Americans, see Tim Fulford's *Romantic Indians: Native Americans, British Literature and Transatlantic Culture 1756–1830.*
3. See John Drew's *India and the Romantic Imagination* for a perspective that does not treat imperial expansion as the starting point for an analysis of the cultural exchange that takes place between England and India. Drew's account approaches the links between India and England as emerging over a timespan that criss-crosses from writing and knowledge production in the medieval and modern periods.
4. William Murray, Lord of Mansfield had famously ruled in 1772 in favor of the slave James Somerset who sought freedom from his master once he reached England from America. Lord Mansfield's judgment considered England a land where slavery was unlawful and in granting Somerset his freedom, made London a sought-after refuge for slaves.
5. See Heffernan's essay also for a discussion of how Wordsworth's portrayal of London differs from the general Romantic attitudes towards city life.
6. This scheme was planned by Coleridge and Robert Southey when they were in college. The plans, which were never realised, entailed emigration to America where they would set up a society based on egalitarian norms like communal property ownership.

7. Lord Clive and Warren Hastings were the first British administrators of Bengal following India's military takeover by the East India Company. The British government would eventually seek to distance itself from the activities of the East India Company whose experience and status as a trading company made them unsuitable for the task of governance. Coleridge's views form part of a growing critique in Britain of the company's hostile, militaristic expansion and administration in India. For a detailed analysis of how the British government would eventually intervene in India's administration by the company and pursue a "reformed" ideal of governance in the subcontinent, see Philip Lawson's *The East India Company: A History.*
8. "Dissenter" is a term that covers a broad set of heteregenous Christian denominations that differ in principles and practice from Anglicanism or the mode of Christianity propounded by the Church of England.
9. See David Brion Davis' *The Problem of Slavery in the Age of Revolution, 1770–1823* for an analysis of how the ideological and cultural apparatus of abolition intersected with the social reality of slavery. Davis' analysis is important for understanding the differential impact of legal judgments, abolitionist campaigns, religious and moral arguments and their representation in literature on slavery in the eighteenth and nineteenth centuries.
10. See Nigel Leask's *British Romantic Writers and the East: Anxieties of Empire* for a detailed discussion on the complexity of relationships between England and Greece, Egypt and India and their manifestation in the works of Byron, Shelley and Coleridge.
11. For a psychoanalytic interpretation of the recurring theme of a threatening Oriental figure in De Quincey's writings, see John Barrel's *The Infection of Thomas De Quincey: A Psychopathology of Imperialism.*
12. This is in specific reference to the concept theorised by the Baron de Montesquieu regarding a despotic mode of governance that was unique to Asia. While the idea of a despotic form of government had been a subject of discussion prior to the eighteenth century, this period of imperial expansion into Asia saw a modification. Asia's climate was seen by the English to be conducive for a form of rule that inhered in only one person (that of the ruler) and

was subject to his whims. See Andrew Warren's *The Orient and the Young Romantics* for a detailed discussion on the influence of British attitudes towards political formations in Eastern countries on Romantic literature.

13. See for instance James Butler's "Travel Writing" where he discusses the gendered aspects of this genre in the Romantic period; Anne Mellor's "Romanticism, Gender and the Anxieties of Empire: An Introduction" where she sets out the gendered aesthetics of looking at Empire in Romantic writing and Vanessa Warne's "'What foreign scenes can be': The ruin of India in Letitia Landon's Scrapbook Poems" (2006) and Jean Fernandez's "Graven Images: The Woman Writer, the Indian Poetess, and Imperial Aesthetics in L.E.L.'s 'Hindoo Temples and Palaces at Madura'" for an extended discussion on female Romantic writers' responses to what they saw as a "masculine" and militaristic imperial project.
14. Avvaiyyar was a female poet of the Sangam period from a pariah caste.

FIVE

THE ROMANTIC SELF

To speak of the "self" in the Romantic period in England means delving into what it meant to be an individual at this historical juncture and how he/she made sense of themselves and their place in this world. Our self or "selfhood" generally refers, in philosophical discussions, to how aware we are of ourselves and how constant this awareness is at every moment of our life and over the course of our lifetime. This may become clearer if we consider the questions asked in disciplines and genres where theories of the self are discussed, namely, autobiography, journals and diaries, memoirs, personal essays in literature and history, and philosophical treatises on how "conscious" we are of our sense of individuality. Some central questions include but are not limited to: Can we become conscious of every part of what makes a person uniquely them? Is each person's sense of self a coherent whole or is it discontinuous and fragmentary? How do we become aware of existing as a self – is it through writing or reading about other selves who have lived? What role does memory, the unconscious, dreams and language play in forming a sense of self? Does the sense of self precede one's birth and entry into the world of language, culture and physical growth or does it develop and transform over the course of our lives?

For our purposes here, in looking closely at the literature of the Romantic period, we can turn to autobiographies and biographies as the more obvious modes through which some of these questions were being engaged with. Even prior to the Romantic period, writing about the self involved having to wrap one's mind around what it meant to have lived a "life", and writers would find that in addition to the autobiography, the novel served as a capacious form for narrating all particulars relevant to an individual. Some of the famous eighteenth-century novels are thus about the lives of various individuals – Robinson Crusoe, Pamela, Tristram Shandy, Moll Flanders – and as such offer minute details of everyday life while simultaneously attempting to capture an entire lifespan. Writing in the Romantic period would continue this interest in and exploration about questions concerning the individual while also taking these in new directions.

Before examining the narration of a self in its various written literary forms, it is important to conduct a brief survey of the sociopolitical contexts in which thinking about the individual occurred in the eighteenth century. As seen in the chapter on revolutions and rights, the late eighteenth century was a period in which the individual was seen for the first time as existing independently of certain pre-established social orders. The perpetuity of monarchical forms of rule were questioned in the wake of the French Revolution and the successful independence of the American colonies from Britain. The Declaration of the Rights of Man and subsequent articulations for the rights of women and slaves would bring a new perspective to how the individual was defined. Abolitionist poetry, for instance, directly responds to this context by forcing readers to contend with the idea that slaves and slave-produced commodities were viewed as one and the same. Abolitionist poetry sought to characterise slaves as persons by representing their point of view in literature and abolitionist campaigns sought to bring back the deliberately erased links between the horrors of the slave trade and slave-produced commodities like sugar. As seen in the chapter on Empire, London was reconfigured as a place that now included individuals from other races and lands and an "English self" had to now be redefined with respect to its daily contact with those unlike itself. The expansion of British dominion in the East would thus place geographical pressures on what and who constituted a British nation and her subjects. Learning the English language would become yet another mode through which one could become an Englishman, despite belonging to lands and cultures that were distributed across the world.

In terms of aesthetics, the Romantic mode in literature is often set apart from the preceding Neoclassical conventions of writing by referring to the ways in which it defines and understands the individual. This is often attributed to the way the individual was seen in relation to divine power before the late-eighteenth century in England. Wordsworth's *Prelude* for example, in narrating the story of the poet's own life, places the individual at the centre of the epic form, previously reserved only for the feats of gods. While Wordsworth's autobiographic poem along with others in the period like De Quincey's *Confessions of an English Opium Eater* and Byron's "Childe Harold's Pilgrimage" (said first to be autobiographical by its readers and then reluctantly corroborated by Byron) belongs to a mode of self-writing prevalent in England since the seventeenth century, it also diverges from its predecessors in several respects. Seventeenth-century autobiographies looked to God as the force that directed the path of the individual's life while Romantic writers sought to remove their protagonists and narrators from any kind of institutional authority in an organised society. The central characters of many famous Romantic works like Childe Harold, Prometheus, Frankenstein and Coleridge's mariner for instance are often misfits and outcasts. In addition to being socially alienated, these Romantic figures are often engaged in a quest or journey whose ambitious scope outlasts them. Illustrated in Coleridge's mariner's tale or the ones narrated by Victor Frankenstein and Captain Walton in Mary Shelley's *Frankenstein* (the novel's subtitle refers to the mythological rule-breaker Prometheus), the quests undertaken by Romantic characters may be spiritual (in the sense that they are reflective about failures and seek a moral code) but are always self-directed and quite explicitly beyond their capacities. In other words, rather than setting limits or seeking to work within limits (understood as the individual's ordained place in the world or even the rules about composing literature), Romantic writers explored the possibilities of exceeding these. Poetic theories like those developed by Wordsworth in his *Preface*, Coleridge in *Biographia Literaria* and Shelley in his *A Defence of Poetry* would emphasise innovation and the renewal of English poetry in contrast to the conformist verse of poets like Alexander Pope and John Dryden.

Even as the autonomous individual who sought to surpass oppressive institutional structures emerged in Romantic literature in the wake of hopeful sociopolitical revolutions in the late eighteenth century, the course taken by these would yet again influence the representations of the self. The bloody turn taken by the French Revolution, Napoleon's rise to power and accession as Emperor as well as the violent and material excesses of Britain's colonial expansion would once more compel English Romantic writers to think of the necessary limits to individual freedom. An expanding market and growing demand for literature, now increasingly viewed as a commodity whose quantity was valued over its intrinsic quality, would push Romantic writers to reconsider their freedom. Moreover, a well-established periodical culture that now controlled information and knowledge about how a literary work ought to be valued threatened to take away the writer's autonomy or self-expression over the meaning of his/her work. It is against these myriad contexts that this chapter will examine the self as it emerges in the writings of the English Romantics.

The Formation of the Individual: Childhood in Romantic Poetry

An important context for the development of ideas about the individual in this period is childhood. One of the genres in which changing attitudes towards the place of the individual in his/her world can be observed is in writing meant for and about children in this period. As Julian Walker and Nelson Hilton have illustrated, William Blake's works like *Songs of Innocence and of Experience* would for the first time systematically overturn the modes through which children were portrayed and addressed in literature. Rather than offer straightforward morals and instructions to child readers, Blake's poems are much more ambivalent in their resolution to complex issues like morality, religion and social inequality. A few other contexts to keep in mind when looking closely at Romantic writers' representations of the early life or formation of the individual are prevailing ideas about the child and its education. Walker notes that in the eighteenth century, the prevailing Christian view about the child was that it came into the world in sin, was innately evil and had to *learn* to become good through religious instruction and discipline. Parallel to this were the views propounded by the philosophers Locke and Rousseau about the nature of the child and its improvement. Locke would argue that the child's mind was a blank slate and capable of being shaped in any way. The duty of the educator was thus an important one and he or she was to inculcate practices of self-improvement that would eventually lead to the making of model citizens. Rousseau, contrary to the Christian doctrine of original sin, believed in the innate innocence of the child who is only corrupted through its exposure to the world of adults. These contrasting views about the early years of human development would occupy many writers of the time while also in turn influencing ideas concerning education.

The Sunday school system, created to make England's working classes literate, would further contribute to ideas concerning the development of individuals in various classes and stations in life. In his "Infant Joy" (1789) and "Infant Sorrow" (1794) from *The Songs* for instance, Blake represents these contrasting views about childhood. What strikes the reader on looking at this pair of poems is how the perspective of the child (even as an infant) is given voice. In "Infant Joy" we see the child emerging from a state of having no name to naming itself "Joy" and it is through this lens that the child's mother views it too – "Sweet joy but two days old, / Sweet joy I call thee" (lines 8–9). In "Infant Sorrow" we hear the child speak in a very different tone – "My mother groand! my father wept. / Into the dangerous world I leapt" (lines 1–2). We do not hear the parents speak at all but the child views its mode of belonging in the world as constraining:

> Struggling in my fathers hands:
> Striving against my swaddling bands,
> Bound and weary I thought best
> To sulk upon my mothers breast. (lines 5–8)

Here, instead of the active entry into language made by the child via the act of naming, the moment of birth is experienced as an extreme awareness of dependency through the use of terms like "struggling", "striving", "bands" and "bound" to refer to parts of the parents' bodies that offer care. Familial support is seen to be an act that is mutually painful given all that has to be done to offer protection for the child from the "dangerous world". Moreover, "groand" and "wept" precede the child's "leaping" into the world, indicating how suffering pre-exists the child.

Poems like "The School Boy" (1789) specifically address the institution of formal education and the impact they have on the child's relationship with his or her natural environment. Blake's schoolboy loves to rise early in summer but hates to "go to school in a summer morn" where "under a cruel eye outworn, / the little ones spend the day / In sighing and dismay" (lines 8–10). The poem's expansive opening scene, with birds singing on "every tree", the sounds of a "distant" huntsman and the skylark singing, soon becomes narrow and confining when speaking of the child's demeanour in school. The child's experience in school is described through various physical signs – he says he sits in a "drooping" manner and that he feels "anxious", "fears" annoy him and cause him to "forget his youthful spring" (line 20). In Blake's view, the schoolboy is severed from all that he could learn in his natural environment when made to learn in the artificial and confining environment of the school. The poem ends with the boy questioning how he is ever to understand phenomena like the changing of seasons and their varying produce if he is not spending his time observing the outdoors.

Blake's representation of his idea of the human in "The Human Abstract" (1794) further consolidates the new mode of looking at the individual during this period. "The Human Abstract" is the corresponding pair for the poem "The Divine Image" (1789) from *The Songs.* In "The Divine Image", man more closely resembles his Christian incarnation where he is created in God's image and is thus seen as partly "divine". Speaking of the abstract qualities of mercy, pity, peace and love, Blake says that these are concretised in the figure of God as well as man. Mirroring the qualities of God and man, Blake argues that God is the "father" who transfers these qualities to man who is the "child" in His care. However, he also posits a multi-ethnic view of man when he suggests at the end of the poem" that

> all must love the human form,
> In heathen, Turk or Jew;
> Where Mercy, Love, and Pity dwell
> There God is dwelling too. (lines 17–20)

Thus, man is here universalised and not viewed as belonging to the Christian faith alone. "The Human Abstract" further complicates this view and the degree to which an individual mirrors the qualities of God. In this poem, Blake suggests that the qualities which we all aspire to – mercy, pity, peace and love – are created and perpetuated through entirely human means. Man and "gods" (referred to in the plural and with a lower case "g") in this poem are viewed as inhabiting distinct domains where the creation of these qualities is attributed to humans alone. In a reworking of how these qualities come about in human life, Blake says,

Pity would be no more,
If we did not make somebody Poor;
And Mercy no more could be,
If all were as happy as we;
And mutual fear brings peace;
Till the selfish loves increase.
Then Cruelty knits a snare,
And spreads his baits with care. (lines 1–8)

In contrast to "The Divine Image", this poem suggests that the qualities we see as divine (pity, mercy, peace) require human social structures to exist. These structures are innately unequal and depict the human as making sense of who he/she is only in the context of other humans – somebody who is poor, those who are not happy, or those we fear. "Care" is seen as a bait through which an individual traps another in order to further a love of himself/herself. The poem ends with a reference to these qualities as well as others they give rise to (humility, mystery, deceit) being part of a tree that "grows in the Human Brain" (line 24). For Blake, this "Brain" is closed off to the "gods of the earth and sea" whose quest for it is unsuccessful. Clearly, an understanding of what it means to be human flows from the human realm alone, with no reliance on the gods. We thus have here a very different version of a person's place in the world where they are the sole author of their nature and make sense of their chief qualities in a world exclusively occupied by "humans".

In his "Ode: Intimations of Immortality from Recollections of Early Childhood" (1807), Wordsworth would again characterise the child as being in a state that he would lose touch with when he reached adulthood. Speaking of the "artifice" of adulthood, Wordsworth says,

with new joy and pride
The little Actor cons another part;

Filling from time to time his "humorous stage"
With all the Persons, down to palsied Age,
That Life brings with her in her equipage;
As if his whole vocation
Were endless imitation. (lines 101–07)

"The little Actor" here refers to the child whom Wordsworth suggests comes into being from an "eternal" state only to then be burdened on its earthly journey by the weight of custom. Adulthood is here again seen to be removed from the domain of the "heavenly" and "immortal" (earlier in the poem Wordsworth mentions that we all come from God and have a sense of "heaven" all around us in our infancy) and all the stages of life are represented as rituals that have a language and grammar that need to be learned. Wordsworth argues that the child must set aside a "natural inheritance" (he calls this "heaven-born freedom") to learn the codes of conduct necessary to survive adulthood. The child thus loses freedom, liberty and a connection with "eternal" states like nature and the divine in order to navigate the earthly world of customs and "business, love, or strife" (line 88).

The Individual in the Context of Revolution

As seen in the chapters on Empire and revolution, plenty of Romantic-era writers would focus on the lives of others, especially on those who were less fortunate. Abolitionist writing and representations of the people, cultures and lands in Asia and Africa are examples of such writing examined earlier in this book. Growing knowledge about and contact with cultures and lands other than England was an important way in which the self was understood at this time. In addition to looking outside England for those unlike themselves, writers would also look at fellow citizens from different social contexts to better understand their own place in the world. For instance, the poor and scenes of poverty both in the rural and urban landscape were a feature of thinking about the self. Poverty and what and who comprised this state was an extensively discussed subject during the eighteenth century. Among the differing attitudes towards poverty in this period were notions about the importance of charity, the human links with the poor that every Englishman shared and the necessity for cultivating independence and morality among the needy. Wordsworth's Simon Lee, George Crabbe's Peter Grimes and Hannah More's Sinful Sally for instance are all characters that portray England's poor in very different ways. While Simon Lee is industrious and continues to work even in his old age, Peter Grimes and Sinful Sally turn to stealing, drinking and work only to further sustain their vices. However, like the figure of the child and the state of childhood, the state of being poor is often utilised as a mode of making sense of the individual and his/her place in society. "Poor" was a catch-all term at the time to refer to a range of individuals who required sustenance from various social institutions to survive. They included soldiers discharged after the war, the elderly, orphans, prostitutes, the sick and disabled. Economic relief was often provided by the Church as well as through the many charitable institutions set up during this time. These institutions relied upon local communities to execute aid to the poor and to this extent, created specific frames for knowing and understanding poverty.

Several Romantic writers would respond to these institutional ideas about the poor, sometimes by furthering the ideas of the church and state and often also by questioning them. Sarah Lloyd has demonstrated that the eighteenth century in England is significant for having added a moral dimension to discussions surrounding poverty. In addition to the many proposals made at this time to tackle the structural or economic reasons for poverty, many writers were also interested in the aspects of human nature that contributed to the sustaining of poverty. This moral dimension is what several Romantic writers would both participate in and critique. For instance, Blake's "The Little

Vagabond" and "Holy Thursday" make explicit references to the church's mode of charity being determined by those who fund this work. The poor who availed relief provided by the church were expected in return to exhibit Christian piety (in terms of attending church and avoiding the vices of drinking for instance) and gratitude towards their social betters (the rich in the community who provided money towards poor relief). Blake criticises this mode of looking at the poor where they exist only *in relation* to their social betters and have no other distinguishing characteristics.

In a different vein, Mary Wollstonecraft in her *A Vindication of the Rights of Men* would argue that the urban poor are a measure of the nation's level of progress towards the ideals of liberty and equality professed by the French Revolution. For her, England's poor are a consequence of the unemployment generated by a market prone to material excesses. She says, "How many mechanics, by a flux of trade or fashion, lose their employment—whom misfortunes (not to be warded off) lead to the idleness that vitiates their character and renders them afterwards averse to honest labour!" (59). The simultaneous framing of the poor through an economic as well as a moral lens is clear here where the cause for poverty may be economic but it is perpetuated by behavioural means. It is the "character" of those who become poor that is of concern to Wollstonecraft in the context of revolution. She further clarifies her interest in England's poor when she says,

> Surveying civilized life, and seeing with undazzled eye the polished vices of the rich, their insincerity, want of natural affections, with all the specious train that luxury introduces, I have turned impatiently to the poor to look for man undebauched by riches or power. But alas, what did I see? A being scarcely above the brutes over which it tyrannized—a broken spirit, worn-out body, and all those gross vices which the example of the rich, rudely copied, could produce. Envy built a wall of separation that made the poor hate, whilst they bent to their superiors who, on their part, stepped aside to avoid the loathsome sight of human misery. (59–60)

For Wollstonecraft, the "civilised" life and any project intended to make a responsible citizenry needed to look at the character of the individual. What is interesting in the quote above is her interest in finding an "undebauched" representative of this individual in England to make the case for why social change is required. Social change is clearly linked in this time of revolution to the improvement of the individual whose moral character is threatened by their social environment. The poor are seen to be linked to their superiors here through some sort of evolutionary chain which the rich are anxious to acknowledge. Wollstonecraft separates the poor as a category unto themselves who can only "rudely" imitate the lives of the rich but lack the material circumstances to sustain the imitation. In separating them thus and "looking to them" for an "undebauched" representative of the individual, she articulates a central Romantic theme: that the poor tell us something about all our characters and "humanness". In combining the poor as the "sight of human misery" and arguing that we ought not to turn away from such a scene, she invites us to look closer at what constitutes the nature of all men and women.

Wordsworth's poetry represents perhaps the richest exploration of the individual in the context of poverty. Several of the central protagonists of his poems ("The Female Vagrant", "Simon Lee, the Old Huntsman", "The Last of the Flock", "The Discharged Soldier", "The Ruined Cottage" and "The Old Cumberland Beggar, a Description") are the rural poor. Even as he mediates stories of the poor in the Lake District (the marginalised, though often making an appearance in Romantic literature, rarely speak themselves) he offers richly detailed portraits of the circumstances of their daily life. His tone is at times that of the ethnographer, offering details about the poor he writes about, like their modes of employment and the consequences of their discontinuation. His poetry not only offers an extensive documentation of the many different causes for poverty in the English countryside but also a unique representation of the individual. His "The Old Cumberland Beggar, a Description" (1800) for instance is accompanied by a preface which suggests that the eponymous beggar belongs to a class that is soon to become "extinct". Wordsworth thus focused on individuals who had been cast out of society on account of material circumstances and were also, for these reasons, likely never to be seen again in the future. His "Simon Lee" and "The Female Vagrant" make mention of the Enclosure Acts of the time that would leave many small farmers and labourers destitute. With no land left to farm and the commons all harnessed towards enhancing agricultural produce, several of England's rural poor would also migrate to London to look for employment. Industrialisation of several processes would result in further unemployment and several workers would even resort to the breaking of machinery. Wordsworth was thus writing at a time when multiple economic transformations were changing the nature of the individual's relationship to their environment and it is in this context that we ought to read his detailed portrayal of the poor.

He often describes his outcast protagonists as solitary figures as evidenced in this extract from "The Old Cumberland Beggar":

> He travels on, a solitary Man;
> His age has no companion. On the ground
> His eyes are turn'd, and, as he moves along,
> *They* move along the ground; and evermore,
> Instead of common and habitual sight
> Of fields with rural works, of hill and dale,
> And the blue sky, one little span of earth
> Is all his prospect. (lines 44–51)

What is interesting in this portrayal of the beggar is the record of what he is able to see – the old man is bent with age and hence cannot look up to survey the "habitual" rural scenery that surrounds him. But it is also tempting to interpret the line, "one little span of earth" that will be his prospect "evermore", as a prophetic vision of what the countryside would become for all who lived there in the wake of growing industrialisation. "Poor Susan" (1800) similarly makes a mention of country scenes "that fade" before Susan, a labourer who was forced to move to the city for work. "The mist and the river, the hill and the shade; / The stream will not flow, and the hill will not rise", says Wordsworth of Susan's vision of the countryside that provides her little comfort in London city (lines 14–15). The poor and displaced in Wordsworth's poetry become records or witnesses of the impact of industrial progress and are themselves on the brink of extinction. Addressing "Statesmen" directly in "The Old Cumberland Beggar", Wordsworth suggests that this figure is not to be seen as useless but rather, as a record of all the acts of charity that sustain him in his community. The community that has helped the beggar survive (since Wordsworth's childhood) also needs him since he is the only visible reminder that charity existed as a tradition. He also makes explicit appeal in the poem to avoid confining the beggar in a poor house – institutions that were set up by the state for the care of the elderly. These institutions for Wordsworth are incorrectly named "houses" since they do not offer the reciprocal communal ties of duty that bind the beggar to the community where he lives.

Wordsworth, like Wollstonecraft, also makes the case that the beggar is tied to all of us through a chain of evolution. It is his "humanness" that requires our attention even as his life circumstances make him a thing apart:

> 'Tis Nature's law
> That none, the meanest of created things,
> Of forms created the most vile and brute,
> The dullest or most noxious, should exist
> Divorced from good, a spirit and pulse of good,
> A life and soul, to every mode of being
> Inseparably link'd (lines 73–79)

Even as man-made laws seek to institutionalise the poor and disabled, Nature's law demands that we see the poor as not being devoid of "life and soul". While we can discern a spectator's gaze in Wordsworth's description and portrayal of the poor which renders them passive objects, there is also here a unique formulation of their connection to what makes us individuals. The Cumberland Beggar is set apart in the poem as a solitary figure who everybody "passes" by or allows "to pass" in his village but is at the same time representative of a stage of life we are all part of in nature. The story of Simon Lee and his wife, recorded in "Simon Lee", similarly ends with a reflection on how this relates to the reader. Wordsworth describes offering help to the poor labourer who can then only repay him with gratitude. This expression of thanks becomes yet again an indication that men are of a kind that more often repay kind deeds with gratitude rather than "coldness". Other writings of the time would also portray cruelty, vice and idleness as emanating from poverty, but these instances continue to be illustrative of the concern with the individual. How this individual could negotiate his place in a community that was riddled with inequality while also being restructured by various political and economic forces was a question that would continue to occupy Romantic writers through this period.

The Individual in the English Landscape

Wordsworth would inaugurate the Romantic tradition of seeing "life" in nature such that the individual and how his experiences were narrated in writing would have to necessarily engage with one's relationship with the environment. The preceding section makes clear that a separation existed in the mind of the Romantic writer between what the city and the countryside represented. The impoverishment of the individual in the context of industrialisation and forced migration to the city was attributed to the loss of an immersion in nature as much as to unemployment and financial ruin. An important context for this continued presence of the theme of nature in Romantic poetry is the Enclosure Acts. Enclosure is the conversion of common lands into privately-owned properties to maximise their agricultural potential. While this was a process that had been going on for a while in England, the eighteenth century witnessed enclosure at a very rapid rate to ensure food production for a growing population. The consequence of enclosure during the Romantic period manifested as growing homelessness and unemployment among smaller farmers who lost access to the "commons". These "commonly" owned resources were dictated by custom and ancestry and were responsible for providing sustenance (in terms of game meat, food for livestock and wood for building for instance) to everyone who lived in a particular village. Enclosure changed this ritual-bound relationship between an individual and their environment by converting land into a commodity. It is precisely in the context of this transition that occurs between nature as tied to the individual through heredity and nature as commodity that a Romantic relationship between the individual and his environment emerges. Just as nature becomes defined as a resource intended for expanding urban requirements, it is also celebrated in Romantic poetry as a tradition meant to be preserved.

In his famous "Lines Written A Few Miles Above Tintern Abbey" (1798), Wordsworth's view of a location he is describing is framed through the lens of "revisiting". Much of this poem is occupied with what Wordsworth's remembers from having visited the abbey near the river Wye five years before. It is also concerned with how much he will remember once he leaves and ends with the reflection that it is likely we all link places with various parts of ourselves. For Wordsworth, his sister Dorothy (who is also traveling with him at the time of the poem's composition) is likely to return from the Abbey with a "fresher" perspective than him since she is visiting it for the first time. Wordsworth himself links the abbey and its surroundings much more with his previous and (imagined) future trips here. What is interesting for us here in the context of the individual is that the description of the landscape surrounding Tintern Abbey offers the possibility for Wordsworth to chart personal growth. By linking his past memory of the place, his current experience there and his reflection on what it will mean to him in the future, Wordsworth uses the landscape to concretise his own existence across time. He says of the Abbey and its surroundings,

> Once again
> Do I behold these steep and lofty cliffs,
> That on a wild secluded scene impress
> Thoughts of more deep seclusion; and connect
> The landscape with the quiet of the sky. (lines 5–7)

While this scene is revisited at a different time, as demonstrated by "once again", certain aspects are unchanged. The "secluded scene" and its impression of a "more deep seclusion" are for Wordsworth the eternal qualities of this place whether in his memory or when borne out by experience. This sense of seclusion seems so important a link to the place that Wordsworth's account of visiting the Wye differs in some respects from that of other travellers. The editors of *British Literature 1780–1830*, Anne Mellor and Richard Matlak, mention in their annotations to Wordsworth's poem that William Gilpin in his *Observations on the River Wye* (1782) spoke of the manufacturing of charcoal on the river bank that produced smoke "frequently seen issuing from the sides of the hills, and spreading its thin veil over a part of them" (572, n. 3). Wordsworth, who no doubt also saw the manufacturing of charcoal on the spot, nevertheless integrates this detail in his poem rather differently. He describes the smoke on this scene as being

> Sent up, in silence, from among the trees!
> With some uncertain notice, as might seem
> Of vagrant dwellers in the houseless woods,
> Or of some Hermit's cave, where by his fire
> The Hermit sits alone. (lines 19–23)

To preserve the "seclusion" of the scene, Wordsworth attaches several meanings to the charcoal manufacture thus emptying it of any associations with manmade intrusion on the landscape. The smoke is "silent" with "uncertain notice" and is attributed to itinerant individuals like "hermits" and "vagrants" who have no claim on the land. While Wordsworth removes the existing inhabitants of the area surrounding the abbey, he simultaneously inserts himself there in "eternal" terms since he always carries the place in his memory.

Wordsworth's memory of the Wye does not only supply geographic specifics but also some learning about who he is as well. When he now thinks about "nature", it reminds him of something that is not curtailed to a specific time and place. Instead, his thoughts about Nature comprise:

> A presence that disturbs me with the joy
> Of elevated thoughts; a sense sublime
> Of something far more deeply interfused,
> Whose dwelling is the light of setting suns,
> And the round ocean and the living air,
> And the blue sky, and in the mind of man:
> A motion and a spirit, that impels
> All thinking things, all objects of all thought,
> And rolls through all things. (lines 95–103)

This sense of nature as being "alive" and capable of being regenerated in the "mind" of man was at the centre of Wordsworth's articulation of his poetic practice. As described in the chapter on gendering Romanticism, the poet in this period was understood as someone capable of creation even in the absence of external stimuli. When confronted with nature, Wordsworth seeks to establish a unity of presence between himself and how he sees his surroundings. He is the "thinking thing" that fuses with nature which forms a part of the "objects" of all thought, thus transcending the particular moment in which he is visiting and experiencing the landscape. The Romantic poet in this case uses the object of discussion to establish a version of themselves that can make claims to immortality. Nature is invested with qualities of an unchanging, eternal and primordial being that the poet lays claim to through the act of poetic creation.

Several other poets in the period would create a self in relation to a landscape or object they were discussing. It is also important to note at this juncture that there were several differences among the kinds of subjectivities (ways of understanding oneself as distinct) found in Romantic writers. While Wordsworth describes a location he revisits and thus links back to his earlier memories, other writers would recreate often-visited tourist sites to impose a version of themselves. Coleridge and Shelley for example would both compose poems about Mont Blanc, a destination frequented by European travellers as part of the Grand Tour of Europe. The Grand Tour, of which the Alps and Mont Blanc were an important part, formed a significant rite of passage in aristocratic education and was extensively described in many eighteenth-century travel accounts. Victor Frankenstein for instance famously retreats to the Alps to ruminate on the consequences of exceeding the limits of his education when he creates his monster. Undertaking travel (both within and outside England) was thus often linked in the period with a psychological transformation of some kind.

Another important context for the self in relation to landscape and nature were aesthetic theories of the picturesque, sublime and beautiful. These aesthetic theories would impact the way travellers framed their experiences and descriptions of what they saw. As detailed in the chapter on gender and Romanticism, Edmund Burke's *A Philosophical Enquiry into the Origins of our Ideas of the Sublime and Beautiful* (1757) was the most influential of the texts that discussed these aesthetic theories. For Burke, the beautiful and the sublime were a dualistic category that also related to the feminine and masculine respectively. Burke was interested in isolating the most fundamental of human sensory experience and, according to him, this is encapsulated by pleasure and pain. Both, he says, are experienced in the service of self-preservation and social relationships. The beautiful is associated with pleasure and social relationships while the sublime is associated with a feeling of terror and states of sickness and pain that are experienced in isolation. Burke would catalogue many objects, physical states and social relationships that evoke a sense of the beautiful and sublime that served as a context for Romantic writers. He is especially influential in terms of having introduced the idea that the aspect of the sublime is responsible for the most powerful of all sensations in the individual. This would fuel a great interest in the writing of the period in states like extreme solitude, madness, pain and a breakdown of reason and provide a vocabulary to discuss them. Immanuel Kant in *The Critique of Judgment* (1790) would continue to maintain this duality between the beautiful and sublime while at the same time addressing their impact on the mind and perception more directly. For him, the beautiful (specifically with regards to nature) offers a sense of boundedness or limitation whereas the sublime has to do with things that are expansive and without boundary while providing only a sense of their totality (qtd. in Trott 80). In other words, the beautiful is within the domain of understanding, but the sublime is something that challenges reason by presenting contradictory states to the mind (providing a sense of totality while also seeming without boundary).

Unlike philosophical origins of the categories of the beautiful and sublime, the picturesque arose within the tradition of painting. English travellers returning from the Grand Tour were inspired by European landscape painters like Claude Lorrain, Nicolas Poussin and Salvatore Rosa and there was a subsequent rise in the demand for landscape painting. English-style aesthetics in landscape painting were then developed by artists like John Constable and J. M. W. Turner to meet a growing demand for certain ways of seeing a landscape. These aesthetic frames would soon be applied to actual English landscapes in the form of "improving" land inside private properties. English landowners would begin cultivating their gardens according to the aesthetic principles of the picturesque to "correct" any natural deficiencies in these spaces. Thus, whether one was in the presence of nature in one's home or in the wilderness, or whether on travels within England or abroad, there was a very well-defined and highly contested set of terms within which to understand what one witnessed. These aesthetic categories are thus primarily about communication (accurately stating one's experience in nature), representation (what kind of formal rules or conventions apply in painting or poetry when describing nature) and our relationship with the world (how we interact with objects in nature and how they impact us). What is of interest to us here is also how these categories allow the creation and understanding of a particular kind of self.

The example of Mont Blanc will allow us to study some representative instances of how travel to specific landscapes evoked a sense of transformation for the self. Coleridge for instance says of Mont Blanc in "Chamouny; the Hour before Sunrise. A Hymn" (1802):

> Oh dread and silent form! I gazed upon thee,
> Till thou, still present to my bodily eye,
> Didst vanish from my thought: entranced in prayer
> I worshipped the Invisible alone. (lines 13–16)

The Burkean sublime is a clear influence here in the manner of describing the mountain. The poet perceives in this object contrary states of "dread" and "silence". His experience too moves from passively "gazing" at the object to becoming physically aware of something larger than what can be understood (the mountain is present to his "bodily eye" but has vanished from "thought") such that he is moved to "worship" it. Rejecting any sense of clarity and definition, Coleridge now uses the term "invisible" to refer to the mountain and significantly, worships it "alone". To Coleridge, Mont Blanc is a reminder of his own diminutive status in the presence of something that he affirms only God could have created. After listing the many astonishing aspects of the mountain and its surroundings, Coleridge no longer "gazes" but instead his head is "bowed low" and then lifted in "adoration" as he "beholds" the scene before him. This is very closely allied with the transformative effects of the sublime as listed by Burke: "Astonishment, as I have said, is the effect of the sublime in its highest degree; the inferior effects are admiration, reverence and respect" (43).

While Coleridge receives answers to the questions he poses about who was responsible for creating Mont Blanc (he imagines in his poem that the surroundings call out that their creator is "God"), Shelley's description of this place is much more ambiguous in "Mont Blanc: Lines Written in the Vale of Chamouni" (1817). In the travelogue accompanying the poem, Shelley uses adjectives like "awe-inspiring", "eternal" and "majestic" to describe Mont Blanc and its surroundings. He does not attribute the "unearthly" quality of the alpine landscape to God as Coleridge does, speaking instead of an "unknown omnipotence" and using various adjectives related to scale throughout the poem to indicate a sense of vastness. For instance, he describes the experience of trying to make sense of the entire expanse of the mountain and says,

> For the very spirit fails,
> Driven like a homeless cloud from steep to steep
> That vanishes among the viewless gales!
> Far, far above, piercing the infinite sky,
> Mont Blanc appears—still, snowy, and serene;" (lines 57–61)

These lines communicate a failure of mental comprehension when faced with the immense scale of the landscape. The use of the terms "driven", "homeless", "vanishing", "viewless" and "infinite" forces the reader to contend with the impossibility of finding a resting place from which to make sense of the scene. Mont Blanc paradoxically appears to be "still" and "serene" amidst the mind's tumultuous movement around it. The poem invokes several aspects of the Burkean sublime when describing different facets of this landscape like its potential for death and destruction and its seclusion and remoteness from human access. Rather than accept submission through the acknowledgement of human diminutiveness like Coleridge, Shelley utilises the feelings evoked by this landscape to describe the potential of human imagination. For him, the incomprehensible nature of the sublime can be harnessed to make sense of the power of the imagination and the poet's capacity for creation. Like with Wordsworth, the sublime also offers Shelley the opportunity to define poetic character and personal growth in a novel way. Consider for instance, the following lines from the poem which sum up Shelley's view of his relationship with Mont Blanc:

> when I gaze on thee
> I seem as in a trance sublime and strange
> To muse on my own separate fantasy,
> My own, my human mind, which passively
> Now renders and receives fast influencings,
> Holding an unremitting interchange
> With the clear universe of things around; (lines 34–39)

Like in the case of Wordsworth and Tintern Abbey, Shelley suggests that the poet is paradoxically central in a landscape that is otherwise sublime on account of its seclusion and inaccessibility to humans. The "human mind" in this landscape "renders and receives", thus implying that what the individual sees is not passively absorbed but inaugurates a continuous process of understanding and communication.

The Self and Romantic Authorship

In addition to aesthetic theories of the sublime, the idea of the poet as central to a landscape is also in line with poetic theories of the time. For instance, Coleridge would argue in his *Biographia Literaria* that the poet's imagination is the result of a conscious assertion of will "which dissolves, diffuses, dissipates, in order to recreate; or, where this process is rendered impossible, yet still at all events it struggles to idealize and to unify" (692). The Romantic poet's ambition thus exceeds the mere reporting, describing and categorising afforded by the aesthetic categories of the picturesque and beautiful. It seeks instead to grapple with "ideals" and the creation of "unity" even where this may be impossible. In his "Mont Blanc" Shelley writes,

> One legion of wild thoughts, whose wandering wings
> Now float above thy darkness, and now rest
> Where that or thou art no unbidden guest,
> In the still cave of the witch Poesy,
> Seeking among the shadows that pass by
> Ghosts of all things that are, some shade of thee,
> Some phantom, some faint image; till the breast
> From which they fled recalls them, thou art there! (lines 41–48)

These lines make the Romantic poetic ambition more explicit in charting a course for the "thoughts" originating in the poet's mind when faced with nature in its sublime form. Thoughts inspired by the mountain are "legion" but do eventually "rest" in the cave of "Poesy". Poetry is thus seen here as having the capacity to offer "rest" to an indeterminate set of thoughts.

However, it is interesting that when these thoughts do enter the cave of poetry, they continue to evade clarity. The poet's perception of the mountain concretised in an individual act of creation (poetry) does not provide a definitive shape to the object described. Even inside the "still cave of the witch Poesy", where, presumably, data received by the poet's senses from the environment can be made comprehensible, he is still "seeking among shadows" and "ghosts", "shade" and "faint" images. The poet-self in this period thus sought to make sense of his place in the world in the context of cognition and perception. The questions evoked by aesthetic theories like the sublime, the beautiful and the picturesque were primarily about how what we saw around us impacted our perception of who we are. Romantic poetic ambition sought to unseat the previous era's (often termed the Neoclassical period) reliance on reason and instead grappled with states of uncertainty, madness, isolation and incomprehension. Shelley would argue in *A Defence* that reason "may be considered as mind contemplating the relations borne by one thought to another, however produced; and the latter [imagination], as mind acting upon those thoughts so as to colour them with its own light, and composing from them, as from elements, other thoughts, each containing within itself the principle of its own integrity" (1184). While reason is acknowledged as a significant contributor to a certain mode of understanding, poetic "imagination" is also linked with the act of "creation". This creation is not linked through a relationship with other things but possesses an internal logic that is unique to it. Shelley's "Mont Blanc" similarly illustrates how Romantic poetry would not only grapple with an expansive exterior (in terms of terrifying and beautiful landscapes) but was also interested in its impact on the human mind. Perception was now seen to be two-way – the poet shaped his surroundings as much as they shaped him. This process, moreover, was not one that was rooted in certainty. The anxiety in Romantic poetry about the inability to adequately reproduce the scale, details and strong impressions left by nature is indicative of an acknowledgment that the individual's perceptions are only partial. Thus, even as the poetic self existed at the intersection of modes of perception and understanding, this self was also internally divided. In other words, while Romantic poetic ambition allowed for the creation of an individual who could surpass the limits of human understanding and seek to "unify" otherwise disparate or unknowable elements in the natural world, it would continue to acknowledge the limits placed on this individual.

Keats would define individual literary achievement in 1817 for instance as "*negative capability*; that is, when man is capable of being in uncertainties, mysteries, doubts, without any irritable reaching after fact and reason" (*Letter to George and Tom Keats* 1263). Keats would also differentiate himself from an earlier generation of Romantic writers in thinking about how the self is articulated in the creation of poetry. In a letter to Richard Woodhouse written in 1818, he would describe the poetic character as being chameleon-like. This letter is interesting for the way in which it sums up Keats' ambition as both belonging to his age as well as wanting to be set apart from it. He says first that he would like to be seen as different from "the Wordsworthian or egotistical sublime; which is a thing per se and stands alone" (*Letter to Richard Woodhouse* 1266). His own notion of the poet is that he "is the most unpoetical of any thing in existence; because he has no Identity—he is continually in for—and filling some other Body—the Sun, the Moon, the Sea and Men and Women who are creatures of impulse are poetical and have about them an unchangeable attribute" (1266–67). Keats here makes a very interesting separation between what the poet creates as the subject of poetry and his own experience and understanding of who he is. He argues that while objects and characters in nature can be "fixed" in the act of writing, the experience and understanding of one's own nature continues to be elusive.

He further destabilises the poet's capacity to "fix" an identity through writing when he says that in seeking to write about his own ambition, he may very well be "in character" and seeking to fit a pre-existing frame to articulate who he is. He describes a version of his ambition thus: "I feel assured I should write from the mere yearning and fondness I have for the Beautiful even if my night's labours should be burnt every morning and no eye ever shine upon them" (1267). But this "assurance" is immediately undercut by the very next line which states: "But even now I am perhaps not speaking from myself; but from some character in whose soul I now live" (1267). Thus, both writing about others and their nature (from observation and through social intercourse with them) and about oneself (based on a reflection of one's poetic ambition for instance) lead to the annihilation of the self. Keats' description of poetic ambition shows a self-awareness about the way a poet's identity and social role was discussed at this time.

As discussed in the chapter on the Romantic public sphere, poetic theories and discussions about the poet's place in society have to be seen in the light of pressures from the periodical market which threatened to destroy the autonomy of the individual writer. Writing at this time was increasingly seen as being directed towards the "other" – understood at various times as either the professional critic, the "faceless" reader or diverse market demands and the trends and styles dictated by these. In this context, Keats' acknowledgment of an instability in how the poetic self-manifests in writing demonstrates a keen awareness of the changes in understanding the individual in early nineteenth-century England.

As demonstrated in the chapter on gendering Romanticism, there are distinct and gendered modes of making sense of the authorial self in this period. In the masculine mode, poetic theories propounded by male Romantic poets would view the capability of creating verse as akin to the creation of life while simultaneously circumscribing this activity as a distinctly male sphere of achievement. The self that is created via these theories is one that seeks no reference to the outside world to generate verse. In this mode, the individual is not only isolated from external stimuli but is confident about the capacity to exert his own will over what he writes. As Anne Mellor (1993) has noted, these masculine and feminine modes arise in the act of writing and are expressed at varying points in male *and* female writers. She describes for instance, the "cross-dressing" carried out by a poet like Keats who expresses a "feminine" mode when he speaks about a self that is not "fixed" but always threatened and engulfed in the process of writing. This "feminine" mode of making sense of the self is also illustrated in Dorothy Wordsworth's journals; many of her entries in

The Grasmere Journals for instance are illustrative of a self that is always aware of her family and the community in which she lives. In contrast to William Wordsworth's portrayal of the poor he encounters as a scene to be "gazed" upon, Dorothy writes of her experience of *being with* those she meets.

In an entry from 3 September 1800, she records her experience of visiting a pauper's funeral in Grasmere. She begins by saying, "I ironed till half past three, now very hot. I then went to a funeral at John Dawson's—about ten men and four women" (604). Even though the description of the funeral takes up most of the entry, she does not place herself in the centre of this event. Setting out for the funeral is listed as one of the many activities in her everyday life including ironing and setting out for a walk that morning with her brother and Coleridge. Once at the funeral, her encounter is with everyone there – she describes the attendee's actions collectively using the pronoun "they" to indicate the rituals that are carried out. Her own reflection on her experience is described thus:

> I was affected to tears while we stood in the house, the coffin lying before me. There were no near kindred, no children. When we got out of the dark house, the sun was shining and the prospect looked so divinely beautiful as I never saw it. It seemed more sacred than I had ever seen it, and yet more allied to human life. The green fields, neighbours of the churchyard, were green as possible and, with the brightness of the sunshine, looked quite gay. I thought she was going to a quiet spot and I could not help weeping very much. (605)

The use of pronouns in this passage is very interesting for the contrast it offers with the descriptions of nature and those present around us examined earlier in this chapter. Even as she begins with "I", the same sentence reflects the presence of others around her in the use of "we" and the phrase "the coffin lying before me". Again, her view of nature is prefaced with "we" but registers a private reflection on the "prospect". What is significant here is that she sees the "sacred" landscape as being so only with the presence of human life. The landscape for Dorothy is not one where she exists alone but very much a *shared* space; the beauty of the fields neighbouring the churchyard are fitting not for her eyes alone but as a final resting place for the pauper about to be buried. The entry is circumscribed by yet another reference to her ironing duties and the time her brothers (William and John Wordsworth) returned home. Dorothy's account of her life as seen in her journal entries thus portrays a self that is grounded in the home (via her domestic responsibilities and relationship with her brothers and friends) and the community. This version of the Romantic self integrates aspects of daily life with descriptions of picturesque beauty without separating the two. Her construction of a self as seen in her journals no doubt ought to be understood in the context of women's material circumstances at the time. She sees her role primarily as the companion of her brother and takes her duties in the household seriously. Nevertheless, her portrayal of a domestic self that is integrated with rather than separate from her home and community offers an interesting variation in how Romantic authors saw themselves.

John Clare, also called the "Northamptonshire Peasant Poet", offers another interesting illustration of heterogeneity in the self as seen in Romantic writing. As Keats' and Byron's contemporary, Clare allows us to see a different kind of Romantic celebrity as well as a different perspective on nature. His *Poems Descriptive of Rural Life and Scenery* for instance made him a celebrity figure but this was premised on his being from an impoverished background. This is a very different kind of celebrity discourse when compared with the scandal and intrigue associated with the aristocratic Byron. Clare was classified as a "natural" genius or someone who crafted beautiful poetry *in spite* of being poor and not having received formal education. Clare's poems also differed from those of Keats' as evidenced by their treatment of the figure of the nightingale. While in Keats' famous ode the nightingale's global and ancient symbolic value is celebrated (he cites its relevance to cultures other than his own that precede his existence), Clare's nightingale is described in its domesticity and very much rooted in the present. In Keats' ode the nightingale is never seen and is only heard while Clare in his "The Nightingale's Nest" (1835) would spend time "creeping on hands and knees through matted thorn / To find her nest, and see her feed her young" (lines 13–14). There is a sense that encountering a nightingale is a very physical act and thus his poem focuses a great deal on how quietly and slowly he needed to move to avoid scaring the bird away as she tended to her young. On seeing the nightingale up close, Clare remarks that "her renown / Hath made me marvel that so famed a bird / Should have no better dress than russet brown" (lines 20–21). These lines appear to question the glamour surrounding the bird as a subject of classical poetry and simultaneously link it with "russet", the colour most often associated with peasants.

Finally, Clare can also be productively compared with the self as seen in Wordsworth to demonstrate the different modes of being "in" a landscape in Romantic poetry. In his "The Village Minstrel" (1821), Clare would use the rural landscape to chart a story of personal growth but in very different terms from Wordsworth. Clare was personally affected by the Enclosure Acts and saw the lands surrounding his childhood home transform drastically as he reached adulthood. The enclosures and their impact on the landscape, including the human and animal life that inhabited it, were a central theme in several of his poems. For him, childhood would come to be associated with the time prior to enclosures when the common land fostered a very different world order. In several poems he recreates the world of oral tales and folk culture (ballads, superstitions, fairs) that bound a rural community together and were eventually lost with the dividing of common lands into private enclosures. In "The Village Minstrel" he narrates the story of Lubin, himself a budding "peasant-poet", whose childhood is radically transformed by the enclosure. What Lubin witnesses of the transformation of his childhood home is described as follows:

> Ye fields, ye scenes so dear to eye,
> Ye meadow-blooms, ye pasture-flowers, farewell
> Ye banish'd trees, ye make me deeply sigh,—
> Inclosure came, and all your glories fell:
> E'en the old oak that crown'd yon rifled dell,
> Whose age had made it sacred to the view,
> Not long was left his children's fate to tell;
> Where ignorance and wealth their course pursue,
> Each tree must tumble down — old "Lea-close Oak," adieu!
> (lines 865–73)

Even as this transformed and transforming landscape is meant to indicate the change that occurs in Lubin, the reader is given a sense of how much Lubin is a part of the landscape around him. The particularity in referring to the oak tree as "Lea-close Oak" indicates that the boy is a dweller in the landscape he speaks of rather than a tourist. The oak's age and its "sacredness" to the view references a local history of the region's ecology whose course was now to be changed by "ignorance and wealth". While Wordsworth's Tintern Abbey mourns the possibility of not always being near the majestic sights of the Wye and necessitating a reliance on memory, Clare's "The Village Minstrel" mourns the loss of a communal and ancestral experience of always being *in* and *with* nature.

This chapter has examined different ways in which writing during the Romantic period in England created a sense of being an individual. For writers and readers, knowledge about differences among individuals, the notion of childhood and aesthetic theories about how a writer/poet's identity is formed would influence how they made sense of themselves. The material conditions in which individuals lived – whether they were men and women and what class or profession they occupied – would also influence how they understood who they were and their relationship with their environment.

Even a prominent Romantic theme like an individual's connection with nature would produce very different meanings for people depending on their material conditions. The Romantic self thus reveals itself as diverse and offers information about a range of contexts that influenced how an individual understood himself/herself and his/her place in the world at this time in England.

Works Cited

Blake, William. "Infant Joy." *British Literature 1780–1830*, edited by Anne K Mellor and Richard E Matlak, Harcourt Brace, 1996, pp. 281.

———. "Infant Sorrow." *British Literature 1780–1830*, edited by Anne K Mellor and Richard E Matlak, Harcourt Brace, 1996, pp. 303.

———. "The Divine Image." *British Literature 1780–1830*, edited by Anne K Mellor and Richard E Matlak, Harcourt Brace, 1996, pp. 280.

———. "The Human Abstract." *British Literature 1780–1830*, edited by Anne K Mellor and Richard E Matlak, Harcourt Brace, 1996, pp. 302–03.

Burke, Edmund. *A Philosophical Enquiry Into the Origin of Our Ideas of the Sublime and Beautiful.*R and J Dodsley, 1757, *Eighteenth Century Collections Online Text Creation Partnership*, 2011, http://name.umdl.umich.edu/004807802.0001.000. Accessed 23 December 2019.

Clare, John. "The Village Minstrel." *Spenser and the Tradition: English Poetry 1579–1830*, http://spenserians.cath.vt.edu/TextRecord.php?action=GET&textsid=36354. Accessed 9 September 2020.

———. "The Nightingale's Nest." *The Rural Muse*, Whittaker and Co, 1835, pp. 30–33, *Archive.org*, 2006, https://archive.org/details/ruralmusepoems00claruoft/page/30/mode/2up. Accessed 14 January 2023.

Coleridge, Samuel Taylor. "Chamouny; the Hour before Sunrise. A Hymn." *Romanticism: An Anthology*, edited by Duncan Wu, 3rd ed., Wiley-Blackwell, 2012, pp. 677–79.

———. Excerpt from *Biographia Literaria*. *Romanticism: An Anthology*, edited by Duncan Wu, 3rd ed., Wiley-Blackwell, 2012, pp. 691–94.

Hilton, Nelson. "William Blake, *Songs of Innocence and of Experience*." *A Companion to Romanticism*, edited by Duncan Wu, Blackwell, 1999, pp. 111–20.

Keats, John. Extract from *Letter to George and Tom Keats*. *British Literature 1780–1830*, edited by Anne K Mellor and Richard E Matlak, Harcourt Brace, 1996, pp. 1262–63.

———. Extracts from *Letter to Richard Woodhouse*. *British Literature 1780–1830*, edited by Anne K Mellor and Richard E Matlak, Harcourt Brace, 1996, pp. 1266–67.

Lloyd, Sarah. "Poverty." *An Oxford Companion to the Romantic Age: British Culture 1776–1832*, edited by Iain McCalman, Oxford UP, 1999, pp. 114–25.

Shelley, Percy Bysshe. "Mont Blanc: Lines written in the Vale of Chamouni." *Romanticism: An Anthology*, edited by Duncan Wu, 3rd ed., Wiley-Blackwell, 2012, pp. 1075–79.

———. "A Defence of Poetry." *Romanticism: An Anthology*, edited by Duncan Wu, 3rd ed., Wiley-Blackwell, 2012, pp. 1184–99.

Trott, Nicola. "The Picturesque, the Beautiful and the Sublime." *A Companion to Romanticism*, edited by Duncan Wu, Blackwell, 1999, pp. 79–98.

Walker, Julian. "William Blake and 18th Century Children's Literature." *British Library*, https://www.bl.uk/romantics-and-victorians/articles/william-blake-and-18th-century-childrens-literature. Accessed 3 September 2020.

Wollstonecraft, Mary. *A Vindication of the Rights of Men and A Vindication of the Rights of Woman*, edited by Janet Todd, Oxford, 1993.

Wordsworth, William. "Lines Written a Few Miles above Tintern Abbey on Revisiting the Banks of the Wye during a Tour, July 13, 1798." *British Literature 1780–1830*, edited by Anne K Mellor and Richard E Matlak, Harcourt Brace, 1996, pp. 571.

———. "Ode." *British Literature 1780–1830*, edited by Anne K Mellor and Richard E Matlak, Harcourt Brace, 1996, pp. 604.

———. "Poor Susan." *Lyrical Ballads with Other Poems*, *Vol 2*, 1800, *Project Gutenberg*, https://www.gutenberg.org/cache/epub/8912/pg8912-images.html. Accessed 30 August 2020.

———. "Simon Lee, the Old Huntsman, with an Incident in Which he Was Concerned." *British Literature 1780–1830*, edited by Anne K Mellor and Richard E Matlak, Harcourt Brace, 1996, pp. 564.

———. "The Old Cumberland Beggar, a Description." *Lyrical Ballads with Other Poems, Vol 2*, 1800, *Project Gutenberg*, https://www.gutenberg.org/cache/epub/8912/pg8912-images.html. Accessed 30 August 2020.

SIX

Science and English Romantic Literature

> Learn from me, if not by my precepts, at least by my example, how dangerous is the acquirement of knowledge and how much happier that man is who believes his native town to be the world, than he who aspires to become greater than his nature will allow.
>
> (Shelley, *Frankenstein,* 48)

> If the time should ever come when what is now called science, thus familiarized to men, shall be ready to put on, as it were, a form of flesh and blood, the poet will lend his divine spirit to aid the transfiguration, and will welcome the being thus produced, as a dear and genuine inmate of the household of man.
>
> (Wordsworth, *Preface to Lyrical Ballads*, 579)

The story of science in the Romantic period in England is one that can take us through the journey of this term's emergence as a field of study distinct from philosophy. Exploring this distinction is useful for us to understand how changes in knowledge systems impact our ways of making sense of the world and our place in it. Since our interest and entry point into this story is via the literary, a couple of caveats are in order. This chapter will aim to unravel how science – understood here as the emergence of a mode of studying the natural world – and those who worked in this field, serves as a context for literature produced in England in the Romantic age. The focus here will thus be on literary responses to science and the history of scientific developments at this time will be alluded to only as they pertain to illustrating an intellectual context to literary and artistic productions.[1] The literary can be situated with respect to science via some of the questions that occupied prominent Romantic figures. For example, it is characteristic of the late eighteenth and early nineteenth century in England that seeking answers from the natural world was not contingent upon belonging to certain professional and specialist spheres within religion or philosophy. Poets, artists, philosophers, mathematicians, chemists, physicists and biologists (though these were not yet "distinct" specialisations at this time as we will see) would all participate in asking questions about the natural world and would write both specialist and general treatises on how they arrived at answers. Physicians like Erasmus Darwin wrote poetry about botany, the chemist Joseph Priestley was outspoken in his support of the French Revolution and religious dissent, and taught grammar at school and lectured on scientific topics to the public. Coleridge's poetic theory of imagination is suffused with his understanding of chemistry and the newly emerging organic sciences of natural history of the time. There is evidence of a "commerce" of ideas that existed between a range of modern subjects like science and literature during this period and little of it remains in how we study Romantic-era writing in the present.

Further complications arise from the use of the term "science" as we understand it in the present. A discussion on science in the Romantic period is unusual because the term itself is not used in the sense we know it today until the 1830s when William Whewell coined the term "scientist". However, it is an important context for English Romanticism because the period between the late eighteenth and early nineteenth century witnessed a transformation in what was defined as science, consequently impacting writers' central concerns during this time. Ideas about nature (in terms of the natural world we inhabit as well as what makes up our essence as humans), religion (with specific reference to God and His relationship with the universe), revolution, the rights of man, and the social place (or value) of knowledge systems would all be impacted by and in turn influence the field referred to as "natural philosophy" or what we now call science. Eighteenth-century debates about what constituted science had to do with both *methods* of study as well as the object of enquiry. For instance, Richard Yeo notes that the term natural philosophy in eighteenth-century England encompassed a wide range of enquiry into "natural knowledge". Encyclopaedias of the time cross-referenced entries on physics, moral philosophy, philosophy, chemistry, botany, optics, mechanics and Newtonian philosophy to give readers a sense of what the term natural philosophy meant. By the end of this period however, encyclopaedias featured categories that are more recognisable to present-day readers: natural philosophy now meant "physical sciences" or "Newtonian" sciences like astronomy, chemistry, mechanics, electricity, optics and magnetism. This was distinguished from "organic" sciences like biology and zoology which were grouped under the broad label of "natural history". So, where earlier in the eighteenth century the term natural philosophy served as an umbrella category for a range of intellectual inquiry into nature, by the early nineteenth century this was no longer tenable.

Differences in methods (experimental and theoretical), objects of study in the natural world (everyday aspects like gravity and force and non-repeatable events like the creation of fossils) and their outcomes (description and classification of local flora and fauna in biology and the universalising of local phenomena in electricity) resulted in fissures within natural philosophy. The establishment of societies that served the interest of specific disciplines like zoology, biology, astronomy and geology in this period illustrates the need for more specialised intellectual affiliations compared to the one offered by The Royal Society which had served to speak for all sciences. Moreover, diverse political and religious affiliations among individual practitioners further divided the intellectual landscape of natural philosophy. This brief overview of the developments within disciplines that sought to quantify and understand the natural world allows us to examine the impact this had on individuals at this time.

Romantic Responses to Newtonian Science; Poetry and the Natural World

Newton's discoveries about motion and gravitation were among the most significant in understanding the nature of the world in the seventeenth and eighteenth centuries and they simultaneously heralded new *methods* of study within natural philosophy. Newton, or Newtonianism as this new branch of study would be called, placed a great emphasis on observable phenomena and an accounting of these through experimentation and mathematical theories. This empirical mode sought to distinguish itself from philosophical modes of study prevalent since earlier centuries where a set of hypotheses about the natural world could be assumed (and believed to be true) even in the absence of any observable evidence. In other words, one did not stop asking questions or attempting to develop a theory about aspects of our natural world if there were no means to design an experiment that could prove its occurrence. Following Newton's laws of motion and his embedding of these and his other discoveries in quantitative and experimental reasoning, the natural world (phenomena like Earth's movement around the sun and the way all matter functioned) was no longer a "second" cause – something that illustrates the existence of a prior entity like the Christian God. Instead, the natural world now became the primary locus of inquiry and was the only conceivable starting point for theories seeking to explain it. Moreover, any questions regarding the nature of phenomena which could not be discerned or proven through experiments were left unanswered within Newtonianism. Even as Newton admitted to the necessity of a Supreme Being or entity to intervene in the continued "decaying" of motion and the slipping of Earth from its axis, his experimental methods had stripped the divine from the natural world of physical matter. The natural world, in the context of eighteenth-century science, was viewed as "mechanically" ordered by a set of laws which humans could only infer but not directly impact. Romantic writers would react to this "emptying" of the natural world through an emphasis on empiricism and rationality by imbuing what they saw around them with a different set of meanings.

A prominent example of Romantic writers responding to these developments within the field of natural philosophy is Blake's engraving of Newton. Titled "Isaac Newton" (1795), the engraving portrays the mathematician as fully absorbed in the process of abstracting from natural phenomena using tools for precise quantification. Blake's Newton is naked and seated on a rock formation covered in colourful algae. He is bending forward and closely scrutinising a roll of parchment. His right hand measures a geometric diagram drawn on the parchment using a compass while his left signals (to himself really since no one else occupies the frame) to a point on the diagram. The engraving subtly contrasts the wide spectrum of colours and complex shapes of the algae on Newton's rock-seat with the white of the parchment Newton draws on and the black space that surrounds him. Newton is visualised as a muscular young man with blonde curls, reminiscent of idealised versions of masculine beauty in the portraiture of an earlier era. Blake's portrait is a response to Newton's heroic status within natural philosophy in the late eighteenth century, where an increasing reliance on empiricism and rationality would become the cornerstone of enquiry into natural phenomena. For Blake, Newton's gaze – fixed as it is on an abstraction of the universe rather than how it appears to individual perception – seeks to look away from things that provide wonder and awe like the skies above him or the rocks below him. Moreover, Newton's nakedness and his presence in an environment with no other human life represents his distance from the world he seeks to study. For Blake, even as Newton seeks to begin all theorising from the rigorous quantifying of natural phenomena that he can see, he removes himself from the natural world and thus attempts to see it as distinct. The scale of the portrait is such that Newton seems towering in comparison with the diagram he measures with his compass.

The idea of Newton and his mode of studying the natural world has thus superseded the object of study itself – understanding Newton's laws is now of greater significance than attempting to unravel what can be known in the natural world. The dark space behind him that is ignored while he scrutinises his scroll (which in turn serves as the only source of illumination in the image), symbolises his faith in precision and an inattentiveness to all things that are unquantifiable. It is important to note that a Newtonian ordering of the world and the consequent primacy accorded to the physical sciences was not without critics in the scientific domain. Rather than merely reacting to, or opposing, a Newtonian version of the natural world, Romantic writers were also frequently paralleling arguments made by other scientists. In 1714, Wilhelm Leibniz, the German philosopher and mathematician had proposed for example, that the universe comprised innumerable "monads" or microcosms of spiritual energy whose creation and dynamic interaction was governed by God. Matter, in Leibniz's view, was thus active rather than acted upon by external force. The chemists Joseph Priestley and Humphrey Davy would similarly insist on a continuity between spirit and matter and would attribute organisation of the "energies" in the universe to a Divine Being. The following lines from Coleridge's "The Eolean Harp" (1795) demonstrate a close affinity with those scientists who see the universe as composed of "active" matter:

And what if all of animated nature
Be but organic Harps diversely framed,
That tremble into thought, as o'er them sweeps
Plastic and vast, one intellectual breeze,
At once the Soul of each, and God of all? (lines 44–48)

Coleridge's poetry at this time, like that of Wordsworth's, as illustrated in their 1798 collection *The Lyrical Ballads*, seeks to order our understanding of the natural world as well. Focusing much more on the *individual experience* of the natural world, Coleridge seeks to use an idea akin to Leibniz's "monads" to explain all life in nature. "The Eolean Harp" casts nature in the role of teacher but learning has to do with individual temperament. Thus, are we all "diversely framed" but become aware of the presence of something outside us and which preceded us when we reflect on our surroundings. This call to "receive" the teachings of nature is articulated in Wordsworth's "The Tables Turned" where he says –

> Sweet is the lore which nature brings;
> Our meddling intellect
> Misshapes the beauteous forms of things;
> —We murder to dissect.
> Enough of science and of art;
> Close up these barren leaves;
> Come forth, and bring with you a heart
> That watches and receives (lines 25–32)

Wordsworth and Coleridge see nature as acting upon us and at the same time, develop ways of articulating how we perceive and ultimately shape nature as well. This form of continuity between forces and modes of combination and opposition among them as being governed by a larger force was thus present in *both* scientific and poetic discourse.

Poetry and Science in the "Household of Man"

Further evidence in poetry for the view that matter was, in fact, "active", can be found in the often-quoted lines from Wordsworth's "Tintern Abbey" where he identifies in nature "a presence that disturbs me with the joy / Of elevated thoughts; a sense sublime" and "a motion and a spirit; that impels / All thinking things, all objects of all thought, / And rolls through all things" (lines 101–03). The echoes of scientific belief contrary to Newton's mechanistic order are evident here. In addition, the idea of a Christian God is here replaced by a "motion" and "spirit" that exists in everything in our natural world. Divinity is thus seen to occur in everything around us and we each possess the capacity to feel and understand this presence.

Prominent aesthetic theories developed by Wordsworth and Coleridge would build further on this system of knowledge, thus merging (in their view) the pursuits of the philosopher and the poet. In his 1800 Preface to *Lyrical Ballads*, Wordsworth outlines what he believes is a poetic theory that seeks to intervene in the conventions thus far established in this form. His Preface is also concerned in many ways with what he sees as the role or social function of the poet. To this end, he outlines several tasks and responsibilities the poet has. The foundation and his primary demonstration of this poetic theory however, rests on proving that this capacity is shared by all individuals. It is with respect to demonstrating a universal quality shared by everyone that Wordsworth speaks of the common goals of Science and Poetry. He says,

> And thus the Poet, prompted by this feeling of pleasure which accompanies him through the whole course of his studies, converses with general nature with affections akin to those, which, through labour and length of time, the Man of Science has raised up in himself by conversing with those particular parts of nature which are the objects of his studies. The knowledge both of the Poet and the Man of Science is pleasure, but the knowledge of the one cleaves to us as a necessary part of our existence, our natural and inalienable inheritance; the other is a personal and individual acquisition, slow to come to us, and by no habitual and direct sympathy connecting us with our fellow-beings. (579)

Wordsworth's articulation of the poet's work here bears many similarities with the ways in which the work of natural philosophers was discussed at this time. First, he separates the categories of the generalist (the poet) and the specialist (the scientist is seen here to build more specialised knowledge). Second, he attempts to situate knowledge about the world in a social context. The "Man of Science" for Wordsworth is primarily individualistic – his understanding of the world relies on methods that require abstraction to the point where they do not inhere in our nature. In other words, training and learning in science takes one far away from the natural world, which, for Wordsworth, is something we all possess knowledge of.

Even as Wordsworth distinguishes between the social purposes of the poet and the man of science, he nevertheless proposes in his Preface a set of universal laws that govern the individual's relationship with nature. It is thus interesting to note how the language and focus of Wordsworth's poetic theory remains comparable with the pursuits of the physical (Newtonian) sciences – that universal patterns are observable across the natural world. Wordsworth states later in his Preface, seeking to find further common cause between poetry and science, that the objects of study in both fields are similar in certain contexts. He attempts to locate a different register of universality in science by unpacking the social contexts of the individual scientist, their observations and discoveries about the natural world. For him, discoveries in science will become the subject of poetry "if the time should ever come when these things shall be familiar to us, and the relations under which they are contemplated by the followers of these respective Sciences shall be manifestly and palpably material to us as enjoying and suffering beings" (579). Wordsworth thus views the scientific discoveries and inquiries of his time as not relating to a material realm as he understands it. What poetry offers to science then, is the opportunity to put on "a form of flesh and blood" as Wordsworth terms it, so as to gain entry in "the household of man". It is likely that he is drawing parallels here between his own vision of the poet speaking "in the language of men" and the necessity for discussions in natural philosophy to include even those not trained in elite institutions or specialist terminology. In his insistence on an inclusive approach to learning and propagating scientific knowledge, Wordsworth echoes the views of the chemist Joseph Priestley. Priestley is an interesting figure to consider in the light of Romantic responses to science in general and Wordsworth's ideas about the Man of Science in particular.

Joseph Priestley best known to us in the present for his isolation of oxygen and several other gases and for discovering photosynthesis. In the late eighteenth century in England however, Priestley presented a very different picture of the Man of Science from what would become the norm in the nineteenth century; his reputation as a revolutionary would almost overshadow his identity as a man of science. He was not only outspoken in his support of the French and American revolutions but was a well-known religious dissenter. He advocated for religious toleration, especially as it pertained to receiving a scientific education. His own education could not be completed at university in England on account of being a dissenter. In 1780, Priestley took up the role of minister at Birmingham and would become a victim of anti-revolutionary sentiments there once revolution broke out in France. His radical activities, which included the celebration of Bastille Day (commemorating the second anniversary of the fall of the Bastille prison) on 14 July 1791 sparked four-day riots in Birmingham in which Priestley's home, laboratory and library were destroyed. Priestley's reputation at this time was linked much more to his political views than his scientific achievements. Popular prints and caricatures like William Dent's *Revolution Anniversary or, Patriotic Incantations*, *A Birmingham Toast* by James Gillray, Bentley and Co.'s *Doctor Phlogiston, the Priestley Politician or the Political Priest*, all published in 1791, portray Priestley in the company of other well-known radicals and show his interest in inciting revolution. Isaac Cruikshank's *The Friends of the People* published in 1792, shows Priestley in conversation with Thomas Paine, thus visually associating him with the most well-known revolutionary of the time. They sit amidst various explosive chemicals like gunpowder, phosphorus, brimstone and electric fluid and appear to be joining forces intellectually as well—behind them are stacks of books that appear to be instruction manuals for organising revolution. In his sermons, Priestley would link the language of chemistry with that of revolution and this would result in the discipline itself taking on seditious overtones in popular media. Priestley, like Paine, would eventually emigrate to America to escape being targeted for his radical views.

While this short account of Priestley can tell us a great deal about reactionary or anti-revolutionary sentiment in Britain, it also gives us insights into the way a Man of Science was viewed in the public sphere. Priestley's radical views also extended to the organisation of scientific knowledge itself – he sought to democratise the process of scientific experimentation by critiquing the expensive infrastructure for experiments used by Lavoisier. Moreover, he argued for the autonomy of sciences like chemistry and electricity, which, for him, were taking natural philosophy in a new direction. Anna Letitia Barbauld's poem "An Inventory of the Furniture in Dr. Priestley's Study" (1773) offers an earlier instance of Wordsworth's vision of science as entering the household of man. For Barbauld, Priestley's practise of science is inextricable from his radical career and this is what makes him an apt subject for her poem. Speaking of Priestley's imminent immortalisation among the present and bygone kings of empires, she suggests that his arena of influence lies amidst the kind of knowledge he gathers and produces. The fact that Priestley's knowledge of the world draws from diverse disciplinary directions is illustrated by Barbauld's detailing in the poem of the presence of classical works of literature, volumes about jurisprudence and religious writings in his library. In her description of his laboratory, it is populated with paraphernalia associated with political organisations as much as with continuing scientific study. "A rare thermometer", she describes,

> by which
> He settles, to the nicest pitch,
> the just degrees of heat, to raise
> Sermons, or politics or plays. (lines 25–28)

The scientific instrument here serves as a means for measuring not only abstract natural phenomena but also the sociopolitical climate of his time. Barbauld suggests that Priestley as a scientist is also well attuned to applying his learning in domains of his life where "sermons, politics or plays" are the better modes of reaching his fellow countrymen. Like the thermometer and jars and phials filled with "lightning keen and genuine", there are several other "instruments" of political action that are included in Barbauld's inventory. She mentions "the shilling touch to pompous folio" and a "blotted proof-sheet, wet from Bowling" to visualise for the reader, the raw material of pamphleteering and giving sermons. Most significant for Barbauld in this inventory is the *potential* they bear to bring about change. She mixes images of experimental science and revolutionary writing and thus seeks to fuse them in their common cause – that of bringing about (a strategic) transformation. The half-formed and completed pamphlets in Priestley's study to her are like "new-made glass, set by to cool, / Before it bears the workman's tool" (lines 33–34). Priestley's "tools" in his study are like "controversial writing" which is "born with teeth, and sprung up fighting". Barbauld's picture of Priestley at work illustrates how the professions of scientist and writer can combine – both use their raw materials to create knowledge that is "born with teeth" or can bring about social transformation when professional practice engages in contemporary concerns.

Chemistry's approach to the natural world, as viewed by practitioners like Priestley and as integrated by Wordsworth and Coleridge in their ideas about nature and our relationship with it, sought to move away from the mechanistic conceptions of Newtonian science. In different ways, they attempted to restore a more dynamic and organic view of nature. While Wordsworth proposed a universal heritage shared by all men that the poet utilised to make his observations on nature, Coleridge attempted to capture how this process occurs in the individual mind. In his *Biographia Literaria* Coleridge attempts to isolate properties of the poetic "imagination" and proposes that it comprises "Primary" and "Secondary" components. Fusing man with the natural world through the notion of the Primary imagination, Coleridge defines it as being "the living Power and prime Agent of all human Perception, and as a repetition in the finite mind of the eternal act of creation in the infinite I AM" (750). Note the difference here from the Newtonian or mechanistic view in which organic life is subsumed under the physical laws of the universe without a capacity to influence or act on them. Additionally, the language of chemistry[2] is evident in his description of the functions of the "Secondary" imagination which he says "dissolves, diffuses, dissipates, in order to re-create" (750).

The publication of Coleridge's theory of imagination coincides with the break made by other fields like geology and biology from the broader category of natural philosophy. While the physical sciences within natural philosophy relied on the predictive capacity of mathematical models and logical reasoning to discern universal laws, the organic sciences of chemistry, geology and biology sought to explain diversity and non-repeating phenomena. This represents a movement in this period towards recording, describing and classifying various aspects of organic life in the broad field of natural history and away from a study of static fields of motion and force in natural philosophy. The fields of study under natural history allowed for an understanding of the world as it unfolded over a unit of time that was not easy to observe for a single individual. Deep time, as the duration in which phenomena like the formation of rocks or the occurrence of volcanoes and earthquakes could be understood, and its illustration of developmental and evolutionary processes that underlie living things in the present required different approaches and instruments of study. Living things could now no longer be understood as submitting to physical laws of force and motion alone. Shelley and Coleridge's poems celebrating Mont Blanc, discussed in the chapter on the self, can also be read as responding to the concept of deep time and an individual's relationship with ancient forms like mountain ranges. Even as Coleridge attributes the creation of Mont Blanc to a "divine presence" and Shelley's poem references a "presence" rather than something explicitly divine, there is a clear insistence on seeing the Alpine landscape as alive rather than as dead matter. Moreover, both poems focus on the interchange or fusing of the speaker's perception of Mont Blanc and the surrounding physical landscape, thus imagining the individual as someone who is responding to and creating the natural world rather than being an impartial observer.[3]

It ought to be clear by now that science as a context for the Romantic period can evoke any one or all of the following ideas: public perceptions about scientific developments, men of science, modes of organising/understanding scientific knowledge and its impact on the individual. Romantic responses to science thus need not always be interpreted as literary figures expressing disagreement with or identifying oneself differently from a Man of Science. Rather, there was continuing intellectual inquiry into questions that were *shared* by scientists and poets/artists alike as well as a commerce (or influencing) of ideas arising from contemporary sociopolitical events and literary and scientific writing. Thus, revolutionary events in France and America as well as divisions within existing forms of knowledge would cause men of science just as much as poets to question all forms of institutional tyranny, especially as it pertained to the state and religion.

Science and Imperial Nature

We can make a small departure here to consider something of importance to a history of science in the period since it pertains to ideas that are significant for literature. Historians of science have looked closely at certain Romantic-era texts that do not receive much attention within literary studies like Erasmus Darwin's *Botanic Garden* (1791) which contains the two poems "The Economy of Vegetation" and "The Loves of the Plants". This text, like those examined before and the context of its writing and readership, offers us plenty of information about the place of science (or some of its branches at the time) in society. Darwin's poems were literary outliers at the time in the sense that they did not find appreciation among contemporaries for their aesthetic merits and employed formal structures (heroic couplets in imitation of Alexander Pope) that had come to be viewed as outdated. *Botanic Garden* also featured copious footnotes that presented scientific research for the educated reader and used a very verbose and embellished style. Seen against the poetic theories of Wordsworth and Coleridge, with their insistence on avoiding embellishments and featuring content in poetry that appealed to the common masses, Darwin's aesthetic and thematic choices do not appear to be "of the time". Nevertheless, *Botanic Garden* was very popular in Britain and can perhaps demonstrate what can sustain our (and whatever did sustain eighteenth-century readers') interest in a scientist composing (bad) poetry. Alan Bewell suggests that the popularity of *Botanic Garden* may have had less to do with Darwin's style and more to do with his celebration of the confluence of science, commerce and empire. For instance, "The Economy of Vegetation" in *Botanic Garden* celebrated technological innovations of the eighteenth century that improved an individual's capacity to harness natural materials. Darwin would also emphasise the creation of something new to cater to the newest trends of his time even as he discussed botany. His attentiveness to how scientific knowledge and technological innovation could be harnessed to create and respond to specific consumers is what explains the popularity of *Botanic Garden*.

This also supplies us with an additional context for science in the Romantic age – that of industry and empire. *Botanic Garden* borrows the taxonomical system for organising plants developed by the Swedish botanist Carl Linnaeus. Linnaeus' system improved on earlier methods of classification by offering a more standard model and explaining the creation of hybrid species. While Linnaeus' system, in accordance with the principles of Enlightenment science, believed it revealed the workings of a divine order, *Botanic Garden* emphasises the importance of hybridisation and acclimatisation among plant forms in the Linnaean taxonomy. In other words, readership for Erasmus Darwin's poetry grew out of the commercial possibilities offered by botany as a discipline, now enriched with a more stable system of enumerating plant life and technological advancements for ensuring their survival in non-native climates and regions.[4]

Eighteenth-century Britain, Bewell notes, had developed a taste for cultivating gardens and this illustrates not only an ecological sensibility but also an imperial cosmopolitanism. Plants became commodities on a global scale at this time and English estates could be populated easily by species from all over the world. This thriving commerce in plants and Britain's imperial expansion necessitated the use of sciences like botany and zoology to learn about, catalogue and control resources that were globally distant. Britain's colonies contained plant and animal life in the form of languages and taxonomical systems that were unknown to Europeans. Classification systems, such as those provided by Linnaeus, allowed for a reliable method of translating knowledge about nature across the globe and technological improvements (like being able to employ alternative sources of heat, light and food for plants) made flora and fauna physically mobile. Travel to and from these colonies all over the world resulted in the redistribution of "life" in various forms, thus blurring the boundaries of what could be considered native in a particular region. Plant life and nature in general, as viewed in *Botanic Garden*, demonstrates this nexus of commerce, botany and empire. It celebrated exoticism in plants and the scientific innovations that allowed species from distant lands to thrive in English gardens. This kind of imperial and economic botany, as seen in Darwin, viewed an individual's relationship with nature very differently from other writers of the time. The idea of a botanical garden, like the Royal Garden established in England in 1759 and subsequent nineteenth-century models for such gardens in English colonies, was emblematic of Empire in illustrating that species from across the globe could cohabit in the climactic conditions of a specific region. In this view, nature could be improved, adapted and acclimatised by the individual's scientific accomplishments and the hybridisation and global interchange of exotic plant varieties is what represents the modern botany of the eighteenth century. The massive imports in foreign plants would impact Britain's ecology in the long term with many invasive species threating those that were native. The commodification of foreign (especially tropical) plants would extend to their visual representations in other popular consumer goods like book covers (frontispieces), ceramic pottery and women's hats.

Dorothy and William Wordsworth's detailed recording of the plant species native to the Lake District ought to be seen against this context of imperial or commercial botany. They celebrate an Englishness they see emerging in the plant varieties of their rural home made possible by the publications of English botanical catalogues that sought to divide "native" and "non-native" species. Their cataloguing of the Lake District's botanical minutiae represents a "nativist" philosophy where plant life is concerned. The Wordsworths' nature poetry thus sought to preserve the link between local communities and their flora and fauna, under threat from the growing demand for a global exchange of plant life. John Clare's celebration and detailing of natural life in his rural neighbourhood and community represents yet another break from the global and commercial interest in botany. Clare imbues the plant species he encounters with personality traits, much like Darwin, but he also links them with the memories and life of the marginalised. His poems about nature touch upon enclosure and deforestation to illustrate the threat to native ecology while also detailing his memories of the rural landscape prior to these events. Developments in botany at the time would thus impact writers in diverse ways and lead to the development of multiple visions of nature itself.

Science and Understanding the Human

As seen in earlier chapters, an understanding of the basis of human nature was also at the centre of Romantic thought. Various branches of existing and emerging knowledge in the eighteenth century would engage with questions about the study of humans. Within medicine, the treatment of and approach to mental health brought about new ways of understanding the relationship between body and mind. Institutions like the York Retreat were established to demonstrate the importance of a "humane" approach in the treatment of the insane. George III's very public diagnosis of failing mental health provided further impetus for the change in perceptions about mental health. Several literary works in the period would focus on the individual psyche – interpreted variously as the workings of the inner mind, our control over emotions and memory, conscious and unconscious states, our behaviour in solitude and the moral code governing our actions. Coleridge and De Quincey's detailed accounting of their dreams and Wordsworth's relaying, through poetry, of sense impressions from memory and the interest in aesthetic categories of the sublime are some examples of literary explorations of various mental states. Neurological theories developed in the late eighteenth century offered a way of grounding illness and disorder in the nervous system. The psychological and physiological were thereby linked, somewhat unsettling the earlier belief in a clear separation of body and mind. The body was no longer viewed as merely belonging to a mechanistic system but was equally rooted in individual experience and perception. For Roy Porter, the Romantic writer was able to demonstrate the "holistic nature of human experience" while also merging the "physical, mental, and the imaginative" (177).

In this context, the novelist Frances Burney's letter (1811) to her sister Esther about undergoing a mastectomy is an illustrative record of how Romantic writers approached the diagnosis, treatment and experience of illness. Burney's letter not only seeks to give her sister an account of being diagnosed with and treated for breast cancer but also offers a "holistic" view of this experience. To begin with, the letter offers the perspectives of several individuals affected immediately by her diagnosis and the decision that she will undergo an operation – she describes her husband's anxiety, her surgeon and attending physicians' fear of failure and their horror at her pain as well as the panic experienced by her nurses. She also describes the anxiety she experiences from being unable to predict the moment of her operation thus: "After sentence thus passed, I was in hourly expectation of a summons to execution, judge, then, my surprise to suffered to go on full 3 Weeks in the same state!" (Burney 115). Eventually, Burney's husband would write to her surgeon requesting a written summons for when her operation could take place. Contrasting her own state before the operation with that of her husband she says that "*consent* was my utmost effort" (115).

Burney's letter very clearly demarcates "states of being" outside that of being diagnosed as a cancer patient – waiting on a date and time for a surgery with no guarantee of a positive outcome likens her to a criminal awaiting execution. She also questions the idea of consent by describing how little control she had over the course of events following her diagnosis. She is eventually given very little warning before the start of the operation and has no means of preparing for it. She has no idea, for instance, what she will be expected to wear and whether she would be permitted female attendants. It is also clear from the letter that Burney is unaware that her entire breast is to be removed. Since this takes place before the invention of anaesthesia, Burney's account is also a significant record of surgical experiences where patients were conscious during operations. For Burney, being conscious still translates to being rendered passive and devoid of any control. She recounts for instance that "7 men in black" comprised the medical retinue that was to carry out her mastectomy and they entered her room without first speaking to her and "without previous message" (116). This crowd of men would further require her to lie down on a bedstead, rather than on an armchair as she was previously informed, and she is made to undress while her female attendants (maids and nurses) are asked to leave when they begin to cry and demonstrate panic. Engaging in a dispute with her doctors over whether the maids and nurses could stay is the only thing that Burney says reanimates her during a procedure in which she struggles to resist the increasingly "militaristic" commands issued to her. Burney would ultimately resign herself to her surgeons' plans when it becomes clear that she is to be conscious during a procedure which is not properly explained to her and over which she has no say. "Hopeless, then", she says, "desperate and self-given up, I closed once more my Eyes, relinquishing all watching, all resistance, all interference, & sadly resolute to be wholly resigned" (116).

Burney's account is not only a fascinating record of the individual experience of medical diagnosis and treatment in this period but also offers insights into the woman's encounter with a male-dominated and masculine practice. Burney also reflects on the writing of an account of illness and surgery by drawing attention to its materiality in the context of how little information she receives from her doctors. "This miserable account", she says, "which I began 3 Months ago, at least, I dare not revise, nor read, the recollection is still so painful" (117). Burney's account is the only one which preserves knowledge about her mastectomy with attention to her own perspective and the context in which she received her diagnosis and experienced the surgical procedure. This "holistic" view, preserved in her account, is as real for her as the experience itself and therefore difficult to read or revise. Burney's account does not offer any insight into the rational processes through which her doctors may have arrived at a diagnosis or plan for cure and instead situates illness almost entirely within the domain of individual experience. Furthermore, what she captures of her attending surgeons focuses on their struggle to maintain control, their fears (she describes their ashen, bloodstained faces) and anxieties over failure and moments of compassion towards her rather than their grasp over knowledge of medical procedure.

Frankenstein: A Convergence of Contexts

Mary Shelley's *Frankenstein*, first published in 1818, is arguably one of the best-known works from the period and the one most associated with scientific discoveries of the time. In Shelley's novel we can discern a variety of themes we have been discussing so far as intersecting with science or natural philosophy in the Romantic period. In narrating the story of a scientist's education and his discovery of the "principle of life" such that he can reanimate dead human matter, Shelley responds to the ethical considerations behind pursuing scientific knowledge. Victor Frankenstein is warned at university for instance that a true scientist is one who acquires knowledge over several branches of science rather than specialising in one. Since his account of creating life is narrated in retrospect, he can preface many of his discoveries with words of caution to the listener. Consider for example his observations on how he arrived theoretically at the possibility of generating life: "Learn from me, if not by my precepts, at least by my example, how dangerous is the acquirement of knowledge and how much happier that man is who believes his native town to be the world, than he who aspires to become greater than his nature will allow" (48). Scientific knowledge is here viewed as something that seeks to supersede one's own nature and Shelley warns that this can have serious consequences for the inquirer as well as his subject. Offering a contemporary example of the consequences of aspiring to become greater than one's nature, Shelley compares Frankenstein's pursuits in uncovering the secret of life to the expansion of empire. Frankenstein remembers that his studies and experiments towards creating life took a great toll on his health – both mental and physical. He says that if you apply yourself to a study that,

> has a tendency to weaken your affections, and to destroy taste for those simple pleasures in which no alloy can possibly mix, then that study is certainly unlawful, that is to say, not befitting the human mind. If this rule were always observed; if no man allowed any pursuit whatsoever to interfere with the tranquillity of his domestic affections, Greece had not been enslaved; Caesar would have spared his country; America would have been discovered more gradually; and the empires of Mexico and Peru had not been destroyed. (51)

There are echoes of Wordsworth here in Frankenstein's claim that the scientist's study of abstract principles takes him away from the "household" of man. Moreover, Shelley also alludes here to the related contexts of science and empire where the aspirations of an individual eventually impoverish him and the community he seeks to control through study.

Anne Mellor has identified this imperial subtext in Shelley's novel as intersecting with the emerging science of ethnology within natural history at the time. Frankenstein and other characters' descriptions of the monster's physical characteristics in the novel, Mellor argues, situates him clearly as belonging to a non-Caucasian race. For Mellor, the ethnological theories of

Johann Friedrich Blumenbach that sought to classify humans into five races (Caucasian, Mongolian, Ethiopian, American and Malay), influence the descriptions of Shelley's monster. Ethnological theories and comparative anatomy, both of which built on Blumenbach's work also intended to historically hierarchise these races and attribute specific qualities to them. These scientific disciplines, arising in the context of empire and the encounter with other races were interested in detailing how life arose and was sustained in regions outside Europe. Descriptions of the creature's "yellow skin", "lustrous" and "flowing" black hair, "black lips" and giant frame in the novel evoke the very categories of analysis employed in ethnology and comparative anatomy. Differences in appearance from the white were attached to specific moral qualities and local environmental conditions (climate, natural disasters and forms of political organisation) in order to produce knowledge about the variety of human life.

These modes of knowledge were also instrumental in establishing the innate inferiority of non-white races thus justifying colonial invasion and domination by Europeans. For Mellor however, Shelley subscribes in *Frankenstein* to the view that the racially different ought to be embraced rather than enslaved. Shelley, in narrating a story about a monster visibly marked as Asian but on a quest for a family in Europe, sides with several other Romantic writers who imagined stories of interracial love set in the context of empire. Thus, while writers like Blumenbach and later William Lawrence, would insist on a hierarchy of racial characteristics, others like Shelley would offer a solution to racial divide (and consequent hatred and subordination of some by others) by proposing sexual union between races. Victor Frankenstein's creature in the novel is thus portrayed as a victim of racial war, at a time when "monogenist"[5] theories still held currency, rather than as an illustration of a specific race being prone to violence or displaying physically grotesque features.[6]

Additional scientific influences for *Frankenstein* can be inferred from Shelley's mention of Erasmus Darwin's experiments with activating dead matter and galvanism, in her 1831 preface to the novel. In early-nineteenth-century Britain, galvanism could refer to the public demonstration of the effects of electricity on the body. More specifically, galvanism could also be a reference to the work of Luigi Galvani and Giovanni Aldini, both of whom were able to show movements in the muscles of human and animal corpses through the application of electricity. Aldini would conduct a public demonstration of the application of electricity to the corpse of a recently hanged convict to illustrate the resulting movements of muscles and limbs. Aldini's demonstration is one of several public shows of the uses of electricity itself. As an emerging science, electricity generated a great deal of public interest through demonstrations of its uses in treating illnesses, reviving the unconscious, performing experiments and even its capacity to entertain guests at parties. Even though Shelley's *Frankenstein* does not describe the exact process through which life emerges, several twentieth-century film adaptations and book covers for newer editions of the novel notably employ electricity as a key component in animating the monster.

Sharon Ruston argues that Galvani and Aldini's experiments with electricity were only one part of a larger concern at the time about modes of distinguishing between the state of being alive and dead. In addition to electricity, societies established for the resuscitation of those who sought to take their own life, medical debates about how to precisely identify death (as distinguished from states like losing consciousness, coma or sleep) and what really separated living organic forms from those that were dead, were all interested in establishing the boundaries of "life". The character of Frankenstein in the novel thus shared his goals with many real-life scientific counterparts. In describing his pursuits towards discovering how life could be created, Frankenstein confesses to studying the process through which the body decays – something that medical practitioners relied on to pronounce the "certainty" of death. When he makes rapid progress towards discovering how life is generated, he recalls that to him, "life and death" seemed like "ideal bounds, which I should first break through, and pour a torrent of light into our dark world" (49). *Frankenstein* thus demonstrates the general public's interest in a discovery that would have, in an earlier age, been firmly relegated to the realm of religion. Moreover, Shelley situates Frankenstein's work of creating life as taking place outside the university and in his home. Scientific experimentation, especially following public demonstrations of the uses of electricity for instance, was no longer confined to formal institutions alone. A more scientifically informed aristocracy could at this time, with some expense towards infrastructure, easily dabble in various branches of scientific enquiry.

As Jan Golinski notes, scientific experimentation in the early nineteenth century in England was also influenced by eighteenth-century Enlightenment values. These values were embodied, for instance, in Joseph Priestley's insistence on a wide dissemination of scientific knowledge with the express purpose of dismantling the institutional hold on methods and modes of communication. Excluded from English universities as a dissenter, Priestley would find moral and financial refuge in provincial associations like the Lunar Society that sought to find practical utility in and spread awareness about scientific knowledge. Lectures and demonstrations about the manipulation of natural phenomena in chemistry would also serve as the basis for establishing credibility in professions like medicine. Shelley and her narrator Frankenstein's anxiety over the undertaking of dangerous research questions in science is thus not only directed towards institutional studies and practice. The context of public medical debate regarding the bounds of life and death demonstrates that both the lay public *and* men of science were in the dark about the generation of life. Moreover, the public culture of science in the nineteenth century was associated with not only the democratic values of Enlightenment but the fear of revolutionary intent as well. For instance, the at-home experiments in nitrous oxide conducted by Humphrey Davy[7] and Thomas Beddoes would attract criticism by political conservatives and the royalist media. Beddoes' public support of the French Revolution, like in the case of Priestley, resulted in the association of chemistry and para-institutional spaces of scientific experimentation with revolution.

Thus, science in the Romantic period, as this chapter has demonstrated, did not exist in the form that we recognise today. Moreover, science and literature, represented by modes of thinking and their practitioners, shared common concerns and questions about the natural world. The lack of separation within scientific disciplines, as grouped under the domains of natural philosophy and natural history, and their preoccupation with questions about the individual and their relationship with the world enabled an interchange of ideas with, and provoked responses in, literary writing. Romantic writers, this chapter has shown, were not just critical or sceptical about scientific practice and discovery. Rather, they often shared in the scientist's or the natural philosopher's enthusiasm in a quest to uncover universal and specific patterns underlying the natural world.

Works Cited

Barbauld, Anna Letitia. "An Inventory of the Furniture in Dr. Priestley's Study." *The Poems of Anna Letitia Barbauld, British Literature 1780–1830*, edited by Anne K Mellor and Richard E Matlak, Harcourt Brace, 1996, pp. 166–67.

Bentley and Company. *Doctor Phlogiston, the Priestley Politician or the Political Priest. BritishMuseum.org*. https://www.britishmuseum.org/collection/object/P_1873-0712-1150. Accessed on 21 September 2020.

Bewell, Alan. *Natures in Translation: Romanticism and Colonial Natural History*. Johns Hopkins UP, 2017.

Brown, Robert. "Psychology." *An Oxford Companion to the Romantic Age: British Culture* 1776–1832, edited by Iain McCalman, Oxford UP, 1999, pp. 361–69.

Burney, Frances. "A Mastectomy: Letter from Frances Burney to Esther Burney, September 30, 1811." *British Literature 1780–1830*, edited by Anne K Mellor and Richard E Matlak, Harcourt Brace, 1996, pp. 114–18.

Coleridge, Samuel Taylor. Excerpt from *Biographia Literaria*. *British Literature 1780–1830*, edited by Anne K Mellor and Richard E Matlak, Harcourt Brace, 1996, pp. 750.

———. "The Eolian Harp". *British Literature 1780–1830*, edited by Anne K Mellor and Richard E Matlak, Harcourt Brace, 1996, pp. 760.

Cruikshank, Isaac. *The Friends of the People*. *BritishMuseum.org*. https://www.britishmuseum.org/collection/object/P_1868-0808-6237. Accessed on 21 September 2020.

Darwin, Erasmus, 1731-1802. *The Botanic Garden.: A Poem, In Two Parts. Part I. Containing The Economy of Vegetation. Part II. The Loves of the Plants: With Philosophical Notes.* 1st American ed., T. and J. Swords, 1798, *Hathi Trust Digital Library*, https://hdl.handle.net/2027/uc2.ark:/13960/t3vt1hg6d. Accessed 22 September 2020.

Dent, William. *Revolution Anniversary or, Patriotic Incantations*. *BritishMuseum.org*. https://www.britishmuseum.org/collection/object/P_1868-0808-6083. Accessed on 21 September 2020.

Eaves, Morris, Essick, Robert N. and Joseph Viscomi, editors. *Newton (Composed 1795)*. *The William Blake Archive*. 1996–2019, http://www.blakearchive.org/.

Fulford, Tim, Peter J. Kitson, Debbie Lee and Deborah Lee, eds. *Literature, Science and Exploration in the Romantic Era*. Cambridge UP, 2004.

Gilray, James. *A Birmingham Toast*. *BritishMuseum.org*. https://www.britishmuseum.org/collection/object/P_1851-0901-538. Accessed on 21 September 2020.

Golinski, Jan. *Science as Public Culture: Chemistry and Enlightenment in Britain, 1760–1820*. Cambridge UP, 1999.

Hadzigeorgiou, Yannis, and Roland Schulz. "Romanticism and Romantic Science: Their Contribution to Science Education." *Science & Education*, vol. 23, no.10: 2014, 1963–2006.

Heringman, Noah. *Romantic Rocks, Aesthetic Geology*. Ithaca, Cornell UP, 2004.

———. "Science and Human Animality in Mary Shelley's *Frankenstein*". *The Wordsworth Circle,* vol. 50, no. 1, 2019, pp. 127–45.

Knight, David. *Humphry Davy: Science and Power*. Cambridge UP, 1998.

Mellor, Anne K. "*Frankenstein*, Racial Science, and the 'Yellow Peril'". *Romantic Science: The Literary Forms of Natural History*, edited by Noah Heringman, State U of New York P, 2003, pp. 173–96.

Porter, Roy. "Medicine." *An Oxford Companion to the Romantic Age: British Culture* 1776–1832, edited by Iain McCalman, Oxford UP, 1999, pp. 170–77.

Ruston, Sharon. "The science of life and death in Mary Shelley's *Frankenstein.*" *British Library*, https://www.bl.uk/romantics-and-victorians/articles/the-science-of-life-and-death-in-mary-shelleys-frankenstein. Accessed 20 September 2020.

Shelley, Mary and James Rieger. *Frankenstein*, *or*, *The Modern Prometheus*. 1818. U of Chicago P, 1982.

Uglow, Jenny. *The Lunar Men*: *The Inventors of the Modern World 1730–1810*. Faber and Faber, 2011.

Wordsworth, William. "Extract from *Lyrical Ballads 1802*." *British Literature 1780–1830*, edited by Anne K Mellor and Richard E Matlak, Harcourt Brace, 1996, pp. 573–81.

———. "London, 1802." *British Literature 1780–1830*, edited by Anne K Mellor and Richard E Matlak, Harcourt Brace, 1996, pp. 599.

———. "Lines Written a Few Miles above Tintern Abbey On Revisiting the Banks of the Wye during a Tour, July 13, 1798." *British Literature 1780–1830*, edited by Anne K Mellor and Richard E Matlak, Harcourt Brace, 1996, pp. 571.

———. "The Tables Turned; An Evening Scene, on the same subject." *British Literature 1780–1830*, edited by Anne K Mellor and Richard E Matlak, Harcourt Brace, 1996, pp. 571.

Yeo, Richard. "Natural Philosophy (Science)." *An Oxford Companion to the Romantic Age*: *British Culture* 1776–1832, edited by Iain McCalman, Oxford UP, 1999, pp. 320–28.

Notes

1. For the importance of what is referred to as "Romantic Science" (knowledge and practice of science unique to this period) to the history of science as well as present-day science education, see Yannis Hadzigeorgiou and Roland Schulz's "Romanticism and Romantic Science: Their Contribution to Science Education".
2. Jan Golinski notes that Coleridge participated in the experiments on the uses of nitrous oxide carried out by Humphrey Davy and Thomas Beddoes. The gas was discovered by Priestley and was later used by Davy and Beddoes in medical and recreational contexts. One of the principal themes in their writings about the effects of inhaling nitrous oxide (titled "laughing gas" by Davy) was its psychotropic properties and the difficulties in objectively recording the euphoric state it induced in patients and users. In poems like "Kubla Khan", Coleridge would carry out his own experiments in the possibility of narrating objectively when inhabiting similarly compromised states of consciousness: dreams, intoxication.
3. See Noah Heringman's *Romantic Rocks, Aesthetic Geology* for a discussion on the "symbolic" economy that existed between aesthetic discussions of landscape and geology in the eighteenth century that explains the recurrence of rocks and mountain ranges as central objects in Romantic poetry. He suggests, for instance, that aesthetic discussions of the physical encounter with landscape and the geological view of the earth's lifetime as being distinct from and capable of exerting an influence on humans are illustrative of a shared understanding (across scientific and literary realms) of the natural world.
4. See Jenny Uglow's *The Lunar Men: The Friends Who Made the Future* for a fascinating overview of The Lunar Society. Headed by Erasmus Darwin, the society comprised other scientist-entrepreneurs like James Watt, Matthew Boulton, Joseph Priestley and Josiah Wedgwood. This group is notable for their interest in merging science, commerce and industry at the start of the industrial revolution in Britain.
5. As opposed to a polygenist view, the belief that all humans belonged to a single race and develop differences from one another owing to the environmental conditions in which they have lived.

6. See also Noah Heringman's "Science and Human Animality in Mary Shelley's *Frankenstein*" for a discussion of how Shelley's creature questioned anthropocentric modes of making sense of the human species within natural history. Heringman suggests that Shelley's creature, in facing the threat of extinction and displaying qualities of "animality" and humanness, questioned the firm boundaries set by philosophers and naturalists of the time between humans and animals.
7. See David Knight's 1998 biography of Davy (*Humphrey Davy: Science and Power*) for a useful account of how the first professional scientist in Britain emerged. Like the literary figure of the author, the scientist (in terms of making a living from practising science) is a relatively new phenomenon during this time. Davy is also known to have produced plenty of poetry and although none of this was published in his lifetime, it is further evidence for the shared sensibilities of literary and scientific professions in the Romantic period.

Timeline

Political/Social events	Year	Literary/Cultural events
Battle of Plassey fought in India between the army of the British East India Company and the Nawab of Bengal. The Company troops win and pave the way for an economic and military takeover of the subcontinent by Britain.	1757	Birth of William Blake; Edmund Burke publishes *A Philosophical Enquiry Into the Origin of Our Ideas of the Sublime and Beautiful*
	1759	Birth of Mary Wollstonecraft; Birth of Helen Maria Williams; Birth of Robert Burns
Boston Massacre	1770	Birth of William Wordsworth
	1771	Birth of Dorothy Wordsworth
Mansfield Judgment passed declaring slavery unlawful in England	1772	Birth of Samuel Taylor Coleridge
	1774	Birth of Robert Southey; Goethe publishes *The Sorrows of Young Werther*
	1775	Birth of Jane Austen
American Declaration of Independence	1776	
	1782	Publication of *Letters of the Late Ignatius Sancho, An African*. Sancho was reportedly born aboard a slave ship and was emancipated following

Political/Social events	Year	Literary/Cultural events
		his employment in London with the Montagu family. Sancho's literary fame was connected to his correspondence with several notable figures of the time including Laurence Sterne and the African American poet Phillis Wheatley. Sancho's condemnation of slavery in his letters was widely circulated.
Asiatic Society set up in Calcutta by William Jones with a view to promote the study of Oriental systems of knowledge	1784	
	1785	Publication of Yearsley's *Poems, on Several Occasions*; Publication of Clara Reeve's *The Progress of Romance*; Publication of Cowper's *The Task*; Birth of De Quincey
	1786	Publication of William Beckford's *Vathek*; Thomas Clarkson publishes the English translation of his prize-winning Latin essay on the abolition of the slave trade, *An essay on the slavery and commerce of the human species, particularly the African, translated from a Latin Dissertation*

Political/Social events	Year	Literary/Cultural events
Impeachment of Warren Hastings on charges of corruption and misconduct as governer-general of Bengal; Robert Barker patents the panorama—a novel style of viewing paintings of landscapes and current events that would become a popular mode of visual entertainment; Formation of the Committee for the Abolition of Slave Trade. Founder-members were largely Quakers, along with a few Anglicans including Thomas Clarkson. The MP William Wilberforce's membership in the group would result in the representation of their interests in the House of Commons.	1787	Ottobah Cugoano publishes *Thoughts and Sentiments on the Evil and Wicked Traffic of the Slavery and Commerce of the Human Species*
Formation of the London Revolution Society	1788	Birth of Byron; Hannah More publishes *Slavery A Poem*; Ann Yearsley publishes *Poem on the Inhumanity of the Slave Trade*
French Revolution begins; Armed citizens "storm" the Bastille Prison in Paris and successfully take control. Seen as a symbol of oppressive monarchical rule, the prison's takeover and ensuing violence is hailed as a victory for the commoner in France and supporters of revolution in England.	1789	Declaration of the Rights of Man; William Blake publishes *Songs of Innocence*

Political/Social events	Year	Literary/Cultural events
The French National Assembly abolishes their nobility	1790	Edmund Burke publishes *Reflections on the Revolution in France*; Mary Wollstonecraft publishes *A Vindication of the Rights of Men*; Helen Maria Williams publishes *Letters Written in France in the Summer of 1790*
Start of armed slave resistance in San Domingo; In England, Bastille Day is celebrated by the Constitutional Society of Birmingham to mark the second anniversary of the fall of the Bastille prison. The chemist Joseph Priestley's home and laboratory are destroyed in a four-day riot sparked by this event in Birmingham.	1791	Thomas Paine publishes *The Rights of Man*, one of the most widely read books of the time; James Gillray publishes his *A Birmingham Toast, as given on the 14th of July, by the Revolution Society*; Erasmus Darwin publishes *The Botanic Garden*
France proclaims itself a Republic; East India Company troops, led by Charles Cornwallis, together with the combined forces of the Marathas and those of the Hyderabad Nizam, lay siege to Seringapatam. Mysore's ruler, Tipu Sultan, is forced to cede about half his territories to the Company and their allies as part of the Treaty of Seringapatam to end hostilities.	1792	Mary Wollstonecraft publishes *A Vindication of the Rights of Woman*; Thomas Paine publishes *The Rights of Man, Part II*; Birth of Percy Shelley; Hannah More publishes *Village Politics*, counter-revolutionary propaganda that sought to refute Paine's *Rights of Man*; Thomas Paine is tried by the English government for seditious libel; Formation of the London Corresponding Society by Thomas Hardy, a radical member of the English artisan class; Formation of

Political/Social events	Year	Literary/Cultural events
		the Association for Preserving Liberty and Property against Republicans and Levellers, an example of local, voluntary societies that sprang up to monitor and curb radical activity in Britain
France declares war on Britain and Netherlands; Suspension of habeus corpus; The wide circulation of *The Rights of Man* and its arguments against monarchical rule were perceived by the government as likely to incite revolution in England. Paine flees to France and is tried in absentia. British courts would sentence him for death at the end of the trial; Louis XVI executed	1793	William Godwin publishes *Enquiry Concerning Political Justice*; Birth of John Clare
Treason Trials begin following the arrest of several prominent English radicals, including Thomas Hardy	1794	William Godwin publishes *Caleb Williams*; Ann Radcliffe publishes *The Mysteries of Udolpho*
The Speenhamland Poor Relief System established to prevent rioting on account of rising bread prices and food shortages during wartime; Stones thrown at George III's carriage while he is traveling to the opening of Parliament. The government responds	1795	Hannah More commences publication of her *Cheap Repository Tracts*. These were created to resemble the street literature of the time – cheap, taking the form of the ballad and moral tale and hawked on the streets to reach the literate poor – to dissuade a popular

Political/Social events	Year	Literary/Cultural events
by passing the Treasonable Practices Act and The Seditious Meeting Act to discourage radical activism.		uprising against government; Birth of John Keats; Goethe publishes *Wilhelm Meister's Apprenticeship*
	1796	Robert Burns dies; Matthew Lewis publishes *The Monk*; Edward Jenner discovers smallpox vaccine
Napoleon invades Egypt in an attempt to establish French naval presence in the Mediterranean. He is eventually defeated by the English naval commander, Horatio Nelson in the Battle of the Nile, an event recorded by several artists of the time.	1798	Wordsworth and Coleridge's *Lyrical Ballads* published; Joanna Baillie's *A Series of Plays* published; Malthus publishes *An Essay on the Principle of Population*; Godwin publishes *Memoirs of Mary Wollstonecraft*
Acts of Union passed, uniting Great Britain and Ireland	1800	Volta builds the first electric battery; Maria Edgeworth publishes *Castle Rackrent*; Wordsworth publishes a new edition of the *Lyrical Ballads* with an expanded Preface
Touissaint Louverture publishes a constitution for Haiti and liberates the island's slaves; General	1801	Maria Edgeworth publishes *Belinda*

Political/Social events	Year	Literary/Cultural events
Enclosure Act passed enabling landowning farmers to enclose village lands without the need for parliamentary regulation. While this would enable increased agricultural production for England's growing population, several landless peasants and smaller farmers had to leave their home of many generations to look for work in the cities.		
Treaty of Amiens results in a temporary cessation of war between England and France; Napoleon is appointed Consul for Life	1802	William Cobbett begins publishing the newspaper *Weekly Political Register*; *Edinburgh Review* founded
Napoleon crowned France's Emperor	1804	Richard Trevithick mounts his steam engine on wheels to make the first steam-powered locomotive. The locomotive makes its first run from the Penydarren ironworks in Wales and establishes that heavy materials can be transported by rail. Gas lighting is adapted for use on the stage for the first time at London's Lyceum Theater.
Nelson leads English naval victory over the Franco-Spanish fleet in the Battle of Trafalgar	1805	Wordsworth's *Prelude* in thirteen books completed (only published posthumously); James Gillray publishes *The Plumb Pudding in Danger*

Political/Social events	Year	Literary/Cultural events
Armed revolt by Indian members of the East India Company regiment against British officers at Vellore. British efforts to standardise army headdress and grooming regulations without accounting for religious and caste diversity in India would result in friction between members of Indian and European regiments.	1806	
Abolition of the Slave Trade Act passed making the slave trade illegal throughout British colonies	1807	Charles and Mary Lamb publish *Tales from Shakespeare*; Wordsworth publishes *Poems in Two Volumes*
America passes The Act Prohibiting the Importation of Slaves	1808	*The Examiner* founded by Leigh Hunt; Blake completes *Milton*; Goethe publishes *Faust Part 1*; Thomas Clarkson publishes *The History of the Abolition of the Slave Trade*
	1809	*Quarterly Review* founded; Byron publishes *English Bards and Scotch Reviewers*; Birth of Alfred Tennyson; Blake sets up an exhibition of his illustrations and publishes a commentary of his displayed works titled *Descriptive Catalogue*
	1810	Anna Barbauld publishes *On the Origin and Progress of Novel Writing*; Walter Scott publishes *The Lady of the Lake*

Political/Social events	Year	Literary/Cultural events
The Prince of Wales is appointed "Regent" when George III is deemed unfit to rule on account of mental illness. This marks the beginning of what is titled the Regency Era. The first "Luddite" riots break out in Nottingham. These riots were characterised by the breaking of a new kind of automated textile loom by skilled textile workers who feared loss of livelihood.	1811	Shelley publishes *The Necessity of Atheism* and is expelled from Oxford as a consequence; Austen publishes *Sense and Sensibility*
	1812	Anna Barbauld publishes *Eighteen Hundred and Eleven*; Charles Dickens born; Byron speaks for Luddites in the Parliament opposing The Frame Work Bill which sought stringent action against those breaking machinery; Byron publishes *Childe Harold's Pilgrimage Canto I and II*
East India Company Act passed ending the company's trading monopoly in India but expanding their role with regards to administration and education in the subcontinent	1813	Austen publishes *Pride and Prejudice*; private publication of Shelley's *Queen Mab*; Southey takes up the post of Poet Laureate
Steam-driven presses acquired by *The Times* newspaper, paving the way for an increase in the availability of printed	1814	Byron publishes *The Corsair*; Austen publishes *Mansfield Park*; Scott publishes *Waverly* anonymously; Wordsworth publishes *The Excursion* which

Political/Social events	Year	Literary/Cultural events
materials; Battle of Paris fought between a coalition of Russia, Austria and Prussia against France. The French surrender and Napoleon is forced to abdicate as emperor and is exiled to the Isle of Elba.		is reviewed unfavourably later in the year in the *Edinburgh Review*
Mount Tambora in Indonesia erupts in what is now considered the biggest volcanic explosion in human history and leads to a series of temporary climactic changes like increased rainfall and a drop in global temperatures; Napoleon escapes from Elba and is later defeated in the Battle of Waterloo. This brings an end to a long period of sporadic wars between England and France; Apothecaries Act passed which sought to regulate and establish standards for the practice of medicine	1815	First collection of Wordsworth's *Poems* published; Austen publishes *Emma*; first printed edition of the *Beowulf* manuscript published
Called the "Year Without a Summer" on account of unusually low temperatures. A harsher winter and limited sunshine impact agriculture and food prices. Spa Field riots take place; Public dissatisfaction exists over prevailing socio-economic	1816	Shelley publishes *Alastor*; *The Examiner* publishes Keats' first poem, "To Solitude"; Coleridge publishes "Kubla Khan", "The Pains of Sleep" and "Christabel" which are all reviewed unfavorably; Byron publishes *Childe Harold's Pilgrimage Canto III*; Percy

Political/Social events	Year	Literary/Cultural events
conditions in England following the many wars with France		Shelley, Mary Godwin, Byron and his physician Polidori travel to Geneva where, forced indoors by bleak weather, they challenge each other to write horror stories. Mary Shelley's story for this challenge later takes the form of her famous novel, *Frankenstein* and Polidori writes *The Vampyre* which would later influence Bram Stoker's *Dracula*.
	1817	*The Black Dwarf* is first published; Keats publishes his *Poems*; *Blackwood's Edinburgh Magazine* founded; Byron publishes *Manfred*; Coleridge publishes *Biographia Literaria*; Death of Jane Austen; Austen's *Persuasion* and *Northanger Abbey* are published posthmously; John Gibson Lockhart publishes the first of the "Cockney School" attacks in Blackwood's; David Ricardo publishes *On the Principles of Political Economy and Taxation*
	1818	Walter Scott publishes *The Heart of Midlothian*; Mary Shelley publishes *Frankenstein* anonymously; Birth of Emily Bronte; Keats publishes *Endymion* and "Isabella"; Shelley publishes his *Ozymandias*

Political/Social events	Year	Literary/Cultural events
Birth of Princess Victoria; Peterloo Massacre takes place. The military violently displaces a peaceful protest for Parliamentary reform held at St Peter's Field, Manchester; Radical publisher Richard Carlile tried for criticising the government's action in the Peterloo incident and publishing Paine's *Rights of Man*	1819	Byron publishes *Don Juan I and II* anonymously; Shelley composes his "England in 1819" and "The Mask of Anarchy" in response to the Peterloo incident although both are only published posthumously in 1849; Radical publisher William Hone publishes *The Political House that Jack Built* to defend the freedom of the radical press
Death of George III and ascension of the Prince Regent as George IV; The Cato Street Conspiracy, a plot to murder the Cabinet is exposed; Radical insurrection led by artisans in Scotland; Start of the trial of Queen Caroline over allegations of adultery	1820	The *London Magazine* is revived; John Clare publishes his *Poems Descriptive of Rural Life and Scenery*; Keats publishes *Lamia, Isabella, The Eve of St Agnes and Other Poems*; Shelley publishes *Prometheus Unbound*
Death of Napoleon; Coronation of George IV	1821	Death of John Keats; Hazlitt publishes *Table Talk*; Shelley publishes *Adonais*; Byron publishes *Don Juan III*; Clare publishes *The Village Minstrel*; De Quincey publishes *Confessions of an English Opium Eater* in the *London Magazine*; Byron publishes *The Blues: A Literary Eclogue*
	1822	Death of PB Shelley; Birth of Matthew Arnold

Political/Social events	Year	Literary/Cultural events
	1824	Death of Byron in Missolonghi during the fight for Greek Independence
The Stockton and Darlington railway line inaugurated and a steam locomotive is used to haul passengers for the first time	1825	Death of Anna Laetitia Barbauld; Hazlitt publishes *The Spirit of the Age*
	1826	Mary Shelley publishes *The Last Man*; Felicia Hemans publishes "Casabianca"
	1827	Clare publishes *The Shepherd's Calendar*; Death of William Blake; Death of Helen Maria Williams
Repeal of Test and Corporation Acts that prevented non-Anglicans from holding office	1828	Hazlitt's *The Life of Napoleon Buonaparte, Part I and II* published
Catholic Emancipation Act passed allowing Irish and English Roman Catholics into Parliament; Lord William Bentinck, as governor-general of British-occupied India issues a regulation declaring the practice of Sati to be illegal; British Prime Minister Robert Peel establishes the Metropolitan Police Service	1829	
Death of George IV and accession of William IV	1830	Opening of the Liverpool-Manchester rail line; Tennyson publishes *Poems, Chiefly Lyrical*

Political/Social events	Year	Literary/Cultural events
Reform Act passed	1832	Death of Goethe; Death of Walter Scott; Shelley's *The Mask of Anarchy* published
Slavery Abolition Act passed, making the ownership and purchase of slaves illegal throughout the British Empire	1833	Death of Hannah More
Poor Law Amendment resulting in changes to the poor relief system in England. This law would stipulate that poor relief would only be offered in workhouses and no longer extended to the able-bodied.	1834	Death of Coleridge; Death of Charles Lamb
India Education Act passed declaring English as the medium of instruction in all but two institutions of learning as well as the language of administration and law in India; Charles Darwin arrives at the Galapagos Islands	1835	Macaulay publishes *Minute on Indian Education* which endorses a focus for British public expenditure in India on education in English rather than vernacular languages
Accession of Queen Victoria	1837	
	1843	Wordsworth accepts the post of Poet Laureate
	1850	Death of Wordsworth; *The Prelude* first published posthumously; Tennyson becomes Poet Laureate

Index